THE ENLIGHTENMENT AND MODERNITY

First published in Great Britain 2000 by
MACMILLAN PRESS LTD
Houndmills, Basingstoke, Hampshire RG21 6XS and London
Companies and representatives throughout the world

A catalogue record for this book is available from the British Library.

ISBN 0–333–71650–7

 First published in the United States of America 2000 by
ST. MARTIN'S PRESS, INC.,
Scholarly and Reference Division,
175 Fifth Avenue, New York, N.Y. 10010

ISBN 0–312–22385–4

Library of Congress Cataloging-in-Publication Data
The enlightenment and modernity / edited by Norman Geras and Robert
Wokler.
p. cm.
Includes bibliographical references and index.
ISBN 0–312–22385–4
1. Enlightenment Congresses. 2. Philosophy, Modern—20th century
Congresses. I. Geras, Norman, 1943– . II. Wokler, Robert, 1942–
.
B802.E545 1999
190—dc21   99–25944
                                                            CIP

Selection and editorial matter © Norman Geras and Robert Wokler 2000
Introduction and Chapter 9 © Robert Wokler 2000
Chapter 8 © Norman Geras 2000
Chapters 1–7, 10, 11 © Macmillan Press Ltd 2000

This book is printed on paper suitable for recycling and made from fully managed and sustained forest sources.

10   9   8   7   6   5   4   3   2   1
09   08   07   06   05   04   03   02   01   00

Printed and bound in Great Britain by
Antony Rowe Ltd, Chippenham, Wiltshire

Contents

vi   *Contents*

Notes on Contributors

Andrea Baumeister is Lecturer in Politics at the University of Stirling. Her research interests lie within the area of liberal political philosophy in general, within which she has a particular interest in the challenges posed for liberal conceptions of citizenship by the politics of difference and cultural diversity.

Vittorio Bufacchi is College Lecturer in the Department of Politics, University College Dublin, and formerly Lecturer in Political Theory at the University of Manchester and Visiting Professor at Yale University. His publications include *Italy since 1989: Events and Interpretations* (with Simon Burgess, 1998), and *Democracy and Constitutional Culture in the Union of Europe* (co-edited with Richard Bellamy and Dario Castiglione). He is currently writing a book on moral motivations and social justice.

Ian Carter is a research fellow in the Department of Political and Social Studies at the University of Pavia, Italy. He is the author of *A Measure of Freedom* (1999).

Alistair Edwards is Lecturer in Political Thought at the University of Manchester. He is co-author (with Geoffrey Roberts) of *A New Dictionary of Political Analysis* and is currently preparing (with Jules Townshend) an edited collection of papers on interpretive problems in the history of political thought for publication by Macmillan.

Norman Geras is Professor of Government at the University of Manchester. His main current research interest is the Holocaust. Recent publications include *Solidarity in the Conversation of Humankind: the Ungroundable Liberalism of Richard Rorty* (1995) and *The Contract of Mutual Indifference: Political Philosophy after the Holocaust* (1998).

Ian Holliday is Professor of Policy Studies at the City University of Hong Kong. His most recent books are *The British Cabinet System* (co-authored with Martin Burch) and *Ashes '97: Two Views from the Boundary* (co-authored with Norman Geras).

Geraint Parry is the W.J.M. Mackenzie Professor of Government at the University of Manchester. He is author of *Political Elites*, *John Locke* and, jointly with G. Moyser and N. Day, *Political Participation and Democracy in Britain*. He is currently working on a history of political and educational thought.

Maurizio Passerin d'Entrèves is Senior Lecturer in Political Theory at the University of Manchester. He is the author of *Modernity, Justice, and Community* (1990) and *The Political Philosophy of Hannah Arendt* (1994), and co-editor of *Habermas and the Unfinished Project of Modernity* (1996) and *Public and Private: Legal, Political and Philosophical Perspectives* (2000).

Hillel Steiner is Professor of Political Philosophy at the University of Manchester. He has contributed articles on liberty, rights and moral reasoning to various philosophy, politics and economics journals and collections. His book, *An Essay On Rights* (1994), was awarded the W.J.M. Mackenzie Prize, and he is the co-author (with M. Kramer and N. Simmonds) of *A Debate over Rights: Philosophical Enquiries* (1998).

Ursula Vogel is Senior Lecturer in Government at the University of Manchester. Her publications include *The Frontiers of Citizenship* (co-edited with M. Moran); 'But in a Republic Men are Needed: Guarding the Boundaries of Liberty', in R. Wokler (ed.), *Rousseau and Liberty*, and 'Gleichheit und Hersschaft in der ehelichen Vertragsgesellschaft: Widersprüche der Aufklärung', in U. Gerhard (ed.), *Frauenrechtsgeschichte* (1997).

Robert Wokler is Senior Research Fellow in the Department of Politics at the University of Exeter and was formerly Reader in the History of Political Thought at the University of Manchester. His most recent publications include *Diderot's Political Writings* (with John Hope Mason) and *Rousseau* (1995), and he is (with Mark Goldie) co-editor of the *Cambridge History of Eighteenth-Century Political Thought*.

Editors' Preface

Most of the papers collected in this volume were presented to a workshop seminar held in the Department of Government at the University of Manchester during the 1994–5 academic session. They are all the work of scholars either currently or recently connected with this department. The aim of the seminar, which was proposed and organized by Norman Geras, was to explore how the Enlightenment and its legacy were perceived by the several contributors to relate to their own current areas of research and, through our discussions, to view this central theme in the light which our different interests and approaches might cast upon it. The volume we have assembled is the outcome of that collective enterprise.

Norman Geras
Robert Wokler

Introduction

Virtually everyone who holds opinions about the most central issues of contemporary ethics or political theory, or indeed about the crises of our civilization as a whole, has thereby felt licensed to pronounce upon the nature of the Enlightenment Project. Whatever principles it might embrace are presumed, by persons who reflect upon such matters, to form the essential core or guiding thread of modernity itself. The Enlightenment Project is the ghost in our machine. Students of eighteenth-century thought across a variety of disciplines may be forgiven their frustration when confronting such global judgements about the subjects of their research, not only because shorthand truth always makes detailed scholarship redundant, but also because it portrays their excursions into what they imagine to be the uncharted past as circumnavigations of the present locked within familiar waters. Why should they set out with their scalpels to clear away the frontiers of knowledge when if they stay at home with sledgehammers they can dispose of the Enlightenment at a stroke? Never mind that *the Enlightenment* is an invention of the late nineteenth century, *the Scottish Enlightenment* a fabrication of the early twentieth century, *the Enlightenment Project*, of more recent pedigree than the Manhattan Project, just a scheme largely devised in the past two decades. What possible bearing can genuine scholarship have upon claims about the conceptual roots of modernity which are writ large and on stilts?

Scholars of Enlightenment thought almost invariably have at least a dual identity. After assembling at symposia and conferences addressed to eighteenth-century themes, they return to their departments of English, French or German language and literature, or of philosophy, music or art. If they are specialists in political thought with academic appointments in the English-speaking world, they may feel not so much schizophrenic as shorn of any identity at all, on account of the great gulf that has arisen in their discipline over the past thirty years since the predominance of political theorists at the University of Chicago, on the one hand, and at Oxford University and the London School of Economics, on the other, has been transformed into the hegemony of Harvard, with respect to political philosophy, and Cambridge, in the history of political thought. That sharp division of labour does not lend itself well, either to the contextual study of Enlightenment political thought or to the conceptual analysis of modernity in terms of its putative Enlightenment roots. The wedge now deemed to separate the history from the philosophy of political argument only obscures the interdisciplinary character of eighteenth-century thought, across boundaries which did not come to be demarcated until after the end of the age of Enlightenment itself.

In the discourses of modernity that figure in the philosophical histories of Voltaire, d'Alembert or Gibbon are embedded frameworks for the understanding of contemporary civilization along lines that lead in our day to the perspectives of Reinhart Koselleck, Jürgen Habermas or Michel Foucault, but which have scant purchase for those who only study political concepts either analytically or alternatively with respect to the initial circumstances of their use. Above all, perhaps, the current gulf between political philosophy and the history of political thought masks the sense in which so many leading eighteenth-century thinkers sought not only to interpret the world but, through their interpretations, to change it. If such moral endeavour may be described as their Enlightenment Project, our manner of fragmenting it by way of our methodological approaches to the study of political thought betrays its most fundamental ideals.

This collection comprises a modest attempt – perhaps even an unwitting effort on the part of some contributors – to repair that breach. No subject in the human sciences offers a more dramatic illustration of the ties that join philosophy and history than the Enlightenment and its legacy. Some of the central questions of psychology and epistemology today still turn around claims regarding the nature of human perception and knowledge first articulated by Descartes, Locke, Berkeley or Hume. In linguistics, Enlightenment doctrines of universal grammar or the origin of languages have been embraced by researchers determined to map the future of their discipline no less than by those who have sought to retrace its past. By way of Kant in particular, modern ethics is seen by most of its current interpreters to have embarked upon a wholly fresh path, disencumbered of the authority of classical or religious dogmas. In economics and other social sciences, Smith and Montesquieu are deemed to have cast our current disciplines in the forms in which they are still studied. Every school child comes to learn that contemporary society was first shaped by the Industrial Revolution of the eighteenth century, and that the modern nation-state is an invention of the French Revolution, generated in turn by an Enlightenment spirit of commercialism and republican ideals of self-rule. A close connection between the theory and practice of the modern state, as advocated in the eighteenth century by writers of all denominations, has also been identified by later critics of totalitarianism who have uncovered its philosophical roots in the doctrines of Rousseau. Still other commentators have attributed the patriarchal character of modernity ultimately to the exclusion of women from the French Revolutionary declaration of the rights of man.

For much of the past two hundred years, before the history and philosophy of politics took their separate paths, most of our principal political and social theorists have followed Hegel, Tocqueville, Marx and Nietzsche in tracing the conceptual or economic underpinnings of modernity to the age of Enlightenment, thereby pursuing themes about the nature of modern civilization and the course of its past or prospective history which were already much discussed by eighteenth-century thinkers themselves. In the twentieth century, the subject of modernity's debt to Enlightenment ideals of progress or to its canons of reason and scientific objectivity has been of central importance to Martin Heidegger and Carl Schmitt in their conservative critiques of atomistic individualism, and to Charles Taylor, Michael Sandel and other radical communitarian opponents of Enlightenment liberalism.

The subject has informed the sceptical realist perspective adopted by Richard Rorty and a variety of so-called post-modernist objections to principles of universal truth. It lies at the heart of the difference between Foucault's anti-Enlightenment account of the despotism of knowledge and power in the modern world, on the one hand, and Habermas's commitment to the open and engaged discourses of the public sphere, on the other. Interpreters of the Holocaust from Max Horkheimer to Zygmunt Bauman have understood modernity's greatest crime as also, in some measure, a legacy of the Enlightenment. Passionate admirers of Isaiah Berlin, such as Steven Lukes and John Gray, take fierce issue with one another around the question of Berlin's debt or opposition to Enlightenment ideals. From a Thomist perspective, Alasdair MacIntyre rejects the political philosophy of John Rawls just because of its Kantian, and hence Enlightenment, presuppositions. It is proving increasingly difficult to open a literary review or even a daily newspaper without confronting the question. Rather too few of the commentators who feel obliged to address it are sufficiently well-informed. If they pause long enough to read these essays, at least some of them may come to feel better insulated from the windy vapours they often emit themselves.

Our first section is devoted to the study of Enlightenment moral, political, educational and scientific principles, with respect both to eighteenth-century debates and their current applicability. Ursula Vogel, in challenging misconceived notions of the abstract universalism of the so-called Enlightenment Project, offers a perspective on its concrete dimensions through some of its travellers' commentaries on the nature of foreigners who inhabit the peripheries of the civilized world. With reference especially to the eighteenth-century discovery and exploration of Tahiti, she shows that the philosopher travellers of the age of Enlightenment, even while subscribing to notions of mankind's nature in general and to a Euro-centric bias in particular, took notice of the distinctive character of savage societies in ways which enriched their perceptions of the variability and diversity of human cultures. Moving from the margins of civilization to the internal dynamics by which it can be acquired, Geraint Parry addresses Enlightenment conceptions of autonomy and self-fulfilment with respect to programmes of instruction designed to emancipate children from religious prejudice and blind conformity. In stressing the spirit of criticism and ideals of active life encouraged by eighteenth-century educationalists, he shows that the Enlightenment promoted a greater plurality of values and more self-reliance than have been allowed by critics who subscribe to Foucault's contention that the same intellectual movement which discovered our liberties also invented our disciplines.

Andrea Baumeister takes to task those critics of Kant's moral philosophy who find that his conception of self-reliant subjectivity leads to the fragmentation of society, contending that, on the contrary, his dictates of the categorical imperative are premised on a notion of moral community which aims to overcome just such fragmentation. Pursuing a line of argument in part inspired by Onora O'Neill, she shows that Kantian claims about the nature of public reason and the development of moral character imply an approach to the cultivation of the virtues which his communitarian detractors have overlooked, from which it follows that his ethics comprise a corrective to, rather than a source of, the impoverishment of modern morality. Hillel Steiner finds Kant's formulation of the same dictates to be linked with his notion of universal justice conceived in terms of a distribution of property rights, which, however, are shown to be without proper foundation as Kant defines them. For in stipulating that such rights can issue from the original common possession of things only through the enactment of the general will, he makes the obligations of forbearance which are entailed by property rights depend upon the agreement of persons who would have had to consent before they were born.

Ian Carter confronts several of the same objections to Enlightenment ethics which Baumeister meets on behalf of Kant, in his case by demonstrating that they may enjoy much the same rational justification as the teleological moral principles which MacIntyre in particular invokes against them. Enlightenment ideals of progress and perfectibility may appear more indeterminate than the specifiable ends of human activity which were portrayed by Aristotle, but allowing for the empirical correlation between progress and freedom, or progress and equality, which liberal thinkers have so often accepted, Carter contends that the merits of liberty or equality can be legitimately upheld just in so far as they are seen to promote those ideals. Alistair Edwards subjects to close critical scrutiny the contention of Friedrich von Hayek, drawn from the Cardinal de Retz by way of Adam Ferguson, to the effect that the social order is an unintended product of individual actions. Hayek's contrast between what he sees as this essentially Scottish approach to social scientific enquiry, on the one hand, and the rational constructivism of Continental thinkers like Rousseau, on the other, is found to be overdrawn, while the strength of unintended consequence explanations of how social institutions operate, Edwards argues, is due less to any hidden hand of spontaneous order than to the inescapability of mistaken knowledge and ignorance.

In our second section, which deals with the conceptual history of modernity, we address a variety of questions about the Enlightenment's putative influence, or lack of influence, in shaping our political thought and culture. Ian Holliday re-examines the English conservative critique of Enlightenment rationalism associated above all with Edmund Burke and Michael Oakeshott, and he argues that the plausibility of the conservative case is as much a matter of sociological understanding as of philosophical principle. Not only did English conservatism offer the first major response to the universalist, empiricist or utilitarian strains of eighteenth-century philosophy as a whole, he observes; in engaging with Enlightenment rationalism over the whole course of its history, it established the traditions which underpin its own identity by way of the different voices it adopted in that conversation. Taking a work of Ralph Miliband as his point of departure, Norman Geras considers some implications of the assumptions that human nature is intrinsically evil, or intrinsically good or vacuous, and he concludes that the only warrantable assumption for socialists is that it is intrinsically mixed. Optimistic psychological claims drawn from the Enlightenment are often upheld by socialists, but particularly on the evidence of the brutalities of our century they are difficult to sustain, he observes, while allowing that modest hopes for the establishment of tolerably contented human existence may be more solidly grounded on realist and pessimistic premises.

Robert Wokler challenges both the proposition that the Enlightenment loved the thing it killed, in substituting a secular religion for Christian absolutism, and the contention that the main philosophical and political principles of modernity since the French Revolution stem from the Enlightenment. If the notion of an Enlightenment Project means anything at all, he argues, it must embrace a commitment to pluralism and religious toleration, while the nation-state that was invented in the course of the French Revolution betrayed not only the cosmopolitan ideals of the republic of letters but also the Roussseauist principles of popular sovereignty from which it appeared to have sprung. Maurizio Passerin d'Entrèves interprets an essay drafted by Foucault on Kant in commemoration of the two-hundredth anniversary of the publication of Kant's *Was ist Aufklärung?*, and he compares its argument closely with two earlier texts which Foucault had completed on the same subject. In investigating Foucault's diverse readings of the tendencies of Enlightenment thought, he suggests that the apparent tensions between them may be reconciled, particularly in the light of the Nietzschean character of his critical ontology, whose fundamental hostility to the age of Enlightenment Foucault never abandoned.

Vittorio Bufacchi examines the normative implications of two main traditions of Enlightenment social contract theory, one deriving from Hobbes and based on a notion of mutual advantage, the other inspired principally by Kant and founded on an idea of social cooperation. In stressing the benefits of cooperation, David Gauthier has adopted the Hobbesian perspective, he argues, while John Rawls, in emphasizing that cooperation must be based on fair terms, has instead followed in the footsteps of Kant, there being no way to reconcile these differences in the manner attempted by Rawls, since they recapitulate the tensions in an Enlightenment Project that never had, nor ever can have, logical coherence. Whatever might be the coherence, or indeed the identity, of that Project, these essays bear testimony to the persistence and significance of claims about its nature, and to the strength of its images and ideals within the edifice of modernity that we inhabit. For better or worse, whether enacted or betrayed, the so-called Enlightenment Project has cast Western civilization under its long shadow over the past two hundred years. Even if it brings modernity to its close, the second coming of Christ, due soon after the publication of this book, may by contrast seem little more than an apocalyptic anti-climax.

Robert Wokler

Part I
Interpreting Enlightenment Principles

1 The Sceptical Enlightenment: Philosopher Travellers Look Back at Europe

Ursula Vogel

> If the scientific and scholarly gain of a few individuals has to be bought at the price of the happiness of whole nations, then it would be better for discoverers and discovered alike if the South Sea had never become known to the restless European.[1]

INTRODUCTION

A central failure of the Enlightenment, it is frequently argued today, lay in its incapacity to deal with human difference and diversity.[2] The consequences of this failure seem nowhere more apparent than in the question of Europe's relationship to non-European peoples and cultures. The alleged insensitivity of eighteenth-century thinking to the intrinsic value of cultural difference is commonly attributed to its universalist frameworks of inquiry – to its abstract conceptions of a uniform and invariable human nature and to the grand narratives of a progressive history of human civilization.[3] What is at issue in this critical portrayal of Enlightenment legacies is not merely the epistemological inadequacy of universalist presuppositions to the task of understanding foreign cultures in their own terms. Enlightenment universalism is seen to have fostered modes of thinking which in the following two centuries would all too often serve to legitimate European global dominance and to conceal the histories of destruction that were entailed in it.[4]

In this chapter I shall attempt to give an alternative account of the Enlightenment's engagement with a world constituted by ethnic and cultural difference. That its perception of this world was mediated through discourses of cognitive and moral universalism is not in doubt; nor that the latter remained anchored in the presumption of Europe's unique role in the history of humankind. That such universalist principles, however, should have implied a dogmatic belief in the uniformity of human nature, of a kind that would have systematically closed off all interest in its

3

diverse forms and concrete contexts, betrays a fundamental misunderstanding. It has had the effect of filtering out, and rendering all but invisible, the distinctive scientific aspirations and the intellectual and practical energies which shaped the Enlightenment's encounter with the world outside Europe. In large part the misunderstanding is due to the neglect of many of the key texts and some of the most characteristic genres of Enlightenment literature. Whether, to name but a few of those texts, we turn to Montesquieu's *Persian Letters*, Rousseau's *Discourse on the Origins of Inequality* or Condorcet's construction of a universal history of the human mind, we can easily see how much moral and political argument in this period owed to empirical knowledge about non-European peoples, especially primitive ('savage') societies at the periphery of the known world: 'No reputable philosophe would theorize on the nature of man without producing some well-chosen references to the American Indian, the Chinese, the African negro or the Hottentot.'[5] The same outward-going interest in distant lands and their inhabitants can be observed in the immense popularity of all kinds of travel literature – from the merely entertaining, titillating presentation of 'the exotic' to the serious work of fiction and the scholarly tract – among the reading publics of the eigteenth century.[6]

In short, any attempt to engage with the legacies of the Enlightenment Project must take account of the dynamic of its *Weltoffenheit*. Given that neither the certainties of religious faith nor the *a priori* constructions of metaphysical systems could any longer provide reliable guidance, philosophical inquiry had to turn to the world given in experience. Openness towards the world expressed itself in restless curiosity as the motivational drive behind the pursuit of knowledge and, on a different plane, in the epistemological imperative that questions about the nature of man and society could only be answered by observing human existence in all its diverse manifestations. 'It was my intention,' wrote Georg Forster (traveller and philosophe who from 1772 to 1775 took part in Cook's second voyage around the world), 'to consider the nature of man from as many perspectives as possible'.[7] Even Kant, usually the key witness in the case brought against the Enlightenment's abstract universalism, advised the moral philosopher of the need to travel, at least in the form of conscientiously following the available travel reports.[8]

No other genre of Enlightenment literature expressed these aspirations more faithfully than the 'philosophical' travel account. A distinctive form of narrative interspersed with general reflections on what the traveller had seen and experienced, this genre emerged towards the end of the eighteenth century in response to the great voyages of discovery that had enlarged the world known to Europeans by the immense terrains of the Pacific Ocean. As a result especially of James Cook's expeditions it could be said that the world as the habitat of human beings had become one, in the sense that all its parts were – in principle – accessible to knowledge and could be connected and integrated in a global perspective on the human species. The philosophical travel account captured the meanings and implications of this historic moment. Its author might be a traveller himself, like Bougainville and Georg Forster. Or, in the manner of Montesquieu, Diderot and Kant, he might be an 'armchair traveller', who used the observations brought back by the voyagers as raw material and inspiration for setting the frame to his philosophical or literary enterprise.

The philosophical travel account was indebted to the spirit of scientific investigation in that it aimed to convey exact and comprehensive informa-tion about a hitherto unfamiliar region of the earth (about its geography, climate, flora and fauna as much as about the physiognomy, behaviour and customs of its native populations). But it moved beyond the boundaries of empirical, factual description in the endeavour to bring the new knowl-edge about the differences and variations among the peoples of the world to bear upon philosophical inquiry into the nature and moral constitution of man as a species being. It is in this context that the observed contrast between primitive and civilized societies became the catalyst of a 'painful' enlightenment[9] – of a critical self-reflection on Europe's own identity.

None of the explorations of the 'New World' of the Pacific islands proved as significant in this respect, alluring and unsettling at the same time, as the discovery of Tahiti. In the main part of the paper I shall use accounts of Tahiti as a kind of case study to consider the constitution of a sceptical Enlightenment. For reasons of space I shall confine myself to two main examples – Diderot's *Supplement to Bougainville's Voyage* (written in 1772, but not published before 1796) and Georg Forster's *Voyage around the World* (1774 in its original English version; 1778 in German). Although the *Supplement* is the work of an armchair traveller, while Forster's 1,000-page volume is based on first-hand experience, the two texts share a number of critical perspectives: in both, savage Tahiti casts radical doubt upon the self-confidence of enlightened Europe, revealing the corruption at the heart of its political systems, its refined morality and civilized forms of sociability. Both envisage the disastrous consequences that the contact with Europe will inflict upon the integrity of Tahiti's native culture. But while Diderot implicated enlightenment itself in the process of irreversible destruction, Forster's critique of civilization salvaged those of its achievements which might in future work to the benefit of all peoples on the globe.

THE GREAT MAP OF MANKIND IN
THE EIGHTEENTH CENTURY

The eighteenth century's perception of the world evolved out of long-standing and varied traditions of thought which recorded the successive stages of Europe's encounter with foreign lands and alien cultures.[10] With its roots in the discourses of Hellenic barbarism, on the one hand, and in the confrontations of Christianity with Islam in the Middle Ages, on the other, Europe's understanding of the geographical and cultural boundaries of the world and of its own central place within it was first radically altered as a consequence of Columbus's discovery of the New World and of the waves of overseas expansion which followed in its wake. The voyages of the Renaissance period transformed the closed, hierarchically ordered cosmos of the Christian transnational community into a spatial universe of as yet uncertain extent.[11] Not only did this epoch witness the most extensive enlargement of the known world in terms of physical space which, as Alexander von Humboldt put it, 'doubled the works of the Creation' for the inhabitants of Europe.[12] It brought the latter face to face with terrains and peoples for which neither the Bible nor the classical authors of Greek and Roman antiquity would provide authoritative guidance. To the extent that first-hand knowledge about the indigenous populations of Asia, Africa and the Americas continued to reach European readers in the form mainly of missionary reports, the understanding of primitive peoples remained until the end of the seventeenth century bounded by concerns central to Christian faith and salvation. Yet, as the travellers and scholars of the eighteenth century were to acknowledge, the expeditions of the Renaissance already laid the foundations of that systematic secular interest in the shape and history of the earth which was to become the hallmark of the scientific endeavours of the Enlightenment period: 'For the first time man knew the globe that he inhabited.'[13]

Voyages around the world in the eighteenth century heralded a second momentous phase in the history of European overseas discoveries. The exploration of the Pacific Ocean by Bougainville, Cook and many others, and the discovery of Australia, New Zealand and the South Sea islands brought one-third of the earth's surface into the orbit of the known world. After Cook's second voyage (1772–5) had laid to rest the long-held belief in the existence of a vast land mass in the southern hemisphere (the *terra australis incognita*) there remained no new continents to be discovered. Much was still left to future explorations, especially as regards the inland regions of Africa, the Americas and Australia. But the cartography of the globe was largely complete.[14] And in this sense the world was known:

> But now the great map of mankind is unrolled at once; and there is no state or gradation of barbarism and no mode of refinement which we have not at the same instant under our view.[15]

In contrast with the Spanish and Portuguese conquests since the sixteenth century, the colonial settlements in North America and the slave trade from the coast of West Africa, contact with the native populations of the Pacific took place under relatively favourable circumstances of inter-cultural tolerance. Due to the decline of missionary endeavour in the eighteenth century the voyages pursued no religious aims. Nor were they directly implicated in, or immediately followed by, military conquest, colonization and economic exploitation. Bougainville's and Cook's vessels sailed under instructions to stake out claims on behalf of their governments; they carried soldiers and military equipment, and instances of violence against natives occurred. But with astronomers, botanists, natural historians, linguists and engravers on board, the prior interest of the journeys lay in the expansion of knowledge.

The knowledge sought by the itinerant scholars (and by their counterparts back home) covered a wide spectrum of objectives. It was to be of use to the seafarer through the exact cartographic delineation of the coastlines of continents and islands, the location of ice masses, the measurement of the depths and currents of the ocean. The inquiries of the natural historian focused on the formation of the planet earth and the evolution and variation of vegetative, animal and human organisms under different circumstances of climate, soil and water supply. The interest in man as part of nature called for detailed observations of the physiognomy and anatomy of native tribes in their relationship to a specific natural environment. Attention to sexual behaviour, patterns of parenting and familial organization, as to modes of subsistence, religious rituals and forms of sociability, similarly contributed to identify the specific characteristics that distinguished each variation of the human species. From this perspective alone – that is, if we consider the wealth of factual information about the native populations of the Pacific that was conveyed in the note-books and published accounts of the travellers[16] – the view of the Enlightenment's lack of interest in diversity can hardly be sustained. Nor should we, on the other hand, overlook the magnitude of intellectual challenges and moral apprehensions that confronted the European observer in the shock experience of extreme forms of otherness. 'For the benefits of the friends of man [*Menschenfreunde*] we have explored a number of hitherto unknown variations of human nature': Forster's concluding remarks on the achievements of his voyage show that the encounter with the unfamiliar and alien was experienced as an enrichment of knowledge and moral horizons alike. But the immediately following reference to the unfortunate savages of the Tierra del Fuogo – 'half-starved, apathetic ... and relegated to the lowest stage of human nature at the borderline to non-rational animals'[17] – also attests to the difficulties of absorbing this experience. The enormous distance that seemed to separate the European from some of his fellow humans threatened to undermine the unity of the human species and to thrust the Enlightenment's central question, 'What is man?', into a vacuum of radical uncertainty.

Confrontations of this kind – to which we might add the observation of cannibalism among the Maoris of New Zealand – go some way to explain the unique space that Tahiti came to occupy in the travel narratives of the late eighteenth century. Filtered through the spell-bound descriptions of virtually all travellers who set foot on the island, the discovery of Tahiti captured the imagination of the European reading public as an event of extraordinary and lasting fascination.[18] Reality and myth combined in many different ways to make the Tahitian islander both the distant ancestor and beguiling hope of European man. Tahiti became the focus of nostalgia for a lost world of human happiness, of utopian speculation and even plans of emigration. It supplied an imagery capable of expressing the widely felt disenchantment with the ills of the modern world and of turning the critical modes of Enlightenment thinking upon the progress of enlightenment itself.[19]

What was it about Tahiti, a small island thousands of miles away from Europe, that could evoke such intense and profound identifications? The more important answers to this question would, of course, have to be sought in Europe, i.e. in the dominant intellectual currents and collective sentiments of the late eighteenth century. But we can get a glimpse of what the real Tahiti, at the moment of discovery, must have been like if we consider those first impressions on which the testimony of all visitors converged.[20] What struck the travellers first – after the hardships of a dangerous and uncertain sea journey and after months spent without sighting land – was the overwhelming natural beauty of the country. All accounts dwell on the beguiling charms of a landscape where coastal regions, inland valleys and distant mountains were suffused with the intense colours of abundant vegetation and where the neatly built abodes of the natives were set out in rich groves of banana, coconut and bread trees. Nature herself, operating through a beneficent climate, seemed to provide human beings with all they needed without exacting the tribute of arduous labour. This favourable impression was matched by the physical beauty of the islanders: their well-built, healthy bodies, their nakedness borne without shame and artificial reserve, their attractive bronze skin colour and melodious language. These physical attributes alone set the Tahitian apart from other savages whom the travellers encountered in the Pacific region, comparing them favourably with the forbidding ugliness of the natives of New Zealand and New Caledonia, who displayed stark similarities with the negroes of West Africa and the Caribbean islands. Above all, the visitors were attracted by the behaviour that the inhabitants of Tahiti showed towards them. The same scene of arrival is replayed in all descriptions: The ships of the Europeans, anchoring at some distance from the shore, would soon be surrounded by countless canoes and cries of 'Tayo' (friend). The uncanny friendliness, childlike trust and innocent curiosity of these savages would become further evident in their willingness to barter the much-needed fresh foodstuffs for iron nails and trinkets of fake jewellery, and to share their meals, huts and – if we are to believe Bougainville and Diderot – their women with the strangers. In short, in the Tahitian islander eighteenth-century Europeans met their *bon sauvage* (whom the previous century had identified with the North American Indian). Here was a 'variation' of the human species sufficiently different to be endowed with all the charms of the exotic and yet, unlike other savage tribes, still similar enough to be adopted by the European as an image of himself.

Tahiti, then, seemed to offer a glimpse of what the human condition of man 'close to the origins of the world'[21] and as yet unspoilt by the trappings of civilizatory progress must have been like. It might be said, of course, that it was the European traveller weary of Europe's decadence who invented the Tahitian as his other and turned his island into a place of ecstatic imagination. However, as we shall see in the following two sections, the most pertinent insights of Diderot's and Forster's accounts and the distinctive features of their sceptical Enlightenment are owed to the fact that Tahiti was a real place. Both understood that Tahiti's discovery and first contact with Europe marked the beginning of an inexorable process that would draw its people into the world determined by the superior power of European civilization. In Diderot these insights took the form of resignation in the face of irremediable loss. Forster was led to a position where he altogether abandoned the presumption that questions about the nature of man and about the future of the human species could ever be answered by reference to a state of primitive simplicity and happiness.

BOUGAINVILLE AND DIDEROT: THE MYTH OF TAHITI

The magic spell that a first encounter with the island of Tahiti could cast even over an experienced traveller of foreign lands is particularly evident in the case of Bougainville. Louis Antoine Bougainville (1729–1811) – aristocrat, soldier, philosophe and naval explorer – was the perfect embodiment of the Enlightenment's explorative spirit, 'balancing a treatise of integral and differential calculus on one side, with a voyage round the world on the other.'[22] Much of his account is given to technical problems of navigation and to the detailed recording of the dangers, hardships and ravaging diseases that the seafarer is likely to encounter in remote parts of the world. The same endeavour to supply an extensive array of useful facts is applied to the description of indigenous populations and of the economic and political strategies of the colonial powers. The imperative of factual veracity leads him into frequent attacks upon the then fashionable genres of merely entertaining travel literature and, with no less indignation, on the distortions of experience that are owed to the speculations of the closet philosophers at home: 'Geography is an exact science and not to be fashioned in the spirit of system without falling prey to fatal errors.'[23]

Yet, it was Bougainville who 'really launched the legend' when he named Tahiti *La Nouvelle Cythère*, after the mythical Greek island of erotic pleasure.[24] His observations may be of interest to us mainly because they supplied the factual material from which Diderot was to fashion the philosophical tale of civilized man's alienation from his natural state. But they are also interesting in their own right in that they highlight the manifold difficulties and misunderstandings that enveloped the traveller as he attempted to give a faithful description of native attitudes and practices which in many instances would appear wholly unintelligible to the eyes of European observers. (Such difficulties were compounded in Bougainville's case by a brief stay on the island of only ten days and, above all, by his ignorance of the native language.) 'We did not trust our eyes': Time and again Bougainville voices the inadequacy of previous experience to establish the meaning of what he sees.[25] Nothing, it seems, has prepared the European traveller for the spectacle of beautiful native women unashamedly displaying their naked bodies and willing, indeed positively encouraged by their menfolk, to grant sexual favours to strangers. Familiar codes of sexual propriety which back home bind sexual desire into the narrow confines of the monogamous marriage are thrown into disarray in the face of the freedom and ease with which the Tahitians follow the promptings of their natural impulses.

What comparisons and analogies were available to the foreigner to incorporate these unfamiliar sights into his own language and modes of thinking? As an educated Frenchman well-versed in classical literature, Bougainville spontaneously recalls names and images that belong to the mythology of ancient Greece. He compares the event of a Tahitian woman stepping on board the *Boudeuse* to the goddess Venus appearing to the phrygian shepherds; he invokes anacreontic songs and dances to capture the graciousness and innocence of the public display of erotic desire. Although further observations would lead him in some instances to correct those first rapturous impressions,[26] the alluring image of a Tahiti situated in the 'elysian fields' remains unaffected.

With these references to the cradle of European civilization Bougainville's 'Tahiti' is set in a discursive tradition and pattern of assimilation which for centuries had played a dominant role in the European traveller's exploration of primitive societies.[27] The gap of cultural difference is bridged and the incomprehensibility of non-European peoples overcome by moving the latter into one's own distant past, be it actual or imagined. Mediated through the imagery that pertains to that past, a relationship between them and us is created. They – the savages at the periphery of the world – represent an earlier and perhaps happier stage of mankind's development which once was ours too.

Diderot's *Supplement to Bougainville's Voyage* construes this relationship in an altogether different manner. Tahiti reminds us not of the ancient Greece of our known history, but of a much earlier stage 'close to the origins of the world'. Although the title seems to suggest that the work would merely add to Bougainville's observations and although these can be seen to have provided a minimal frame of factual information, the *Supplement* bears little resemblance to the original travel account. Bougainville's description of events, adventures and curiosities is transformed into a philosophical satire on the morality of civilized society.[28] As in other works, Diderot uses the literary form of the dialogue (here, in fact, of a double dialogue) as the most suitable vehicle to consider a philosophical question from multiple standpoints and to indicate the incompleteness and ambivalence of any one of them.[29] The work consists of four parts, each of which develops a different perspective upon the moral implications and practical consequences of the encounter between Europe and 'Tahiti' – between civilized and natural man. An initial conversation between two philosophers, A and B (Diderot's alter ego), about Bougainville's explorations and their contribution to the expanding knowledge of nature and man, is followed by the 'old man's farewell' which carries Diderot's impassioned indictment of the devastating abuses which the European intruders have inflicted upon Tahiti. The third and main part of the *Supplement* recounts a dialogue between the ship's chaplain and Orou, the wise Tahitian native, about the true foundations of a sexual morality which would be in tune with man's natural dispositions and unencumbered by the religious and institutional fetters of civilized society. The concluding conversation between A and B reflects on the irreconcilable divisions between civilized and natural man and on the practical implications that should be drawn from this knowledge. There is, in the end, no universal standpoint from which the antagonism could be resolved.

In the involuntary erotic adventures and trials of 'the good chaplain' – who struggles in vain to uphold the demand of celibacy imposed by his religion – Diderot portrays the contrast between Europe and 'the most savage people on earth'[30] as a conflict about the meaning and practice of sexual love. What on Tahiti is a physical appetite satisfied spontaneously and without secrecy has in civilized Europe become chained by a myriad of artificial moral and religious precepts. The chaplain's unsuccessful struggle against his natural impulses is replicated in his conversations with Orou and in his inability to refute the latter's radical interrogation of the morals and customs of Europe. In this context Diderot does not confine himself to denouncing particular institutions and practices, such as the indissoluble marriage, the adultery laws and, more generally, the hypocrisy inscribed in civilized society's codes of sexual etiquette. In a mode of radical abstraction which follows in the footsteps of Rousseau's *Discourse on the Origins of Inequality* he tears away from the core of human nature all and any additions that have entangled natural sexual desire in refined sentiments and affections. Other thinkers of the Enlightenment, like Condorcet, Adam Smith, and Georg Forster, took the gradual refinement of manners in the process of civilization as heralding a move towards greater equality between the sexes and an improvement of the status of women.[31] For Diderot, by contrast, nothing but the basic biological imperatives which direct physical passion towards the sole end of procreation are left standing as authentic, unadulterated nature. Like male and female in other living species, the young men and women of Tahiti simply follow the path that nature has outlined for them: 'They eat to live and grow; they grow to multiply.'[32] From the age when their bodies are mature and their sexuality has awakened they are at complete liberty to consummate their passion: 'let the good and simple inhabitants multiply without shame in the light of the day under the open sky'.[33] If the freedom that pertains to the expression of sexual desire and to the choice and change of sexual partners among the Tahitians deserves the name of a natural *morality*, it is because this unconstrained pursuit of natural human impulses accords with the demands of public utility. Against Tahiti, where numerous healthy and able-bodied children count as the most cherished good of the community, all of Europe's legal and moral regulations as well as the common standards of physical beauty stand revealed as so many artificial rules that thwart both individual and public happiness. Where women, instead of being the property of their husbands, are free to take new lovers, the 'tyranny of man'[34] sanctioned by monogamous marriage must appear as the greatest threat to liberty. Tahiti's women are treasured – and deemed beautiful and attractive – to the extent that their bodies suggest the promise of bearing strong and healthy offspring. Terms such as 'adultery' which in Europe carry the stigma of sin and crime are unknown on Tahiti. Even the taboo of incest fades away as but a distortion of a perfectly natural and innocent practice. (By the same token, on the other hand, sexual acts doomed to be unfruitful – intercourse during menstruation or with a woman beyond childbearing age – fall under public censure and even harsh punishment, like exile and enslavement.)

How much of this picture is owed to the real Tahiti? How closely does it reflect the knowledge available at this time? Diderot's *Supplement* betrays little of the traveller's ambition to convey all the details and nuances of what he has experienced. Bougainville's more balanced observations, for example, of the patriarchal structure of marriage based on a husband's far-reaching powers over his wife, and of the severe punishment which the latter's act of adultery will incur on the island,[35] do not enter Diderot's vision. Nor does he seem to entertain the doubts which trouble Forster, namely whether what is perceived by the eye of the foreign observer corresponds to the local, native meaning of a given custom. Orou is not a genuine native at all. Like Usbek in Montesquieu's fictional *Persian Letters*, he speaks in the unmistakable voice of the Enlightenment philosophe. The same confusion of perspectives occurs when the Tahitians are described as a 'people wise enough to have stopped their development at an early stage'.[36] Such wisdom could not possibly be attributed to the youthful savage tribe still in the infancy of the human race. It is a wisdom derived from the disillusionments and the self-knowledge of 'old age'.

And that is, of course, the point. In promising to show that the myth of Tahiti 'is not a myth',[37] Diderot is not concerned to convey specific factual knowledge about a particular people and its unique ways of life. He is concerned to reveal the truth about civilized Europe. The confrontation with the otherness of primitive society serves the purpose of exposing, and undermining, the false sense of superiority that Europe derives from its advanced civilization. That, however, is only possible because, unlike the savage tribe in the South Sea, the Tahitians of Diderot's fable are in an important way like us. They are, that is, what we would be had we been fortunate enough not to be drawn into the turmoils of progressive historical change. Conversely, there is the danger that they will one day be forced to be what we now are.

It is from this latter perspective that Diderot addresses the real relationship between Europe and the newly discovered world of primitive nations. The universalist principle of a common humanity and of the common destiny of the human race which, as we have just seen, impedes the understanding of primitive cultures in their own terms of reference is used to defend their identity in terms of their entitlement to their freedom, to their soil and their own ways of life. In the 'old man's farewell' Diderot launches a devastating attack not only on the political practices of European colonialism but also on the illegitimate intrusion entailed in the restless dynamic of discovery and expansion.[38] Occupation of land, plunder and the transmission of venereal diseases have laid a trail of destruction which will eventually lead to the subjugation and enslavement of the indigenous populations. Commercial relations, economic improvement and, in the last instance, the advance of knowledge have left an equally fatal legacy that is bound to subvert the self-sufficiency and moral integrity of the native culture: 'We have no wish to exchange what you call ignorance for your useless knowledge. Everything that we need and is good for us we already possess. ... Do not fill our heads with your factitious needs and illusory virtues'.[39] Enlightenment seems to turn on itself as Diderot questions the very expectations and hopes which he had once invested in the project of the *Encyclopédie*: 'to assemble knowledge ... so that our descendants, in becoming better informed, may at the same time become more virtuous and content'.[40]

GEORG FORSTER: THE REAL TAHITI

> The traveller who makes his way around all four continents will nowhere find that charming tribe that dreamers promised him in every forest and every wilderness.[41]

At the time when Diderot worked on the review of Bougainville's book, Georg Forster was sailing towards Tahiti on board Cook's ship the *Resolution*. In many respects his account of the South Sea island reads like a 'Supplement to Cook's voyage', betraying the same fascination with 'the uncorrupted children of nature' and the same mood of disenchantment towards the corrupt world left behind in Europe. Unlike Diderot, however, Forster had actually seen Tahiti with his own eyes and, in contrast with Bougainville's short stay on the island, he had had the opportunity of more extensive and repeated observation. He thus arrived at a sharper perception of the particular features of Tahitian society; and this appreciation was further enhanced by his familiarity with other primitive peoples in the Pacific region. Confronted by the considerable differences of physical appearance, language and forms of sociability that set the Tahitian apart from the native of New Zealand and New Caledonia,[42] Forster sought the explanation in different degrees of civilization. The need to place Tahiti – and any other savage society – in a context of historical development led him to abandon the divide between natural and civilized man as an erroneous assumption that could not serve the philosopher's interest in the nature of man.

In many ways Forster was the Enlightenment's philosopher traveller *par excellence*. He combined wide-ranging scholarly interests in both the sciences and the arts with the public commitment and ability of the man of letters to communicate knowledge in a lucid and accessible form. A scholar of considerable reputation – botany was his favourite discipline – he hailed the voyages of his time as pioneering expeditions into the still unknown terrains of nature and 'the history of man'.[43] Extensive travelling in Europe when still in his teens and the trained eye of the natural historian enabled him to study the social and cultural practices of primitive peoples in the same spirit of scientific curiosity and with the same attention to detail that he applied to the plants, minerals and geological formations of their natural environment. The truth of what travellers reported from foreign countries, he insisted, could only be guaranteed by the scrupulous honesty of an observer willing to let factual evidence prevail over established certainties. Yet while his explorations were thus to be driven by the quest for the most extensive information, the philosophical traveller had at the same time to search for the connecting threads that would bind the separate facts into an integrated picture of the whole: 'It was my intention to consider the nature of man from as many perspectives as possible and to find a standpoint which would allow for a comprehensive view.'[44]

Forster – and in this he but represents the distinctive aspirations of the Enlightenment scientist and philosophe – was in no doubt that the endeavour to study 'human nature in all its given forms'[45] required a supportive framework of universalist dispositions. The first was a kind of moral obligation – to safeguard the inclusiveness of observation and the impartiality of judgement in the face of unexpected and, at first impact, disquieting deviations from the familiar forms of human existence: 'All peoples of the world have the same claim on my good will.'[46] This impartiality, however, depended in the last instance upon a sentiment of universal benevolence: upon the sympathetic dispositions of a 'friend of humanity'.[47]

The first arrival at the shores of Tahiti – narrated in one of the finest pieces of German eighteenth-century prose – echoes Bougainville's enraptured impressions: 'We found that Monsieur Bougainville had not gone too far when he described this country as an earthly paradise.'[48] In Forster's description, too, the beauty of the island combines with the abundant generosity of nature under a felicitous climate and with the attractive appearance and amiable behaviour of the inhabitants to evoke all the charms of the exotic which for the European readers of this time made the South Sea a place of yearning. This first picture of the Tahitians conveys the happy simplicity of a life without want and worry: In the youthful health and serene comportment of an old man Forster finds proof that here people grow old, free from the burdens of misfortune and pain that are the predicament of old age in civilized nations;[49] women's much longer period of fertility similarly points to a life that knows of no deprivation and sorrow;[50] the observer is as struck by the undistorted expression of feelings of joy and grief in these 'uncorrupted children of nature' as by their acts of friendship and noble magnanimity towards strangers. Although his response to the manifestations of Bougainville's paradise of sexual love is visibly more reserved (as one might expect from a Protestant German's more austere notions of propriety and distrust of sensuous pleasure), he notes approvingly that 'these good people follow the impulse of nature without inhibition'.[51] On Tahiti the procreative impulse is not fettered by the adverse conditions of poverty, deprivation and anxiety which weigh on the state of marriage in civilized countries.[52] Even the unseemly lascivious behaviour that the women of the lower classes display towards the European sailors and which reminds him of the ubiquitous presence of vice in Europe's big cities must count as innocent among the Tahitians, given the naive simplicity of their moral notions and a habit of dressing that tends to emphasize the naked body rather than disguise it.[53]

As these examples show, Forster's understanding of the customs of this savage people draws on the contrast with Europe; and more often than not the comparison works to the disadvantage of the latter. But unlike Diderot (and Rousseau), he does not allow his judgement to take the side of natural simplicity and innocence against the flawed conditions of life in civilized society. Rather, the comparison serves him to establish the contextual meanings of human behaviour for both Europe and Tahiti. The destabilization of certainty which the traveller experiences in the course of the journey affects not only the self-understanding of the European. It equally turns against the cherished preconceptions of primitive society. For, as Forster's familiarity with Tahitian life grows, the shadow of disappointed expectations soon overlays the idyllic images of the first contact. On his daily excursions into the inner regions of the island he comes across instances that reveal the existence of a hierarchical system of rank, property and power where he, like Bougainville before him, had hoped to find an enclave 'of frugal equality in the sense that all classes were sharing more or less the same diet, the same pleasures, work and leisure. How fast did this beautiful vision dissolve.'[54] He finds out that the long fingernails worn by some men with visible pride mark out a group of people who do not work but live off the toil of others.[55] The offensive spectacle of a grossly obese man being fed by several servants recalls the privileged parasites in civilized countries who devour the fruits of the industrious citizen's labour.[56] Tahiti's bloody wars against neighbouring islands and, above all, the common practice of infanticide among the warrior class of the Errioys, shatter the pleasing first impressions of savage man's naturally gentle and peaceful character.[57]

Bougainville's *Nouvelle Cythère* and Diderot's refuge of a natural sexual morality do not fare much better. The Tahitian women who crowd in on the decks of the ship at night, and the men who encourage them to entertain the ship's crew, are not messengers of Venus, the goddess of hospitality (and, by implication, the Orou who offers his wife and daughters to the chaplain is not giving a gift of pure friendship). Forster detects in such dealings the unmistakable signs of prostitution – of commercial exchanges in which sexual favours are traded for much-desired European goods, such as iron tools, false pearls and pig meat (which on Tahiti was reserved to the class of the nobles).[58]

How to make sense of the real Tahiti? Forster's attempt at explanation turns in the first instance to the degeneration of indigenous habits and morals that the contact with the Europeans has brought about. Like Diderot, he depicts a vicious cycle of new desires for hitherto unknown goods, calculating commercial reasoning, theft and murder, which has been triggered by the arrival of the foreign intruders. In some passages where he reflects upon the irremediable damage that Europe's overseas expansion has inflicted upon the moral culture of savage peoples Forster goes so far as to wish that all relationships initiated by the voyages of discovery could be undone:

One should sincerely wish that the contact between the Europeans and the inhabitants of the South Sea islands was broken off in time before the corrupt manners of the civilized nations can contaminate these innocent people who live so happily in their ignorance and simplicity. But it is a sad truth that philanthropy [*Menschenliebe*] and the political systems of Europe do not accord with each other.[59]

Indeed, and as we have seen in Diderot's case, self-doubts of this kind are not confined to the corrupt politics of Europe. They extend to the conditions and costs of the project of enlightenment. If the benefits of expanding in knowledge can only be purchased for the happiness of whole nations, it would have been better – for both the dicoverers and the discovered – 'had the South Sea never become known to the restless European'.[60]

A different judgement, however, derives from the insight that some of the disturbing features that blight the image of a state of natural ignorance and simplicity must have preceded the arrival of the Europeans. The inequalities of the class system, the effects of private property and the scourge of venereal diseases have no doubt been compounded by overseas trade and inter-cultural contact. But their origins, Forster insists, are owed to the internal dynamic of a process of development which envelops Tahiti, as it does all human societies. The comparison with primitive peoples in other regions of the globe and in other periods of history reveals that all known societies have structures that prefigure those of civilized society: 'Show me the savage who has no idea of mine and thine.'[61] The direct experience of the traveller, combined with the reflections of the comparative anthropologist, expose the myth of Tahiti for what it is. What is at issue in this process of deconstruction is not merely the belief that in eighteenth-century Tahiti the European could actually still encounter man in an unadulterated natural state. Neither Diderot nor Rousseau would have held such a belief. But Forster goes one step further. He contests the legitimacy of any philosophical construct which separates human nature from the process of civilization and which finds in the life of the savage the indication of a state of greater human happiness.

In a barely veiled attack on Rousseau[62] he denounces the sophistry that philosophers have deployed to praise the advantages of an original savage state by casting it off against the ills of modern civil society. Such a view, Forster maintains, can only be held by people who have not actually seen human nature in *all* its variations. Knowledge of the harshest, least developed conditions of human existence, such as those suffered by the 'unfortunate' Pesserahs in the Tierra del Fuogo, should leave no doubt that 'we in our civilized state enjoy immeasurably greater happiness'.

Forster learns in the course of his journey that the European's perception of primitive cultures has to free itself from two constricting preconceptions. The first, and in his eyes far more damaging one, centres in the presupposition that the present political systems of Europe and its social and religious institutions could serve as the universal norm by which to judge non-developed societies. As things are, nothing entitles the European to a sense of moral superiority. Europeans will condemn the savage who eats human flesh as a monster while they themselves let thousands of human beings be slaughtered on the battle-field at the whim of a tyrannical ruler or the caprice of his mistress.[63] (Only a few years after the publication of the *Voyage* Forster would translate his radical critique of the *ancien régime* into a lasting commitment to the cause of revolutionary republicanism.) Secondly, however, in order to understand the institutions and practices of primitive peoples as they have evolved and changed over time we also have to abandon the myth of the 'charming tribe in the wilderness' and, with it, the idea that the process of civilization entails the denaturation of man.

This second emphasis enabled Forster to distinguish between the genuine benefits of civilization and the abuses to which it had given rise. The destructive effects of Europe's colonialist policies upon native peoples clearly belonged in the latter category. The advances in the sciences and arts, the development of manufacture, commerce and sociability, by contrast, could count as benefits of potentially universal value. In thus comparing and ordering the 'variations' of the human species by their different degrees of civilization Forster's observations remained Eurocentric and informed by the values of the Enlightenment. He would find evidence of an ascending line of development among primitive peoples in the enhanced skills of overcoming the adversities of their natural environment, in the evolution of agriculture, in peaceful social association and – the most frequently cited proof – in the dynamic driving towards greater equality between the sexes. One can, on the other hand, argue that goods of this kind are valuable not only within limited cultural contexts. The tangible improvement of the human condition that Enlightenment thinkers associated with the idea of civilization – and the real benefits that newly discovered peoples might derive from the contact with Europe – are recounted in Forster's concluding comments on the achievements of his voyage:

From this perspective our recent voyage was important … even if had had no other merit than that we left behind *goats* on Tahiti, *dogs* on the Friendship Islands and the New Hebrides, and *pigs* in New Zealand and

New Caledonia. It is certainly much to be wished that voyages of discovery of this kind, given to benevolent and truly useful purposes, should be continued in future.[64]

CONCLUSION: UNIVERSALISM AND
THE RECOGNITION OF DIFFERENCE

This chapter has looked at eighteenth-century voyages of discovery and their reflection in the accounts given by 'philosopher travellers'. The exploration of the South Sea islands, and the encounter with Tahiti in particular, has served as an example to show how the Enlightenment responded to the experience of cultural difference. Two centuries later, these responses are in many ways no longer adequate to the demand of conceptualizing transcultural relationships in an era of globalization. But to acknowledge this is not the same as to accuse the Enlightenment for having failed to face the reality of a multi-cultural world. As we have seen in the example of the philosopher travellers, the opposite was the case: arguments about human nature, controversies about the distinctive character of modern civilization, about Europe's past and future role in the world, were profoundly shaped by an outward-going interest in the diversity and variability of human existence.

It is true that universalist presumptions and the Eurocentric bias inherent in them prevented Enlightenment thinkers from fully coming to terms with the identity of foreign cultures at the periphery of the civilized world: to consider all peoples on the globe as but so many variations of a homogenous human species or as all part of a single story of civilization would often result in seeking the distinctive character of savage societies only in those features in which they were similar to or different from us (the Europeans). From this perspective, one would miss out on the uniquely local contexts of primitive customs, languages and religious traditions which bore no resemblance to anything Europeans were familiar with. We should, on the other hand, not use 'universalism' and 'Eurocentrism' as self-explanatory categories of judgement on the Enlightenment's engagement with other cultures. Neither the assumption of a common human nature nor the understanding of Europe's special place in the world had the status of unquestionable certainties. Rather, in the course of a voyage around the world the question of what is natural, i.e. given in the constitution of a human being, met with ever new challenges and the continuous need for boundary revision. Thus, observation of the sexual customs on Tahiti led Diderot and Forster to understand that shame and guilt were not, as assumed in the moral codes of civilized nations, universally inscribed in human nature, but were the product of social conventions. Conversely, when Forster witnessed the distressing incident of cannibalism among the Maoris of New Zealand he had to contend with the widely-held belief that such abhorrent practices cast the savage out of the domain of a common humanity. Considering the circumstances which might force primitive men into cannibalism and comparing the examples reported from various parts of the world, he came to the conclusion that it was, as such, not unnatural – and not a sign of a subhuman species – to eat human flesh.

We have also seen that the contact with primitive societies and the reflection on what made them different from civilized Europe acted as a catalyst of self-doubt that might even extend to the central hope which sustained the project of enlightenment, namely that the increase in knowledge would lead to greater virtue and happiness. If, as we see it today, it is one of the conditions of successful transcultural communication to be able to relativize one's own cultural identity, then the legacies of the sceptical Enlightenment would seem to point in just that direction.

The same applies to the political commitments in which Enlightenment universalism expressed itself. They base themselves, first, on the recognition of the irreversibility of historical processes which have brought all parts of the world into a system of interdependence and communication. Secondly, they take account of Europe's special role in making the world one – through discovery, conquest, enslavement and exploitation of non-European peoples. From the self-critical stance compelled by the knowledge of past legacies derives the notion of Europe's special responsibility for the future of global relationships. This future is conceived – by Diderot, Condorcet and Forster – in the form of a benevolent trusteeship which makes it incumbent on an enlightened Europe, as the most developed and most fortunate region, to promote the conditions of social progress in other parts of the world. It is a vision which clearly falls short of present conceptions of transcultural dialogue. The Enlightenment was not able to see all nations, each from its own centre of identity, as equal partners in a world-wide system of mutual interdependence. (Although we have to consider here that the differences that separated 'civilized' from 'savage' societies in the eighteenth century were much greater than those by which we today distinguish 'developed' from 'developing' countries.)

Finally, the political resources of Enlightenment universalism in relation to non-European peoples depended crucially upon a sentiment of universal sympathy. When Diderot and Condorcet described the project of peaceful colonization in terms of mutual friendship, or when Forster demanded that the new knowledge about primitive societies be used by the 'friends of man', they invoked a term with distinctive qualities and with an important function in Enlightenment discourses. To be a friend of humanity meant to seek extensive and impartial knowledge about other cultures, however remote and different from us. It also meant, as a matter of political practice, to recognize their claims on us. There seems to be no equivalent of 'friendship', in the sense of universal sympathy, in the present languages of politics. It is a point worth stressing when we consider the legacies of the Enlightenment.

NOTES

1. Georg Forster, *Reise um die Welt*, in Gerhard Steiner (ed.), *Georg Forster: Werke in vier Bänden* (Frankfurt am Main: Insel Verlag, 1967), vol. I, p. 332.
2. See Dorinda Outram, *The Enlightenment* (Cambridge: Cambridge University Press, 1995), p. 79; Tzvetan Todorov, *On Human Diversity: Nationalism, Racism and Exoticism in French Thought* (Cambridge, Mass.: Harvard University Press, 1993), ch. 1.
3. See Linda Nicholson, 'Introduction', in Nicholson (ed.), *Feminism/ Postmodernism* (New York and London: Routledge, 1990), pp. 1–16.
4. See Doris Kaufmann, 'Die "Wilden" in der Geschichtsschreibung und Anthropologie der "Zivilisierten"', *Historische Zeitschrift*, vol. 260, 1995, p. 53; Ulrich Beck, *Was ist Globalisierung? Irrtümer des Globalismus – Antworten auf Globalisierung* (Frankfurt am Main: Suhrkamp Verlag, 1997), p. 136.
5. P.J. Marshall and Glyndwr Williams, *The Great Map of Mankind: Perceptions of the New Worlds in the Age of Enlightenment* (Cambridge, Mass.: Harvard University Press, 1982), p. 212.
6. See Ralph-Rainer Wuthenow, *Die erfahrene Welt: Europäische Reiseliteratur im Zeitalter der Aufklärung* (Frankfurt am Main: Insel Verlag, 1980), pp. 16ff, 207ff; Marshall and Williams, *Great Map of Mankind*, ch. 2.
7. Forster, *Reise um die Welt*, p. 17.
8. Kant, 'Anthropologie in pragmatischer Absicht', in Wilhelm Weischedel (ed.), *Immanuel Kant: Werke* (Frankfurt am Main: Suhrkamp Verlag, 1964), vol. 12, p. 400.
9. 'Extracts from the *Histoire des Deux Indes*', in John Hope Mason and Robert Wokler (eds), *Denis Diderot: Political Writings* (Cambridge: Cambridge University Press, 1992), p. 197.
10. See Urs Bitterli, *Die 'Wilden' und die 'Zivilisierten': Grundzüge einer Geistes- und Kulturgeschichte der europäisch-überseeischen Begegnung* (München: C.H. Beck, 2nd edn, 1991); Jürgen Osterhammel, 'Kulturelle Grenzen in der Expansion Europas', *Saeculum*, vol. 46 (1), 1995, pp. 101–38.

11. See Benedict Anderson, *Imagined Communities: Reflections on the Origin and Spread of Nationalism* (London–New York: Verso, rev. edn, 1991), pp. 12–19.
12. Quoted in Wuthenow, *Erfahrene Welt*, p. 41.
13. Condorcet, *Sketch for a Historical Picture of the Progress of the Human Mind*, trans. June Barraclough (London: Weidenfeld and Nicolson, 1955), p. 104.
14. See Urs Bitterli, *Alte Welt – neue Welt: Formen des europäisch-überseeischen Kulturkontaktes vom 15. bis zum 18. Jahrhundert* (München: C.H. Beck, 1986), p. 191.
15. Edmund Burke in a letter to William Robertson; quoted in Marshall and Williams, *Great Map of Mankind*, p. 93.
16. 'For no other region do we have such detailed and thoughtful accounts of the indigenous inhabitants over a short period of time': Marshall and Williams, *Great Map of Mankind*, p. 258.
17. Forster, *Reise um die Welt*, pp. 997ff.
18. See O.K.H. Spade, *Paradise Found and Lost* (*The Pacific since Magellan*, vol. 3) (Minneapolis: University of Minnesota Press, 1988), ch. 11.
19. See Uwe Japp, 'Aufgeklärtes Europa und natürliche Südsee. Georg Forsters "Reise um die Welt"', in Hans Joachim Piechotta (ed.), *Reise und Utopie: Zur Literatur der Spätaufklärung* (Frankfurt am Main: Suhrkamp Verlag, 1976), pp. 10–56; Wuthenow, *Erfahrene Welt*, ch. 4.
20. See Forster, *Reise um die Welt*, sections 8 and 9; for extracts from Louis Antoine de Bougainville, *Voyage Autour du Monde* (1771), see Wuthenow, *Erfahrene Welt*, pp. 212–25; for the accounts given by other travellers, see Marshall and Williams, *Great Map of Mankind*, ch. 9; Spade, *Paradise*, ch. 11.
21. Diderot, 'The *Supplément au Voyage de Bougainville*', in Hope Mason and Wokler, *Diderot: Political Writings*, pp. 35–75; quote at p. 40.
22. Diderot, *Supplement*, p. 36.
23. Bougainville, *Voyage*, quoted in Wuthenow, *Erfahrene Welt*, p. 213.
24. Spade, *Paradise*, p. 237.
26. For the relevant passages from Bougainville's *Voyage*, see Wuthenow, *Erfahrene Welt*, pp. 213–25.
26. See Marshall and Williams, *Great Map of Mankind*, p. 267.
27. For the enduring impact of the classical tradition upon European accounts of primitive peoples, see Wolfgang Haase/Meyer Reinhold (eds), *The Classical Tradition in the Americas, vol. I, part 1: European Images of the Americas and the Classical Tradition* (Berlin–New York, 1994); for the part played by this tradition in the discovery of Tahiti, see Marshall and Williams, *Great Map of Mankind*, pp. 270ff, 277.
28. See the full title of the work: 'Supplement to the voyage of Bougainville, or dialogue between A and B on the appropriateness of attaching moral ideas to certain physical actions that do not accord with them', Hope Mason and Wokler, *Diderot*, p. 35.
29. See the editors' Introduction to Hope Mason and Wokler, *Diderot: Political Writings*, pp. xv–xxi.
30. Diderot, *Supplement*, p. 67.

31.   For Condorcet, see *Progress of the Human Mind*, pp. 27–8; for Forster: *Reise um die Welt*, pp. 753, 772, 779ff, 812, 852, 862; for Adam Smith and the Scottish Enlightenment: Jane Rendall, 'Virtue and Commerce: Women in the Making of Adam Smith's Political Economy', in Ellen Kennedy and Susan Mendus (eds), *Women in Western Political Philosophy* (Brighton: Wheatsheaf Books, 1987), pp. 44–77; Silvana Tomaselli, 'The Enlightenment Debate on Women', *History Workshop*, 20 (1985), pp. 147–9.

32.   Diderot, *Supplement*, p. 44.

33.   Ibid.

34.   Diderot, *Supplement*, p. 70.

35.   Bougainville, *Voyage*, in Wuthenow, *Erfahrene Welt*, p. 221.

36.   Diderot, *Supplement*, p. 66.

37.   Diderot, *Supplement*, p. 41.

38.   See Diderot, *Supplement*, pp. 41–5.

39.   Diderot, *Supplement*, p. 43.

40.   Diderot, 'Encyclopédie', in 'Articles from the *Encyclopédie*', Hope Mason and Wokler, *Diderot*, pp. 21ff.

41.   Georg Forster, 'Cook, der Entdecker', in Forster, *Werke*, vol. 2, p. 181.

42.   See Forster, *Reise um die Welt*, pp. 189–221, 688–702.

43.   Forster, *Reise um die Welt*, pp. 11ff; 'Cook, der Entdecker', pp. 189–224.

44.   Forster, *Reise um die Welt*, p. 17.

45.   Ibid., p. 923.

46.   Ibid., p. 18.

47.   Ibid., p.12.

48.   Ibid., p. 254.

49.   Ibid., pp. 265ff.

50.   Ibid., p. 310.

51.   Ibid., p. 587.

52.   Ibid., p. 329.

53.   Ibid., p. 307.

54.   Ibid., pp. 275ff.

55.   Ibid., p. 265.

56.   Ibid., p. 276.

57.   Ibid., pp. 617ff.

58.   Ibid., pp. 307ff.

59.   Ibid., p. 281.

60.   Ibid., p. 332.

61.   Forster, 'Cook, der Entdecker', p. 181.

62.   Forster, *Reise um die Welt*, pp. 923ff.

63.   Ibid., pp. 447ff.

64.   Ibid., p. 21.

2 Education Can Do All
Geraint Parry

'Education can do all' (*l'éducation peut tout*) is one of the most celebrated phrases in the history of educational thought. It comes from the title of chapter I of section X of Helvétius' *De l'homme, de ses facultés intellectuelles et de son éducation* (1772; citations are from the 1773 edition). The remark seems to encapsulate the transformative ambitions of Enlightenment thought. Education could be seen as a means of imprinting truth and virtue on the minds of the rising generation and extirpating prejudice at its roots. The potential of education had been expressed by Helvétius in an earlier passage in the book:

> If I can demonstrate that man is, in fact, nothing more than the product of his education, I shall doubtless reveal an important truth to the nations. They will learn that they have in their hands the instrument of their greatness and their felicity, and that to be happy and powerful, it is only a matter of perfecting the science of education. (Helvétius 1773: I, 3)

This excitement at the possibilities afforded by education permeates eighteenth-century writings on the subject and is one of the Enlightenment's most important legacies. The Age of Enlightenment was also an Age of Pedagogy. The very term 'enlightenment' implies an educative task of enlightening, and Kant's celebrated definition of it as an exodus from a condition of immaturity or tutelage to one of autonomy points to a process whereby mankind is led or leads itself to a new understanding of the world. However, the same confidence that education could 'do all' also gave rise to programmes, based on novel techniques of teaching, designed to achieve the re-socialization of populations so that they would find their own happiness in the pursuit of the interests of the state. As the remark of Helvétius appears to imply, education could be the means whereby peoples might be mobilized in the pursuit of the typical goals of modernity – progress, power and prosperity.

It is therefore not surprising that the onslaught in recent times on what critics of the Enlightenment term the 'Enlightenment Project' should have included education amongst its targets. As one recent study of postmodernism and education puts it:

> Education is very much the dutiful child of the Enlightenment and, as such, tends to uncritically accept a set of assumptions deriving from

Enlightenment thought. Indeed it is possible to see education as the vehicle by which the Enlightenment ideas of critical reason, humanistic individual freedom and benevolent progress are substantiated and realised. (Usher and Edwards 1994: 24)

Following the Enlightenment, the task of education has been widely perceived as assisting rational human beings to realize their potential, to exercise moral agency, to become autonomous. However, virtually every one of these terms of educational thought has become, in a favourite word of postmodernism, 'problematized'. Usher and Edwards go on to cite another commentator as stating that the postmodern critique 'stabs at the heart of the most cherished ideals of Western culture [particularly that of personal autonomy] as an educational goal' (Lovlie 1992: 121, cited in Usher and Edwards 1994: 25).

Hence Enlightenment education is complicit in the various alleged failures of the whole Enlightenment Project. These failings are many. Whilst the Enlightenment, it is said, presented itself as emancipating human beings from prejudice and uncovering natural man, in reality this new subject was a construct of which education was an artificer. To produce this subject required discipline in certain modes of thinking and behaviour which were to become norms. Amongst the objectives of such education was to empower those who conformed to those norms in order that they might master nature in the name of progress. In the pursuit of these goals, however, the Enlightenment, and those educated in its wake, are accused of having ignored plurality and diversity, of having propounded an abstract individualism which neglects the manner in which people are embedded in communities and cultures and, worst of all, of having been the source of a utopian conception of technological control over the social order which culminated in the horrors of twentieth-century totalitarianism. The upshot of these attacks (admittedly an amalgam of different critiques) is, according to Peter McLaren, a leading figure in contemporary 'critical pedagogy', that:

> The Faustian dream of imposing master codes of Enlightenment reasoning (in the guise of a Western hyper-rationalism) on the indeterminacy of social and cultural life has become a nightmare ... (McLaren 1995: 17)

Amongst the most plausible of these identifications of an Enlightenment Project is that presented by Michel Foucault. Unlike many other accounts of the Enlightenment in this literature, Foucault's work is based on some genuine research into the practices and mentalities of the period (Foucault

1991). It has received support from other historically aware postmodernist writers such as Zygmunt Bauman (Bauman 1992). Foucault's arguments have, moreover, found favour with major scholars of the period such as James Tully (Tully 1993: 179–241). There are also distinct affinities with the work of the notable historian of the early modern era, Gerhard Oestreich (Oestreich 1982). Although Foucault's *Discipline and Punish* is ostensibly concerned with, as its subtitle indicates, the 'birth of the prison', it contains an extensive discussion of schools as institutions of discipline. Its crucial chapter takes, as the peg on which to hang its argument, Bentham's Panopticon which, as well as being a model for a well-supervised prison, was also appropriate for a school (Bentham 1983: 106). Indeed, one commentator has declared that

> Foucault really discovered something very simple (but highly unfamiliar nonetheless) – the centrality of education in the construction of modernity. (Hoskin 1990: 29)

The key to Foucault's work in this area is his coupling of power and knowledge in a reciprocal relationship. Knowledge is dependent on the exercise of power and in turn legitimates power.

> Each society has its regime of truth, its general politics of truth: that is, the types of discourse which it accepts and makes function as true... (Foucault 1980: 131)

The way in which this power–knowledge relationship is operationalized is through disciplines. Foucault exploits the dual, but related, meaning of 'discipline' as both a mode of regulation or control and a body of knowledge. In the sense of a systematic body of knowledge, a discipline orders this knowledge, sets certain boundaries to it and lays down rules for its acquisition. These are norms which the noviciate must accept in order to be recognized as a master or mistress of that knowledge. He or she must, in the time-honoured phrase of British universities, 'satisfy the examiners'. Hence the effectiveness of a discipline is not so much through the use of coercion as it is a result of the subject's commitment to its norms.

Although disciplines had existed for centuries in monasteries and armies, Foucault contends that 'in the course of the seventeenth and eighteenth centuries the disciplines became general formulas of domination' (Foucault 1991: 137). It is in this period that the 'disciplinary society' is created. This is a society permeated with disciplinary institutions, including not only prisons and armies but new modes of factory production and schools. These disciplines produce docile subjects, i.e. those taught through the disciplines and, indeed, produced by them (Foucault 1991: 194). Such products are subjected to surveillance, inspection and examination. The consequence is that the period of the Enlightenment, instead of being one of emancipation of the autonomous agent, is portrayed as an era in which individuals were more comprehensively and subtly controlled. The autonomous agent is in reality a subject produced by disciplinary society who will, moreover, ideally discipline himself or herself to obey the norms which are inculcated.

In the remainder of this essay I wish to look at the educational thought of the Enlightenment in order to uncover how far the Foucauldian story of education as discipline is plausible, or whether the traditional emancipatory picture survives as the more accurate account of its legacy. Or perhaps it is a bit of both. Foucault himself noted, without sufficient further exploration, that

> The Enlightenment, which discovered the liberties, also invented the disciplines. (Foucault 1991: 222)

That Foucault's observation has considerable force appears to gain support from the fact that in exploring both the liberties and the disciplines the same Enlightenment texts are often at issue.

In part, however, Foucault's claim that the Enlightenment and its legacy of modernity is permeated by disciplinary practices gains credence from the ambiguities in the idea of discipline. Eighteenth-century programmes of positive education can be seen as systems of discipline intended to produce ordered but progressive populations. At the same time the belief in the emancipatory power of education was also accompanied by the conviction that this could not be achieved without its own form of discipline. The Enlightenment was a project of education – something recognized from the outset not only by its protagonists but, quite explicitly, in Edmund Burke's conservative critique (Burke 1987: 130). The critical spirit it sought to disseminate involved learning a disciplined manner of thinking which its advocates believed necessary to successful emancipation. Yet to the critics of the Enlightenment, then and now, the effect of this combination of discipline and critique has been both to subvert older disciplines and the social order they underpinned and to install a new set of disciplines which delegitimized alternative ways of thinking and feeling. A new intellectual elite was alleged to have emerged which threatened to exercise a hegemony over thought which could extend into a form of absolute political domination justified by its employment of the findings of modern knowledge in the pursuit of the 'real' or 'enlightened' interest of the subjects.

ENLIGHTENMENT EDUCATION AND DISCIPLINE

This essay will take the more overtly disciplinary story first and then the emancipatory. For both it is necessary to start with John Locke, since the *Essay Concerning Human Understanding*, *Of the Conduct of the Understanding* and *Some Thoughts Concerning Education* together formed the foundation works of eighteenth-century educational theory. *Some Thoughts Concerning Education* of 1693 was in its fifth edition by 1705 and was reprinted some twenty times during the century, apart from its inclusion in Locke's collected works. Pierre Coste's French translation appeared in 1695 and went through repeated printings. The Italian version came out in 1735 and was in its sixth edition by 1792, and German, Dutch and Swedish translations were also rapidly made available. Although in itself an occasional work, indebted to Montaigne and Comenius, the prestige of *Some Thoughts* was, of course, due to its coming from the pen of the author of the *Essay*. Moreover the *Essay* is itself replete with illustrative examples drawn from the learning processes of children.

The positive role of education (and the kernel of a disciplinary interpretation of the educational project) is stated in the opening paragraph of *Some Thoughts* – a paragraph cited repeatedly in educational treatises throughout the century:

> of all the Men we meet with, Nine Parts out of Ten are what they are, Good or Evil, useful or not, by their Education. (Locke 1989: para. 1)

It is education which makes the great difference amongst mankind. Consistently with the *tabula rasa* doctrine of the *Essay* the educator is able to consider the child 'only as white Paper, or Wax, to be moulded or fashioned as one pleases' (Locke 1989: para. 217).

The meaning which Locke gave to the ancient *tabula rasa* metaphor was that at birth the child possesses virtually no ideas of the world and none concerning logical or moral principles (Locke 1979: 2.1.2). The mind acquires ideas from experience which comes, initially, from external objects whose features are conveyed to us through the senses and, secondly, from reflection on the internal operations of the mind. The child's experience in the womb may result in its gaining certain ideas of hunger, thirst and warmth (Locke 1979: 1.2.4) but otherwise the newborn child's understanding is formed as a result of its gradual coming to familiarity with the qualities of external objects. Children are additionally equipped with a capacity to experience pleasure and pain. The great variety of external factors which surround the child ensure that a 'variety of *Ideas*, whether care be taken about it or no, are imprinted on the Minds of

Children' (Locke 1979: 2.1.6). At first these ideas are like 'floating Visions' and 't'is pretty late' before children get ideas of their own minds and begin to reflect and put order and constancy into their thoughts (Locke 1979: 2.1.8).

This brief résumé is perhaps enough to suggest three profound implications for education – egalitarianism, malleability and control, and developmentalism.

The egalitarian implication is that differences between human achievements are nine-tenths due to the different opportunities persons have of experiencing a variety of external stimuli. What differentiates the country gentleman (for whom Locke wrote his educational thoughts) from the day-labourer is not any natural gifts but the greater opportunities to employ them. The vast bulk of the poor lack the leisure to cultivate their minds and are condemned 'by the natural and unalterable State of Things in this World and the Constitution of humane Affairs' to labour to fill their stomachs (Locke 1979: 4.20.2; also *Reasonableness of Christianity, Works* VII: 157–8). Even amongst the gentry, those most exposed to the variety of affairs are more knowledgeable than those who confine themselves to hunting and drinking claret. This also implies that differences between people are attributable to the extent to which they employ or neglect their understandings. One task of education will be to develop the practice of the mental faculties in constructing complex and abstract ideas.

The second implication follows from the first and can be summed up in the title of John Passmore's famous paper as 'the malleability of man' (Passmore 1965; see also Passmore 1970: 149–89). The careful management of the child's experiences could shape its understanding in the directions desired by parents, tutors and the society at large. The extent of such management might, in principle, be almost unlimited since all experiences are educative. When Enlightenment theorists write of the power of education they refer to the total effect of the environment in shaping the mind. In stricter terms, however, it would imply the control of a more specific environment – the choice of teacher or school, of playmates and friends, of reading, travel and all exposure to example or what nowadays would be called 'role models'. All of these matters are considered by Locke and his successors.

The third implication is that such management must take heed of the stages in the mental development of the child. It does not develop reflection for some time. The child is living in a foreign country and needs a guide who will gently steer its natural curiosity (Locke 1989: para. 120). Children have to learn gradually to apply themselves. It is counterproductive to teach them beyond their capacities. What moves children, and adults, is pleasure and pain. The tutor should seek to make learning gentle and pleasurable. Hence Locke's influential, if not entirely original, advocacy of play as a means of education. Learning should not be a burden to the child. It should be 'cozened' into it (Locke 1989: para. 149).

This itself can be regarded as a form of discipline. Thus Bourdieu and Passeron argue that to

> overwhelm one's pupils with affection ... is to gain possession of that subtle instrument of repression, the withdrawal of affection, a pedagogical technique which is no less arbitrary ... than corporal punishment or disgrace. (Bourdieu and Passeron 1977: 17)

It is as the child grows older, Locke argues, that more formal learning becomes possible and that it can be increasingly treated as an adult agent.

The essential element in education is not, however, the acquisition of knowledge but the inculcation of habits. These are habits of study, habits of behaviour and habits of virtue in general. Habits have to be learned but cannot be acquired by rote. The objective is to make certain behaviour second nature. The prime way of developing such habits is through repeated practice, whether of study or of moral conduct (Locke 1989: para. 64). It is just like dancing on a rope – a matter of hard work. In some cases the same fault must be overcome in study as in morality, such as the tendency to inattention or 'sauntering'.

But what is the measure of mastery in any field? For the most part it is the good opinion of society. In morality the ultimate test of the good is to be found in the law of nature. This should guide all human conduct. It cannot be identified with any human consensus on proper behaviour, since Locke always reminded his readers of examples of societies which seemed to ignore the instructions of natural law. Nevertheless, Locke asserted that the *terms* 'virtue' and 'vice' are in all societies those used to describe conduct which is considered praiseworthy or blameworthy. They are employed according to the 'Law of Opinion or Reputation' (Locke 1979: 2.28.7–12). In *Some Thoughts* Locke states that 'though it be not the true Principle and Measure of Virtue ... yet it is that which comes nearest to it' (Locke 1989: para. 61).

In the *Essay* opinion and reputation are described as a process which 'by a secret and tacit consent' sets up the standards of behaviour in societies. People may hope to reconcile themselves with God for their crimes or may expect to avoid the civil law, but no one escapes 'the Punishment of their Censure and Dislike, who offends against the Fashion and Opinion of the Company he keeps'. The condemnation of his club or his society is more than anyone can suffer (Locke 1979: 2.28.12). For these reasons reputation

> being the Testimony and Applause that other People's Reason, as it were by common Consent, gives to virtuous and well-ordered Actions, it is the proper Guide and Encouragement of Children ... (Locke 1989: para. 61)

Hence Locke recommends the use of praise and loss of esteem as the means of inculcating habits, rather than physical punishment or even trying to instil rules (Locke 1989: para. 56).

Children find pleasure in receiving their parents' approval and experience pain when it is withheld or when they suffer shame or disgrace. The regular use of these methods will guide the child into behaviour which will be commended by society at large. This has a double effect when children are praised in public (though they should not be similarly shamed). In turn this policy implies that persons should take care in selecting the company they keep so that their circle will reinforce the habits acquired at home:

> we are all a sort of Camelions, that still take a Tincture from things near us: Nor is it to be wonder'd at in Children, who better understand what they see than what they hear. (Locke 1989: para. 67)

These passages therefore give support to a Foucauldian interpretation of Locke's objectives advanced by some recent scholars. James Tully, in an essay dedicated to the memory of Foucault, argues that the love of reputation is 'the basis for subtle, detailed, and closely supervised governing of drill and repetition' (Tully 1993: 232). Uday Singh Mehta suggests that Locke is seeking to internalize feelings of shame and guilt and that his 'pedagogical project' articulates attempts to 'mold or homogenize individual reason' (Mehta 1992: 157). Still more forcefully:

> For Locke, individuals are formed by embedding them within, and by their internalizing, the minutiae of a complex constellation of social structures and conventional norms. (Mehta 1992: 170)

On such evidence Locke is contributing to a project which will unite self-love and love of the social. It is one in which reputation and opinion play crucial roles as regulators of human conduct. Moreover Locke's significance lies in his being the source of a parallel movement in France and Britain in educational ideas. In France Locke's influence was mediated by Condillac and reaches Helvétius and other proponents of positive education. In Britain the mediator was Hartley and the ultimate disciples include Priestley, Catharine Macaulay, Bentham, down to James Mill. Both Condillac and Hartley modified Locke by arguing that all ideas, including those Locke attributed to reflection, originated in sense impressions. This radical sensationalism permitted a still more radical assessment of the positive potential of education.

Helvétius in *De L'Esprit* (1758) and *De L'Homme* (1773) argued that sensation and memory are the causes of all ideas. Self-love and interest prompt us to pay attention to certain sensations and seek to recall them because of their pleasurable effects. All conduct is reducible to this desire to experience pleasurable sensations. Morality is the pursuit of the public interest or the happiness of the greatest number (Helvétius 1773: II, 10–11). Private happiness and morality can be aligned to ensure that we discover a pleasurable sensation in the pursuit of the public good.

The power of education arises because of its capacity to restructure the sensations a person experiences in ways beneficial to society. Humans at birth are equal in their lack of ideas. Hence, 'Quintillian, Locke and I say' that inequalities in understanding are the consequence of the single cause of education (Helvétius 1773: I, 78). Whilst no one receives exactly the same education, because experiences in life are never precisely identical, the skilled educator can employ the methods of nature to achieve specific objectives. By the repetition of striking sensations certain ideas can be implanted in the memory. Tastes can gradually be fixed through the combined operation of environmental factors which include rank, wealth, associations, friends and reading, as well as mistresses!

The supreme educative responsibility is that of government which is, and should be, the major influence on manners. Morality is the science of living in peace. For this a public (i.e. school) education is preferable to domestic education. The family bond should yield to the love of country which can more effectively be promoted in schools, provided the state is prepared to spend enough to pay for good teachers. The school can expose the child to a consistent set of stimuli. It might do this by a moral catechism, the repetition of which would engrave useful precepts and principles on the mind (just as religious catechisms are used to engrave the most ridiculous beliefs). Ultimately the objective would be a moral dictionary which could fix the meanings of words and would show principles of morality to be as demonstrable as those of geometry. Everyone would share the same ideas of morality because all would see the same relations between objects. Once translated in all the languages it would destroy scholasticism and metaphysics (Helvétius 1773: II, 168–70).

Here, it seems, we have the outlines of Foucault's panopticism – a public education in virtue, the sovereign as lexicographer (an idea which Hobbes had already propounded). In 1763 La Chalotais, likewise building on premisses derived from Condillac, had proposed his widely admired system of national education based on the 'inalienable and imprescriptible right' of every nation to instruct its members. The 'children of the state' should be taught only by citizens of the state and from state-approved text-books (La Chalotais 1932: 53). Philipon De La Madelaine declared that 'children belong more to the republic than to their parents' (Philipon De La Madelaine 1782: 12). The most extreme, totalizing implications of such theories were to be drawn in the French Revolutionary era by Michel Le Pelletier in his *Plan d'Education Nationale* with its proposals for compulsory state boarding schools for all children. They would be received 'from the hands of nature' at the age of five and given back 'to society' at twelve, having been taught in conditions of absolute equality and austerity the rudiments of learning and the basics of morality. Away from its parents, the child's existence belongs to society, and 'the material ... never leaves its mould' (Le Pelletier 1793: 8–10; 22). The object was a complete regeneration and the creation of a 'new people'. The as yet unfulfilled potential of education was deplored by Helvétius:

> Man is too often unknown to him who governs him. However to direct the motions of the human puppet it is necessary to know the strings by which he is moved. Deprived of this knowledge it is not to be wondered that his motions are often so contrary to those the legislator requires. (Helvétius 1773: I, 4)

The parallel movement in ideas in Britain was to draw some different policy conclusions from this shared confidence about the power of education. Distinctive to British educational philosophy was its employment of the doctrine of the association of ideas which David Hartley had derived from Locke (whilst giving it a rather different turn). According to Hartley sensations are the result of vibrations in the brain transmitted through the ether. Ideas are the product of repeated sensations which leave traces in the brain. Certain powerful and repeated sensations are associated together, and any one of these will trigger off corresponding ideas. Sensations may be pleasurable or painful. Consequently there will be regular associations of ideas such as those of fire, heat and pain. Children come to learn these. The acquisition of language to designate ideas results in associations of ideas with words.

If it were possible for persons to be exposed to precisely the same impressions and experiences the differences between them would disappear. Alternatively, if it were possible to work backwards from the affections and passions through to the associations which lay behind them we could, Hartley suggests, learn

> how to cherish and improve good ones, check and root out such as are mischievous and immoral, and how to suit our manner of life, in some

tolerable measure, to our intellectual and religious wants. And as this holds, in respect of persons of all ages, so it is particularly true, and worthy of consideration, in respect of children and youth. (Hartley 1749: 52)

The young could be deconstructed and reconstructed to experience those sensations and produce those ideas consistent with virtue.

Hartley offered educationalists an exciting technology to effect mental and moral transformation. Catharine Macaulay justified adding to the many writings on education on the grounds that they could now be founded on the discoveries of modern philosophy of the mind. Without this the tutor could not manage the mental faculties so as to 'invariably produce volitions agreeable to the laws of virtue and prudence' (Macaulay 1790: ii). Joseph Priestley argued in the same vein that political knowledge is based upon the knowledge of human nature derived from 'Mr Hobbes, Mr Locke, and, above all, Dr Hartley' (Priestley 1780: 27). Their discoveries had established that the differences in moral values between individuals and societies are the consequence of habituation since childhood. Hence the end of education, Priestley says, is to

inculcate such principles and lead to such habits, as will enable men to pass with integrity, and real honour through life, and to be inflexibly just, benevolent and good... (Priestley 1780: xiii)

This is achieved by what he terms 'artificial education' which communicates knowledge more rapidly and consistently than 'natural education', i.e. the experience of ordinary life. The repetition of sensations and associations should commence early in childhood because later ideas have to fight against those already implanted. Here Priestley is led in a direction strongly opposed by Locke (and by Rousseau). It is not the case (as Locke had claimed) that one cannot teach a child ideas until it has reached a condition when it is capable of understanding them. Children see things and hear words before grasping their significance. This can be used to prepare them for a fuller understanding. So, accustoming the child to such outward forms as kneeling in church gradually imposes on its mind that some form of reverence is due to divine power. Similarly, bonfires on the Fifth of November in Britain accustom the child to an 'abhorrence of arbitrary power' before it can understand the period and circumstances the festivities commemorate (Priestley 1780: 87–9). Priestley admits without qualms that

in this method, we take an unfair advantage of the imbecility of the rational faculties, and inculcate truth by such a kind of mechanical prejudice as would enforce the belief of any thing... (Priestley 1780: 90)

To this implied objection Priestley responds that *all* education of children involves 'prejudicing them in favour of our own opinions and practices' (Priestley 1780: 90). The first stage in education must be to habituate children to authority, rewarding positively evaluated conduct and penalizing that which is condemned by right-thinking society. Once again the pleasure–pain calculus is consulted by the educator to ensure support for what Priestley terms 'competent authority'.

Developments in the German-speaking countries were the outcome of a confluence of a number of more varied streams of ideas. They added up to perhaps the most formidable instance of the disciplinary perception of education. Locke's educational writings were but one of the influences which went to make up, along with Rousseau and La Chalotais, the eclectic amalgam which constituted German progressive education, best represented by Johann Bernhard Basedow. He was an educational entrepreneur, founder of an advanced school in Dessau admired by Kant, and author of a vast range of treatises, including what would nowadays probably be described as an 'integrated learning package' of textbooks with illustrated supplements and manuals for teachers and parents (as well as a text on the education of princes – which could be construed as a 'niche market' in eighteenth-century Germany).

Basedow was in many respects a typical *Aufklärung* figure of the second or third rank – totally unoriginal but absorbing and reproducing many of its mildly liberal, vaguely progressive outlooks (albeit too progressive for his conservative critics). Although a fervent cosmopolitan, he was able to accommodate this with support for state supervision (*Staatsaufsicht*) of education, as an aspect of the nation's general responsibility for morality. He proposed a state council which would have the function of advising on the upbringing, in the widest sense, of subjects (Basedow 1771: 384–422). Civic virtue and happiness, he argued, depended on education which could not be left in the hands of churches which are partial associations within the state. Included in the council's educational remit are not only schools but almshouses, orphanages and theatres – every institution capable of influencing morality. In Rousseauian spirit the council should establish annual festivals of the fatherland for which schools should prepare the children with patriotic stories and songs and at which prizes should be awarded to deserving children. The council should also be responsible for approving the textbooks to be used in the nation's schools.

Basedow's teaching books provided the appropriate moral grounding (as well as an encyclopaedic introduction to most of the curriculum). Games offer opportunities for lessons in good conduct – with some sample 'scripts' suggesting, in total contrast to the spontaneity wished for by

Rousseau, how the 'games' should proceed. Stories, accompanied with copperplate illustrations, explain the concept of property, crime and punishment and the role of 'fathers of the country' as wise men caring for the families of the nation (Basedow 1774). In moral education the aim is not to teach children to fear God, or to pursue perfection, but to persuade them that their own happiness will be found through obeying parents, cultivating the favour of those who can influence their fate and doing good to others. Once again the guiding principle is the unity of self-love with social utility.

Whatever the sources of Basedow's progressivist position, in very many respects its conclusions coincided with the treatment of education by the theorists of Prussian and Austrian 'enlightenment absolutism'. To the degree that these regimes were theorized it was by an amalgam of traditional ideas of Christian patriarchal rule, Pietist theology and eighteenth-century rationalism. The result was the most comprehensive theoretical exposition of the disciplined, supervised state. Although the elements of the theory may seem to be in tension, recent scholarship has shown the degree to which they were mutually reinforcing (Melton 1988; Raeff 1983; Tribe 1988; Oestreich 1982; Neugebauer 1985).

Traditional patriarchalism viewed the country as a landed estate under the benevolent care of its ruler who concerned himself with his resources, including the social and moral well-being of his personnel, or subjects. To this, Pietist theology added a powerful and austere conception of the distinctive callings of the ruler and of the estates of the realm. The rationalist proto-utilitarian philosophy of Christian Wolff saw the state as an association created to promote human happiness which included the welfare of the subjects. Elements from each of these approaches came together in 'Cameralism', the distinctive German theory of the absolutist, authoritarian, welfare state best represented in Prussia by Justi and in Austria by Sonnenfels.

The Cameralist state is the prime instance of what Michael Oakeshott has described as an enterprise association (a corporation which has a purpose) rather than a civil association under the rule of law with no purposes of its own (Oakeshott 1975). From the purpose of the promotion of the happiness of individuals and of the collectivity, the Cameralists derived a top-down disciplinary system which would stimulate economic growth, care for the poor and infirm, ensure a healthy environment (clean air, well-planned towns, etc.) and raise the revenues for the defence of the realm (Parry 1963). Education fell within what was understood as the 'police' function of the state and was often coupled with religion as measures to ensure public morality (Justi 1760: para. 277; Sonnenfels 1768: I, 106). Religion explained that the subjects had a duty under God to uphold the political order and perform the obligations of their station. Education was aimed at making useful subjects by developing the skills needed by society and teaching the inhabitants to identify their own good with that of the state (Justi 1755: I, 348–61). Sonnenfels would have liked a 'political catechism' for schools laying out the duties of citizens (Sonnenfels 1768: I, 117).

All this remained firmly within a functionalist defence of the system of estates. One consequence was that, as also for the most part amongst the French *philosophes*, a commitment to education for all children did not mean that all children were to receive the same education, but instead one fitted to their standing, function and calling. In the case of the poor this meant restriction to the 'three Rs' at best.

The Pietist input was designed to reinforce this conception of the calling of each person and rank in the social system (Oschlies 1969). Fulfilment of a calling required that one was fully and internally committed to seeing one's specific vocation as part of the divine order. Pietist education was developed in Halle from 1695 by August Hermann Francke in his schools and orphanages. For Francke education commenced by breaking the will of the child, as it carried original sin, and reforming it (Francke 1733). Once the will was broken nothing could in principle impede the educational project. The major danger was corruption from the environment which had therefore to be as strictly controlled as possible both within the classroom and outside, supplemented by constant inspection and especially excluding parental interference (Oschlies 1969: 110–12). However the object was not to teach simply by rote but to engage the pupil's full understanding and commitment. Thus Francke's catechism was taught Socratically with questions intended to discover whether the child had genuinely grasped its meaning. This understanding would then extend to the structure of authority in the state.

The importance of education to the absolutist regimes lay therefore in its possibility of supplementing the coercive discipline of the state by self-discipline (Melton 1988: xxi–xxii). In a so-called age of enlightenment likely to be sceptical of authority, it would teach the new generation to respect the functions of government in a new way. The Physiocrat Le Mercier de la Rivière, in his treatise on public instruction written for the King of Sweden, perceived the issue with particular clarity. Moral man is an entirely artificial creation since what counts as morality is what is honoured by public opinion. Self-love (*amour-propre*) drives us to seek public esteem:

> Thus it is by means of *amour propre* that opinion becomes in reality the Queen of the World, a despotic power which governs us at its will.
> (Le Mercier de la Rivière 1775: 33)

Education will instruct new subjects how they will find happiness by conduct which society honours. An educational apparatus which stretches from political catechisms in schools to public parks and monuments will tie knots which will bind the subjects to the state and replace coercion by consent. Once shown this route, the citizens will rush to find their happiness in the state and it will no longer be necessary to 'employ against them force and violence, torture and the gallows' (Le Mercier de la Rivière 1775: 42).

The evidence that education was seen as an apparatus of discipline and surveillance in the period of the Enlightenment appears formidable. Pedagogy seems concerned with refining the technology whereby malleable subjects can be persuaded to discover their happiness by conforming, with an appearance of consent and autonomy, either to the standards of public opinion or to those propounded by the absolutist state. The discipline of the state might appear the more concentrated and overt, but that of opinion will be the more pervasive and perhaps the more absolute. Is this, therefore, the Enlightenment Project? Before reaching that conclusion it is necessary to look back at other dimensions of Enlightenment pedagogy, even sometimes to other passages from the same authors.

ENLIGHTENMENT EDUCATION AND EMANCIPATION

Locke is again at the source. Earlier, emphasis was laid on those texts in which Locke wrote of habituating the child to conform to the standards of conduct upheld by opinion and reputation. But other passages in *Some Thoughts*, the *Essay* and the fervently expressed *Conduct of the Understanding* offer a different impression. Here we find a powerful onslaught against received opinion, particularly in intellectual matters but also in politics. Locke explicitly rejects education of students which 'amounts to no more, but making them imbibe their teachers' notions and tenets by an implicit faith' (Locke 1890: section 41). Pupils must examine whether any association of ideas arises from agreement in the ideas themselves or only from habit and custom. Teachers are often reluctant to encourage this.

> Would it not be an insufferable thing for a learned Professor, ... to have his Authority of forty years standing wrought out of hard Rock Greek and Latin, with no small expense of Time and Candle, and confirmed by general Tradition, and a reverend Beard, in an instant overturned by an upstart Novelist? (Locke 1979: 4.20.12)

This is just like parties which cram tenets down men's throats and will not permit them to search for truth (Locke 1979: 4.3.20). Truth cannot be settled by parties or by the votes of the majority (Locke 1979: 4.20.17). This is to neglect one's own understanding.

On this reading the connecting link in Locke's work is 'assent' or, in the political writings, 'consent'. The *Essay* is concerned with the grounds upon which assent may be given to propositions about the world; the *Second Treatise* with the conditions in which rational persons would consent to place themselves under government. The educational writings are directed to the ways to prepare the child's mind so that it can properly grant or withhold assent to statements about nature, morality, religion and politics which it will encounter as an adult. Locke's political thought is predicated on the existence of moral agents who have attained to maturity and passed from the command of their parents.

In morality and politics we are concerned therefore with 'persons' – intelligent 'Agents capable of a Law, and Happiness and Misery' (Locke 1979: 2.27.26). They have liberty, which consists in the power to suspend the execution of their desires and to pause for deliberation before acting (Locke 1979: 2.21.8). They can 'look about' and examine the good and evil of conduct (Locke 1979: 2.21.67). Not only is this a capacity, there is an obligation to employ it. Someone who neglects this liberty and acts hastily is responsible for any subsequent errors (Locke 1979: 2.21.56). In *The Conduct* Locke repeatedly returns to the need to avoid the character flaws which are likely to lead to failures of deliberation. The task of education is to teach the child to use its human capacity for liberty. This entails cultivating habits of deliberation. Parental power over children, Locke says in the *Second Treatise*, is a 'Discipline necessary to their Education' (Locke 1960: II, para. 65) arising from their 'nonage'.

This puts a different complexion on Locke's discussion of habit (for an excellent treatment see Schouls 1992). Locke is facing up to the conundrum of liberal education of how to 'produce' an autonomous agent (Locke 1989: para. 46; compare Kant 1899: para. 29). Autonomy cannot be achieved either by a completely libertarian education or by compulsion. The child has to learn a discipline – that of suspending its desires and using its liberty to deliberate. This will not occur unless the very young child is required at first to acquire the habit of yielding its desires to the authority of adults, which it does initially in response to the manipulation of esteem (Locke 1989: para. 112). As the child becomes older and more capable of reflection it should be given reasoned explanations for the restraint on its desires, until eventually the habit becomes a practice of denying oneself and following one's own reason, which is the 'great Principle and Foundation of all Vertue and Worth' (Locke 1989: para. 33). The transition from habit to practice can be effected in various ways, such as the child being brought into adult conversation, asked for advice, its reasons listened to and discussed (Locke 1989: para. 98). The passage cited above, in which Locke describes reputation as the proper guide of children, ends with the highly significant qualification, 'till they grow able to judge for themselves, and to find what is right, by their own reason' (Locke 1989: para. 61).

From this point onward, as Locke makes clear again and again in Book IV of the *Essay*, in *The Conduct* and elsewhere, opinion, reputation, tradition, the interests of religion, of scholars or of parties should count for virtually nothing against the individual's assessment of the probabilities of the truth of propositions. It remains true that Locke is educating children to a particular mode of reasoning about the world, but it is one which struggles against the constantly threatening straitjacket of orthodoxy. On this reading, which is how many in the Enlightenment and amongst their eighteenth-century critics viewed Locke, it was an education of empower-ment (Schouls 1992: 213–17 and *passim*). The business of a child's educa-tion was not, Locke said, so much knowledge as such, but

> to give his mind that freedom, that disposition, and those habits that may enable him to attain any part of knowledge he shall apply himself to, or stand in need of, in the future course of his life. (Locke 1890: section 12)

Turning to Locke's successors in the line of 'positive' education, we have again to qualify in part the apparent emphasis on the methods of dis-cipline and supervision. This is because, well in advance of their critics, the liberals of the Enlightenment feared some of the consequences of their own theoretical positions. In Continental Europe they were often seeking to emancipate education from the supervision of the church, but they did not all wish to replace this with a new form of authoritarianism. Helvétius insisted that since the form of government was the chief educative influ-ence over youth, a reform of education presupposed a reform of the political structure. His proposal for a moral catechism could only be con-templated in a free society where truth could be examined with impunity (Helvétius 1773: II, 169–70). A moral vocabulary should be the outcome of a free exchange of opinions amongst people for whom the public good was already the supreme law – persons who were able to be concerned for the general happiness because a more equal division of property had made their stake in the community more proportionate. Under despotism, opin-ion cannot be the standard of virtue because only the opinion of the despot, based on his own self-interest, counts. Large states should be bro-ken up into federations in order to prevent a ruling group undermining the liberty of expression essential to an education for the public good. State support for education should not imply monopoly control.

Similar reservations were expressed, but more strongly, by British educationists. Both Catharine Macaulay and Joseph Priestley, were clear in their opposition to those (often themselves republicans or commonwealthmen) who called for state education to restore lost civic virtue. Priestley's critique of state education in the name of toleration and plurality was directed against John Brown who, in *Thoughts on Civil Liberty, on Licentiousness and Faction* (1765), had argued that faction in Britain would be overcome if there were introduced in the manner of Sparta 'a prescribed Code of Education to which all the Members of the Community should legally submit' (Brown 1765: 157). In his rejoinder Priestley accepts that faction would be prevented but at the cost of uniformity. Recognizing, as usual, the power of education he concludes

> Education, taken in its most extensive sense is properly that which *makes the man*. One method of education, therefore would produce only one kind of men; but the great excellence of human nature consists in the variety of which it is capable. (Priestley 1993: 45)

The variety of Athens is a more appropriate model than Sparta, where the state required the sacrifice of natural rights, amongst which Priestley includes rights to educate one's children. Brown, by contrast, complained that according to liberal opinion in Britain every member of society not only had the right to his own principles but also to the same privilege to communicate them to his own children (Brown 1765: 20). In Sparta, however, 'no Father had a Right to educate his children according to the Caprice of his own Fancy'. Instead, public offices initiated the children early 'in the Manners, the Maxims, the Exercises, the Toils, in a Word in all the mental and bodily Acquirements and Habits which corresponded to the Genius of the State' (Brown 1765: 46). But for Priestley the model of education most congruent with Britain's mixed constitution was a plural one in which parents educated their children in their own beliefs, thus preserving the balance between the various sets of opinions in society. Education is therefore 'a branch of civil liberty' (Priestley 1993: 52).

Accordingly, Priestley wanted a modern education suited to those who will take up an 'active life', which includes 'all those stations in which a man's conduct will considerably affect the liberty and property of his countrymen' (Priestley 1780: 194). The old learning was no longer appropriate to a modern society. Traditional humanist studies should yield to useful topics such as modern history, constitutional law, modern foreign languages, political science, the natural sciences and the principles of commerce. The method of instruction should encourage student participation by allowing questions and discussion and by the writing of student theses. The stations of Priestley's pupils (mainly non-conformist middle-class professionals and property owners excluded from Oxford and Cambridge) carried patriotic duties to protect liberty. He warned that Britain's commercial position was threatened by 'our more intelligent and vigilant neighbours', which meant that in 'this critical posture of affairs, more lights and superior industry are requisite' in the political class (Priestley 1780: 189). No man can be an 'unconcerned spectator' in 'a free country, where even private persons have much at stake'.

Catharine Macaulay's republican position is similar. The utility of education to the state is counterbalanced by a concern for liberty and plurality. Ancient education, such as proposed by Plato, treated man as 'the slave to his country' and would appeal to those 'legislators who would form man for the use of government and not government for the use of man' (Macaulay 1790: 15). She acknowledged the appeal of an education designed to further the prosperity of society, as against the view that a man has a natural and inalienable right to bring up a child as a 'Turk, Christian, rogue or honest man as suits his purposes'. The decisive argument against state education was not the rights of families but the experience that governments could not be trusted not to misuse the new science of character formation (Macaulay 1790: 18–20). This combination of optimism over the positive powers of education coupled with suspicion about the dangers of leaving such power in the hands of the state was to be a feature of this stream of British educational thought down to John Stuart Mill.

AN EDUCATIONAL PROJECT?

In all this can one detect an Enlightenment Project which has placed its stamp upon modernity? If the Age of Enlightenment was an Age of Pedagogy the project should be discoverable in its treatment of a topic which seems to involve both the liberties and the disciplines which Foucault said were part of the Enlightenment.

The answer, it is suggested, is that there was an Enlightenment Project and that, rather conventionally, it was what both its eighteenth-century protagonists and their eighteenth-century critics, such as Rousseau, Herder or Burke, thought it was. The project was one of emancipation from old disciplines. In education it sought to replace the old *imitatio* of humanism by a spirit of criticism. Certainly its critical tendencies were restrained by fears of the total destruction of the social order. Nevertheless, contemporaneous conservatives immediately perceived the threat and recognized it in the educational writings, as everywhere else. The schoolmaster Vicesimus Knox fulminated against the speculative theories of Locke and Rousseau which had undermined classical disciplines founded on practice and experience. French levity, precipitate innovation and levelling principles were threatening existing establishments (Knox 1781). The German Burkean Ernst Brandes attributed the collapse in social hierarchy and, especially, in patriarchal authority in large part to the Rousseauian-Basedowian revolution in pedagogy symbolized by the introduction at Basedow's school in Dessau of the familiar version of 'you', *Du*, instead of the respectful *Sie* in relations between parents and children. From there it had permeated family life (Brandes 1809: 38, 49, 80).

Was this critical human being indeed an artificial construct, as critics of the Enlightenment have always asserted? There must be force in this claim, even when seen from the perspective of the Enlightenment itself. Despite their appeals to 'nature', the artificiality of civilized man was recognized by his defenders. The very point of education was to print on the mind of the child the manners and modes of thought of polite society. The extreme case of man as a construct was to be found in Helvétius. It was, of course, too extreme for Diderot – a sympathetic critic and at the same time a central Enlightenment 'projector'. Diderot's review of *De L'Homme* concluded that education could do 'a great deal' but not 'all' since human beings did possess certain innate dispositions and moral orientations (Diderot 1875: 356–7). Rousseau perceived even more critically the way in which positive education constructed man. It was indeed a means whereby a corrupt society moulded its future generations in its own image by a system of supervision and control. That Rousseau's own 'negative' education introduced its own barely concealed disciplines raises profound issues about an education for autonomy (for a further discussion see Parry 1995). Kant, who in some respects sought to harmonize positive and negative theories of education, insisted in his educational treatise that human beings were unique in that, unlike other animals, they had to learn to be themselves – they had to learn to be human. As he puts it:

> Man can only become man by education. He is merely what education makes him. It is noticeable that man is only educated by man – that is, by men who have themselves been educated. (Kant 1899: 6)

Just as in Locke, the first step for Kant is discipline if the lessons of humanity are to be learned. Thus one of the prime objects in sending children to school was to learn to sit still. Again, as is implicit in Locke, discipline operates in two ways. The external discipline of parents and school is temporary, but the acquired self-discipline needed in submitting oneself to laws is a permanent precondition for moral judgement.

Is this so-called autonomous, yet constructed, agent the deracinated individual identified by conservatives since Burke? There is truth in this allegation as well, but a truth which the Enlightenment at least in part acknowledged. The projectors did seek to extract the individual from traditional disciplines and communities. Some believed that human beings could still be held together as a result of natural endowments of sociability, moral sense and sympathy. For those who rejected this possibility the tie that bound the parts that otherwise might fly apart was forged by education. Some sought to achieve this through a revival of classical republican civic virtue. More common was an education which taught that, in Pope's words, 'true self-love and social were the same' and that private advantage was to be found in the promotion of public good. The mechanism, as has already been indicated, was the operation of enlightened opinion on the individual's desire for esteem (the bourgeoisification, as it were, of the aristocratic idea of honour). Such a mechanism of reputation might well threaten to produce that subtle, diffuse discipline of normalization in manners of behaviour and in modes of reasoning which Foucault identifies. At the same time, if this account of the importance of opinion and reputation has any validity, it points to a concern for cohesion and, perhaps, even 'community' in Enlightenment thought which has been neglected amongst the welter of accusations of the crime of abstract individualism.

It has to be admitted that an extreme version of the process of normalization can be found in the German theories of *Aufgeklärte Absolutismus* in which Foucault's panoptical state may readily be discerned, at least in its aspiration and mentality. The broad outlines and the minute detail of human welfare were discoverable by reason, and it was a short step to concluding that these could be taught to experts who, in turn, could realize these objectives through government policy and could additionally, by constant supervision and discipline, mobilize subjects to support the strategy. Education became an aspect of what was understood as the policing function, producing what that critic of the Enlightenment, Michael Oakeshott, saw as the realization of the state as an 'enterprise':

> Enlightened government was, then, the most comprehensive version of a state understood in terms of *universitas* and of government as teleocratic engagement to have appeared since the emergence of Europe as a manifold of states. (Oakeshott 1975: 308)

It was a theory of the disciplinary society in which autonomy played a minimal role. But should this be seen as the *telos* or as the *reductio ad absurdum* of the Enlightenment? Kant's anti-paternalism can be viewed as a powerful rejection of this entire project (however circumspect he might have been in his own dealings with this state in practice).

How far, finally, did these processes of normalization, whether diffuse or more overt, produce a rationalist, universalist, cosmopolitan consensus? Once again this criticism originated amongst conservatives and pre-romantics, especially in Germany, such as Hamann, Herder and Justus Möser. And once again there is a considerable degree of truth in the allegation (if it should be seen as an allegation). Despite the critical and apparently tolerant spirit of Enlightenment thought, it appeared to endorse, and consequently to teach, only certain modes of reasoning, whilst rejecting alternative forms of thought and expression. Nevertheless, more consideration needs to be given to the extent of this alleged closure and to how far it was historically contingent rather than inherent in Enlightenment thought.

Many of its modern as well as contemporaneous detractors have ignored the degree to which the Enlightenment displayed curiosity about the varieties of human culture. In accusing the Enlightenment of indifference to local communities they have, for example, neglected the constantly repeated treatments of patriotism, which many eighteenth-century thinkers believed to be compatible with cosmopolitanism. Thus Basedow, in calling for the singing of patriotic songs in schools, insisted that these should contain no denigratory remarks about neighbouring nations (Basedow 1771: 407). Dr Johnson's famous comment was not an attack on patriotism but on scoundrels. Montesquieu's analysis of cultural particularity was admired by Enlightenment projectors and critics alike. Liberals such as Helvétius, Priestley and Macaulay were sufficiently concerned about the threat to plurality in the name of identity that they opposed state control over education (even though others vehemently advocated it).

It is not, then, difference as such that the Enlightenment neglected – its advocates sought to accommodate it. Perhaps, however, they neglected certain ways of thinking about and defending difference. By means of education the Enlightenment 'created' and then defined humanity in terms which supposed certain procedures of assessment, deliberation and judgement, and these procedures were indeed disciplines which ruled as impermissible other modes of argument. Hence the effrontery, as well as the sarcasm, of Burke's proclamation that 'in this enlightened age I am bold enough to confess that we are generally men of untaught feelings; that instead of casting away all our old prejudices we cherish them ... and to take more shame to ourselves, we cherish them because they are prejudices' (Burke 1987: 76). Hence also why Novalis had declared that Burke had written a revolutionary book against the Revolution.

Nevertheless, defenders of the Enlightenment Project can point to its extraordinarily broad church (if that is not too odd a term to employ). Some of its alleged closures – to the poor and to women – might be regarded as historically contingent, and there is scarcely a shadow of a doubt that the Enlightenment was less closed to these sectors of society than were its immediate critics who in this respect look unpromising sources of liberating inspiration. More importantly, there are good reasons why Enlightenment theories of education have exercised so powerful an influence on the subject, as is acknowledged by virtually all its modern critics in educational philosophy. As Usher and Edwards put it:

> Of course, one could argue that the Enlightenment story of a sovereign (autonomous and agentic) subject is not only a goal but a necessary feature of any educational practice. (Usher and Edwards 1994: 29)

They go on to argue, however, that despite its apparently emancipatory message, it contains oppressive consequences. Enlightenment education propagated a desire for rational control and certainty and helped to compel consensus. This essay has suggested, by contrast, that much of this criticism involves a caricature of the Enlightenment. There was a 'Project', but it was one which embraced a greater plurality of beliefs than recent critics have been prepared to acknowledge. The Enlightenment recognized that its conception of humanity was something which had to be consciously fashioned. What Locke and his successors sought to develop was a person who could stand back, deliberate, criticize and choose whether or not to consent. From this has arisen an associated caricature of autonomy, as Stanley Benn argued in his last, posthumously published, book. Benn suggested that autonomy was not an 'end-state', but a 'disposition' to examine incoherences in a person's cultural inheritance. As Benn put it:

> just because the tradition that values autonomy is also a rationalist tradition, it cannot require that the autonomous person conjure his *nomos* out of thin air, adopting it by a kind of random fancy, kicking aside the *nomoi* of his culture, its traditions, as so much clutter. (Benn 1988: 220)

On this account autonomy was a 'conscious ideal' developed in response to rifts in European culture after the Renaissance and the Reformation which required that human beings defined what they believed (Benn 1988: 182). If this is so, the Enlightenment notion of autonomy becomes ever more appropriate to a so-called postmodern age characterized by multiple cultural fissures. To cite Benn again: 'Autonomy is an ideal for troubled times' (Benn 1988: 183).

REFERENCES

Basedow, Johann Bernard (1771) *Agathokrator: oder von Erziehung Künftiger Regenten*, Leipzig.

Basedow, Johann Bernhard (1774) *Das Elementarwerk*, Dessau.

Bauman, Zygmunt (1992) *Intimations of Modernity*, London, Routledge.

Benn, Stanley (1988) *A Theory of Freedom*, Cambridge, Cambridge University Press.

Bourdieu, Pierre and Passeron, Jean-Claude (1977) *Reproduction in Education, Society and Culture*, Oxford, Blackwell.

Brandes, Ernst (1809) *Ueber das Du und Du zwischen Eltern und Kindern*, Hanover.

Brown, John (1765) *On the Female Character and Education, Sermon Preached in the Asylum for Female Orphans*, London.

Burke, Edmund (1987) *Reflections on the Revolution in France*, ed. J.G.A. Pocock, Indianapolis, Hackett.

Chalotais, Louis-René de Caradeuc de La (1932) *Essay on National Education*, in F. de la Fontainerie, trans. and ed., *French Liberalism and Education in the Eighteenth Century*, New York, McGraw-Hill.

Diderot, Denis (1875) *Oeuvres complètes de Diderot*, ed. J. Assezat, Paris, Garnier.

Foucault, Michel (1980) *Power/Knowledge: Selected Interviews and Other Writings 1972–77*, Brighton, Harvester.

Foucault, Michel (1991) *Discipline and Punish: the Birth of the Modern Prison*, Harmondsworth, Penguin.

Francke, August Hermann (1733), *Kürtzer und einfältiger Unterricht etc*, Halle.

Hartley, David (1749) *Observations on Man, His Frame, His Duty, And His Expectations*, 6th edn, London, 1834.

Helvétius, Claude Adrien (1758) *De L'Esprit*, Paris.

Helvétius, Claude Adrien (1773) *De L'Homme, de ses Facultés Intellectuelles et de son Éducation*, Londres.

Hoskin, Keith (1990) 'Foucault under Examinations: the Crypto-educationalist Unmasked', in S.J. Ball, ed., *Foucault and Education*, London, Routledge.

Justi, J.H.G. von (1755) *Staatswirthschaft*, Leipzig.

Justi, J.H.G. von (1760) *Die Natur und das Wesen der Staaten*, Berlin, Stettin and Leipzig.

Kant, Immanuel (1899) *Kant On Education (Ueber Pädagogik)*, trans., Annette Churton, London, Kegan Paul, Trench and Trübner.

Knox, Vicesimus (1781) *Liberal Education or, a Practical Treatise on the Methods of Acquiring Useful and Polite Learning*, 3rd edn, London.

Le Mercier de la Rivière, P.P.F.J.H. (1775) *De L'Instruction Publique ou Considérations Morales et Politiques sur la Nécessité, la Nature et la Source de cette Instruction. Ouvrage demandé pour le Roi de Suede*, Stockholm.

Le Pelletier, M. (1793) *Plan D'Education Nationale*, Paris.

Locke, John (1890) *Conduct of the Understanding*, ed. Thomas Fowler, 3rd edn, Oxford, Oxford University Press.

Locke, John (1960) *Two Treatises of Government*, ed. P. Laslett, Cambridge, Cambridge University Press.

Locke, John (1979) *An Essay Concerning Human Understanding*, ed. P.H. Nidditch, Oxford, Oxford University Press.

Locke, John (1989) *Some Thoughts Concerning Education*, eds John W. Yolton and Jean S. Yolton (Clarendon Edition of the Works of John Locke), Oxford, Oxford University Press.

Lovlie, L. (1992) 'Postmodernism and Subjectivity', in S. Kvale, ed., *Psychology and Postmodernism*, London, Sage.

Macaulay, Catharine [Catharine Macaulay Graham] (1790) *Letters on Education, With Observations on Religious and Metaphysical Subjects*, London.

Madelaine, Philipon de la (1783) *Vues patriotiques sur l'Education du Peuple*, Lyon.

McLaren, Peter (1995) *Critical Pedagogy and Predatory Culture: Oppositional Politics in a Postmodern Era*, London, Routledge.

Mehta, Uday Singh (1992) *The Anxiety of Freedom: Imagination and Individuality in Locke's Political Thought*, Ithaca, Cornell University Press.

Melton, James Van Horn (1988) *Absolutism and the Eighteenth-Century Origins of Compulsory Schooling in Prussia and Austria*, Cambridge, Cambridge University Press.

Neugebauer, Wolfgang (1985) *Absolutistischer Staat und Schulwirklichkeit in Brandenburg-Preussen*, Berlin, Walter de Gruyter.

Oakeshott, Michael (1975) *On Human Conduct*, Oxford, Oxford University Press.

Oestreich, Gerhard (1982) *Neostoicism and the Early Modern State*, eds Brigitta Oestreich and H.G. Koenigsberger, Cambridge, Cambridge University Press.

Oschlies, W. (1969) *Die Arbeits- und Berufspädagogik August Hermann Frankes (1663–1727)*, Witten, Luther-Verlag.

Parry, Geraint (1963) '"Enlightened Government" and its Critics in Eighteenth Century Germany', *Historical Journal*, IV, pp. 178–92.

Parry, Geraint (1995) 'Thinking One's Own Thoughts: Autonomy and the Citizen', in R. Wokler, ed., *Rousseau and Liberty*, Manchester, Manchester University Press, pp. 99–120.

Passmore, John (1965) 'The Malleability of Man in Eighteenth Century Thought', in E.R. Wasserman, ed., *Aspects of the Eighteenth Century*, Baltimore, Johns Hopkins Press.

Passmore, John (1970) *The Perfectibility of Man*, London, Duckworth.

Priestley, Joseph (1780) *Miscellaneous Observations Relating to Education. More especially as it respects the Conduct of the Mind. To Which is Added, An Essay on a course of Liberal Education for Civil and Active Life*, Cork.

Priestley, Joseph (1993) *Essay on the First Principles of Government*, in P. Miller, ed., *Priestley, Political Writings*, Cambridge, Cambridge University Press.

Raeff, Marc (1983) *The Well-Ordered Police State: Social and Institutional Change through Law in the Germanies and Russia, 1600–1800*, New Haven, Yale University Press.

Schouls, Peter A. (1992) *Reasoned Freedom: John Locke and Enlightenment*, Ithaca, Cornell University Press.

Sonnenfels, Joseph von (1768) *Grundsätze der Polizey, Handlung und Finanzwissenschaften*, 2nd edn, Vienna.

Tribe, Keith (1988) *Governing Economy: the Reformation of German Economic Discourse 1750–1840*, Cambridge, Cambridge University Press.

Tully, James (1993) 'Governing Conduct: Locke on the Reform of Thought and Behaviour', in James Tully, *An Approach to Political Philosophy: Locke in Contexts*, Cambridge, Cambridge University Press.

Usher, Robin and Edwards, Richard (1994) *Postmodernism and Education*, London, Routlege.

3 Kant: the Arch-enlightener
Andrea T. Baumeister

In the eyes of numerous contemporary critics modern society is in the midst of a profound moral and political crisis. Although writers such as Alasdair MacIntyre, Charles Taylor and Michael Sandel[1] differ in their precise diagnosis of the nature and extent of what is commonly refered to as the 'malaise of modernity',[2] they concur in the belief that this crisis is the product of the flaws inherent in modern liberalism, which is widely regarded as the dominant intellectual tradition of our time.

To these critics the agnosticism about the good life which underpins liberal pluralism is symptomatic of an impoverished and distorted conception of morality. Once questions regarding the good life are seen as incapable of resolution, morality is reduced to the question of right and subsequently becomes primarily concerned with rules. As Taylor notes, on such a conception

> the task of moral theory is identified as defining the content of obligation rather than the nature of the good life ... this excludes both what it is good to do, even though we aren't obliged ... and also what it may be good (or even obligatory) to be or love.[3]

For MacIntyre this prioritization of the right over the good does not only characterize the philosophy of contemporary liberals such as John Rawls and Ronald Dworkin, but is indicative of modernity at large. As such, it lies at the very heart of the 'malaise of modernity'.[4]

According to many critics of contemporary liberalism the marginalization of the good has given rise to a distorted picture of human agency, of man as detached from his environment, and has resulted in moral fragmentation and disarray. Thus, Taylor argues that the emphasis modern liberals place on individual choice and self-determination has made them blind to the important role of the wider community in the development of individual identity. According to Taylor, this failure to acknowledge the significance of wider moral frameworks has produced an intellectual climate in which individuals are preoccupied with their own lives at the expense of a concern with and awareness of greater religious, political and historical issues which transcend the self.[5]

Given the close link that is commonly held to exist between contemporary liberalism and the ideas of the Enlightenment, it is not surprising to find that for many critics the roots of this modern malaise are to be found in the Enlightenment. MacIntyre, for example, contends that the fragmentation and displacement of morality can be traced to 'the Enlightenment's systematic attempt to discover a rational justification for morality'.[6] For MacIntyre the Enlightenment is characterized by two important developments: the evolution of science and philosophy led to the rejection of Aristotle's metaphysical biology, which in Aristotle's work provides the background for his teleological conception of ethics. Furthermore, the increasing secularization of culture from the seventeenth to the nineteenth century encouraged a critique of both Protestant and Catholic theology and thus undermined the established Christian understanding of man's goal or telos. According to MacIntyre, these developments culminated in the rejection by Enlightenment thinkers of the teleological view of human nature. In place of the Aristotelian conception, the philosophers of the Enlightenment attempted to formulate a purely rational justification of morality based simply on considerations of human nature as it happens to be. However, the men of the Enlightenment had inherited a conception of human nature and a set of moral injunctions which had been developed within the context of a teleological framework. Therefore, as the prevailing moral injunctions had originally been intended to transform man-as-he-is to man-as-he-could-be, there was an inevitable tension between the conception of nature and moral injunctions. Consequently, the attempt by Enlightenment philosophers to establish a rational link between the existing conception of human nature and the prevailing notions of morality was bound to fail. For MacIntyre this doomed attempt to construct a 'universe empty of telos'[7] quite predictably gave rise to the moral fragmentation and disarray characteristic of the 'malaise of modernity'. In this context, MacIntyre and Sandel regard Kant very much as the arch-villain. Thus, MacIntyre claims that:

> In Kant's moral writings we have reached a point at which the notion that morality is anything other than the obedience to rules has almost, if not quite, disappeared from sight.[8]

For Sandel it is in Kant's philosophy that we find the roots of the distorted picture of human agency which Sandel regards as characteristic of modern deontological liberalism:

> The [Kantian] concept of a subject given prior to and independent of its objects offers a foundation for the moral law that, unlike merely empirical foundations, awaits neither teleology nor psychology. In this way, it powerfully completes the deontological vision. As the right is prior to the good, so the subject is prior to its ends.[9]

In this paper I will endeavour to defend Kant against at least some of these charges. Here I will not set out to refute the eminent criticism which has been levelled against his theory since Hegel's famous critique.[10] Nor will I question MacIntyre's account of the Enlightenment as such – although it is undoubtedly open to question.[11] Instead, I wish to focus on Kant's own understanding of enlightenment as expressed in his essay 'What is Enlightenment?' My discussions will be guided by two related concerns: the fragmentation of the good and the role of an ethics of virtue.

With these concerns in mind I will explore three potentially controversial aspects of Kant's essay 'What is Enlightenment?': the distinction between the public and the private use of reason, Kant's definition of enlightenment, and his emphasis on intellectual rather than civil freedom. I will argue that rather than bringing about moral fragmentation, Kant's philosophy is best regarded as a response to a fragmentation which has already taken place. Here I take my cue from a suggestion by O'Nora O'Neill[12] that the dictates of the categorical imperative are best seen as an attempt to re-establish at least the possibility of community. Not only can Kant's philosophy be seen as a response to fragmentation; his conception of morality does, in my opinion, assign a significant role to an ethics of virtue. Apart from examples of Kant's concern with moral character, such as his discussion of practical and pathological love, his very conception of freedom reflects a deep concern with 'how we are'. The picture of morality Kant draws for us is by no means as impoverished as the arguments of contemporary critics of the Enlightenment tradition may lead us to believe, but actually retains important elements of an Aristotelian ethics. Thus, if Kant is to be regarded as the key Enlightenment figure he is usually held to be, the heritage that the Enlightenment has to offer us may be far richer than is frequently recognized. So, while critics of contemporary liberalism may be correct in pointing to the dire consequences of the prioritization of right, the origins of the 'modern malaise' may well be far more recent.

PUBLIC REASON AND THE SEARCH FOR COMMUNITY

The public use of man's reason must always be free, and it alone can bring about enlightenment among men; the private use of reason may quite often be very narrowly restricted, however, without undue hindrance to the progress of enlightenment. But by the public use of one's reason I mean that use which anyone may make of it as a man of learning addressing the entire reading public. What I term the private use of reason is that which a person may make of it in a particular civil post or office with which he is entrusted.[13]

The distinction Kant draws in 'What is Enlightenment?' between public and private reason may at first appear rather odd. After all, it is usually the use we make of our reason in the private sphere which is associated with the type of agnosticism regarding the good considered as typical of modernity by critics like MacIntyre. However, if we reject the kind of characterization of Kant's project offered by modern critics such as MacIntyre, this apparent puzzle can be resolved quite readily. Careful attention to the role the notion of community plays in Kant's philosophy suggests that rather than aiming at the destruction of moral community in the name of reason, Kant is already keenly aware of the dangers of fragmentation. On such a reading, what makes Kant modern is his readiness to face the question of how we are to respond once we no longer have a shared conception of human nature and its telos. Kant's response to this dilemma is not characterized by a rejection of the notion of community, but by the recognition that 'the problem of moral action and social bonds must be faced anew once revealed religion and metaphysics have lost their authority'.[14]

Although, at one level Kant's response to the 'breakdown of the old order' can be seen as an acceptance of the brute fact of diversity and disagreement, it is also undoubtedly the case that Kant welcomed the rejection of at least some of the elements of the previously established conception of human nature and its telos. Thus, Kant explicitly rejects Aristotle's conception of the human telos and the Aristotelian reading of nature which underpins it. However, the rejection of specific elements of the previously shared conception of human nature and its telos does not imply a rejection of the importance of moral community as such. Besides, even MacIntyre, whose work is informed by a deep sense of nostalgia, does not defend the content of Aristotle's conception of the human telos. Instead, MacIntyre argues that what has to be retained is the Aristotelian teleological framework and the emphasis this places on shared goals and understandings. While in the following section I will explore the extent to which Kant retains an Aristotelian framework, it is helpful to first of all trace the role community plays in Kant's thought.

As George Lucas[15] notes, in many of his political writings, including 'What is Enlightenment?', 'Perpetual Peace' and 'Theory and Practice', Kant is clearly preoccupied with the questions of how to establish 'a moral community encompassing individuals of good will'.[16] Central to the strategy Kant adopts in his attempt to construct such a moral community is the notion of universalizability. By urging us to base our actions on fundamental maxims which in principle can be adopted by all, Kant implores us to act in such a manner as 'not to preclude the possibility of open-ended interaction and communication'.[17] For Kant universalizability is vital if we are to hold on to at least the possibility of moral community. Only if we do not exclude others at the outset does community remain possible.

Once we acknowledge this concern with the possibility of rational community, Kant's distinction between the public and private use of reason can be seen to be quite consistent. What characterizes Kant's conception of private reason is that it is based upon the acceptance of some form of external authority. Thus, the clergyman, the tax official and the officer are by virtue of their post or office committed to accepting and implementing the policies and decisions of the organization of which they are a member. However, such a use of reason will always remain partial, since it will only be accessible to those who are prepared to accept the external authority upon which it is based. In the absence of widespread agreement, the private use of reason can therefore be highly divisive. By relying on external authority, private reason will always exclude those who cannot accept this authority.[18]

Public reason, on the other hand, is, according to Kant, aimed at the 'entire reading public'. It does not invoke any external authority and should therefore in principle be accessible to all. By advocating the free use of public reason, Kant is arguing in favour of the kind of 'open-ended interaction and communication' which is essential if we are to safeguard the possibility of moral community. Therefore, in encouraging us to have the 'courage to use our own understanding'[19] Kant is urging us not to allow ourselves to be led by external authority. As O'Neill notes, if there is to be genuine communication we all have to speak in our own voice, since 'otherwise understanding and agreement will be spurious, mere echoings of what the other or the many assert'.[20] This emphasis on the possibility of moral community is further highlighted by Kant's insistence that enlightenment is not merely an individual undertaking but constitutes a public endeavour. It is only once the entire public has emerged from its self-incurred immaturity that 'the moral community of individuals of good will' becomes a real possibility.[21]

Kant is therefore keenly aware of the need for moral community. Although, for Kant, enlightenment or the 'courage to use our own understanding' is clearly synonymous with autonomy, by equating enlightenment with autonomy he does not wish to undermine the importance of moral community. Quite the contrary. While for current advocates of autonomy, being autonomous is tantamount to the choice of personal goals and life-styles, for Kant autonomy implies acting in accordance with the principle of universalizability. Given the link he establishes between universalizability and moral community, being autonomous in Kantian terms means acting on the basis of principles which at least do not preclude the possibility of moral community. While this clearly falls short of full moral community, once fragmentation has taken place, it may well be the best we can hope for.

However, although moral community clearly plays an important role in Kant's thought, it undoubtedly is the case that his conception of community differs from that adopted by modern communitarians such as MacIntyre. While Kant sets out deliberately to build a moral community based upon rational principles, communitarians such as MacIntyre stress the extent to which community membership is a given rather than something that is deliberately constructed or chosen. We are born into communities and our very identity is shaped by our interactions with others. Whereas Kant urges us to safeguard the possibility of moral community by deliberately adopting principles which are universalizable, MacIntyre argues that in a well-ordered community members execute their tasks without reflection. For MacIntyre, choices in a well-ordered community are akin to moves in a game with well-defined rules.[22] While there may be disagreements in such a community, these are always limited and are contained within an agreed framework. However, whereas MacIntyre suggests that it is the loss of community in this unreflective sense which characterizes modernity, it is questionable whether there ever has been a form of life in which social roles structure action to such an extent that no reflection is required. As Martha Nussbaum notes, although MacIntyre deeply admires the ancient Greek *polis*, in the Greek *polis*

> nothing seems to have happened without an argument … The speeches in Thucydides … show, whether historical or not, the sort of extended and frequently very abstract reflection that was taken to be the sort of thing political actors would say.[23]

For Nussbaum this lack of agreement is underlined by Aristotle's discussion of eudaimonia in the *Nicomachean Ethics*.[24] There Aristotle argues that, although all human beings strive towards *eudaimonia*, there is no agreement as to what constitutes eudaimonia or the good life. Furthermore, by no means all communitarians share MacIntyre's nostalgia. On the contrary. The stress writers such as Taylor and Sandel place on the need to build new communities based on open participation, dialogue and non-discrimination, appears to echo Kant's aim to deliberately construct a new moral community.

Once Kant's interest in the possibility of moral community is seen as a response to fragmentation, his concerns are not dissimilar to those which preoccupy contemporary critics of modernity. MacIntyre, for example, recognizes that the establishment of community requires not only an emphasis on those qualities which contribute to the realization of the common good or goods, but also an awareness of which type of actions are liable to 'destroy the bonds of community in such a way as to render the doing or achieving of good impossible in some respect at least for some time.'[25] Given that these latter conditions have to be met before a viable community can be established, Kant's emphasis on the preconditions for community is not surprising. If we no longer have a shared conception of human nature and its telos, if revealed religion and metaphysics have lost their authority, we first of all have to re-establish the conditions which make genuine communication and cooperation possible.

In contemporary discourse autonomy has become synonymous with agnosticism about the good for men and as such may well undermine the possibility of moral community. Therefore, the worries of critics like MacIntyre may be well placed as far as contemporary liberalism is concerned. However, to equate this contemporary conception of autonomy with Kant's notion of moral autonomy is to misconceive Kant's project.

THE 'COURAGE TO KNOW' AND MORAL VIRTUE

Sapere aude! Have courage to use your own understanding.[26]

In his reflections upon Kant's essay 'What is Enlightenment?', Foucault suggests that Kant's definition of enlightenment as 'the courage to know' indicates that for Kant enlightenment is both 'a process in which men participate collectively and an act of courage to be accomplished personally'.[27] In urging us to have 'the courage to know' Kant is asking us to develop a particular type of moral character which enables us to be independent of external authority. As I suggested earlier, for Kant, it is only under these circumstances that the kind of genuine communication vital to the possibility of moral community is feasible.

Yet, the idea that enlightenment may involve the development of a particular type of character may seem at first rather strange. After all, what characterizes modernity, according to critics such as MacIntyre and Taylor, is the failure to address questions of moral character or virtue. Furthermore, for many critics the root of this neglect of virtue can be found in the philosophy of Kant. For Kant morality is synonymous with obedience to moral law and this suggest a preoccupation with rules rather than virtues. However, as Robert Louden observes, this obedience to moral law

> is obedience to rules not in the narrow-minded pharisaic manner for which rule ethics is usually chastised by virtue theorists, but in the broader, classical sense of living a life according to reason.[28]

For Kant, to act morally is to act only on the basis of maxims which are in accordance with the moral law. Therefore, in order to gain a better understanding of Kant's conception of a 'life lived according to reason', it is important to clarify the notion of a maxim. Here O'Neill quite rightly stresses that we cannot simply equate the Kantian notion of maxim with our specific intentions. As Kant recognizes, human beings do not possess perfect self-knowledge and often lack a clear insight into their own motives. Consequently, we are often not aware of or are mistaken about our motives. According to Kant, we cannot even be sure that we have ever acted in a truly moral manner. Furthermore, not all acts are based upon a specific intention. At times our actions are unplanned or negligent. Yet, for Kant all action is based on maxims. Thus, even actions which are without specific intentions, such as unplanned or negligent actions, are founded on a maxim. Given this discrepancy between maxims and specific intentions, O'Neill concludes that 'it seems most convincing to understand by an agent's maxim the underlying principle by which an agent orchestrates numerous more specific intentions'.[29] According to Louden, these underlying principles are probably best understood in terms of a moral disposition which enables us to resist the pressures of chance and desire. However, this is not to suggest that moral disposition is synonymous with habit. After all, to act morally is to act in a principled manner rather than merely on the basis of reflexes. Now, if maxims are best conceived in terms of our underlying principles, then Kant's conception of maxims is much more akin to the idea of virtue than that of rules. On the basis of his conception, 'to have maxims of a morally appropriate sort would be a matter of leading a certain sort of life, or being a certain sort of person'.[30] Therefore to act morally is not merely a question of making your outward behaviour conform to certain principles, but implies acting on the basis of a genuine moral disposition.

While the discussion so far suggests that considerations of virtue play a significant role in Kant's theory, his critics may none the less remain unconvinced. The main stumbling-block here appears to be Kant's insistence that only action from duty can have moral worth. However, for advocates of a virtue ethics the most praiseworthy acts are those which an agent truly wants to do. Yet, as Louden points out:

> Kant's notion of action as *aus Pflicht* means in the most fundamental
> sense not that one performs a specific act for the sake of a specific rule
> which prescribes it … but rather that one strives for a way of life in
> which all of one's acts are in harmony with moral law.[31]

Kant's discussion of practical and pathological love provides a good
example of the importance he attaches to virtue and his rather sophisticated conception of motivation. While for Kant pathological love refers to
love from inclination, practical love is an expression of an attitude of
benevolence as a matter of principle, based upon the recognition of our
duty to be benevolent. Thus, whereas pathological love is based upon a
natural predisposition, practical love rests upon principles which have
been consciously adopted and developed. Although Kant recognizes that
pathological love cannot be commanded, he maintains that it is our duty to
develop an attitude of benevolence *vis-à-vis* others in general. Here it is
important to recognize that Kant does not merely urge us to perform kind
acts, but expects us to develop a genuine attitude of kindness. Kant therefore urges us to acquire the moral disposition or virtue of kindness.
Furthermore, according to Susan Mendus,[32] Kant's conception of practical
love rests upon a rather sophisticated account of the relationship between
inclination and duty. For Kant all men are blessed with some degree of
emotional love. This emotional love is, in Kant's opinion, a necessary pre-
requisite for practical love, since without the sense of fellow-feeling inherent in emotional love it would be difficult for us to recognize the duty of
benevolence. Also, as Barbara Herman[33] quite rightly notes, in cases of
benevolence and charity it is, from a Kantian perspective, desirable to
encourage the appropriate emotions, since this not only provides the agent
with a sense of internal unity but also ensures that we develop the kind of
awareness of and sensitivity to others which helps us to maximize the
instances in which we may be of help to others. It is therefore our duty to
cultivate love from inclination, as this helps us to develop an attitude of
kindness and benevolence in general.[34]

As Kant's conception of practical love suggests, the development of
our moral disposition and character is integral to his conception of morality. In his 'Lectures on Ethics' Kant reminds us that our duties to ourselves are prior to our duties to others. Our first duty to ourselves is to
order our life so as to ensure that we are fit to perform all moral duties.
This implies the development of a specific moral character. For Kant,
only if we develop this moral character will we be able to act in a truly
moral manner.

This emphasis on moral character is arguably reminiscent of an Aristotelian ethics, and indeed on Patrick Riley's[35] reading Kant retains important elements of an Aristotelian approach. While Kant clearly rejects Aristotle's reading of nature and the Aristotelian conception of the highest good, he does agree with Aristotle that 'there is indeed something "for whose sake everything else is" and that those who neglect final causality "eliminate the Good without knowing it"'.[36] As Barbara Herman[37] notes, for Kant, just as for Aristotle, the subject matter of ethics is the good and the aim of ethical inquiry is to identify the unconditional good or final end. For Kant the highest good consists in respect for persons. This provides good will with an objective end that is the source of the categorical imperative. Since, just like Aristotle, Kant is keen 'to avoid an infinite regress in which nothing is more than a means',[38] he retains the Aristotelian notion of final ends. For Kant, not only is the teleological standpoint a necessary supposition with regard to nature; in relation to morality we actually know reason-ordained ends. Thus, while contemporary critics such as Sandel and MacIntyre attempt to draw a clear distinction between teleology and deontology – with Kant as the defining exemplar of the latter – Kant's approach does not readily lend itself to such a classification. In their attempt to read Kant's philosophy in strictly deontological terms, Sandel and MacIntyre distort his enterprise by ignoring the teleological strand in his work. Yet, as Riley quite rightly notes, this strand

> is a crucial part of Kantian morality: Kant says in the *Grundlegung* that we ought to subordinate relative ends or purposes to respect for rational beings as objective ends; he says in the *Tugendlehre* that morality would be destroyed if there were no objective ends for a ... 'good will' to will; he insists in Religion within the limits that reason 'proposes' objective ends (that is respect for persons) that we 'ought to have'. And the whole *Critique of Judgment* is devoted to finding 'bridges' between the realms of Kantianism by discovering (or rather reading in) telos everywhere.[39]

The extent to which Kant's philosophy contains teleological as well as deontological elements is further underlined by his approach to freedom. Thus, the concern with moral character, so apparent in Kant's 'Lectures on Ethics', also informs his discussion of freedom.

THE 'FREEDOM OF PERSONALITY'

Argue as much as you like and about whatever you like, but obey! This reveals to us a strange and unexpected pattern in human affairs...

A high degree of civil freedom seems advantageous to a people's *intel-lectual* freedom, yet it also sets up insuperable barriers to it. Conversely, a lesser degree of civil freedom gives intellectual freedom enough room to expand to its fullest extent.[40]

Kant's emphasis in 'What is Enlightenment?' on intellectual rather than civil freedom is quite typical of his neglect of civil freedom which has puzzled and at times appalled both his admirers and his critics and has led to the suggestion that there is a marked discontinuity between Kant's critical and political writings.[41] However, if Kant's conception of freedom is seen within the context of a regard for virtue, his discussion of freedom is far from inconsistent.

From Socrates and Plato onwards man has been seen to be fundamentally affected not only by the power of what he can do, but also by the nature of what he likes to do. Thus, 'freedom of personality' – the self-mastery which enables an individual to make her will what she truly wishes it to be – has long been seen as a vital aspect of freedom.[42] D.E. Cooper[43] refers to this capacity to resist one's own material whims and desires and to lead a life according to rational principles as 'Promethean' freedom. Cooper's conception of Promethean freedom is characterized by the following three elements, all of which, I will argue, have a place in the Kantian account of freedom.

Firstly, Protheans emphasize that *only* desires which are directed towards our own thoughts, attitudes and the formulation of our own mind are desires which are truly under our control and cannot be thwarted by outside factors. Kant's understanding of the free will as independent of all material grounds of determination can be seen as an expression of this notion. In line with Promethean freedom it equates freedom with inner-directedness rather than the exercise of control over material possessions. Secondly, Promethean freedom stresses the need for self-discipline in the sense of submitting ourselves to a system of order we have chosen ourselves. The emphasis here is on freedom as the mastery of our whims, caprices and passions. Furthermore, such a self-chosen system provides a structure for choice and thus gives us the means for effective and significant choices. Without such a system we would find ourselves easily disorientated in a world of great diversity, and stranded between choices. Self-discipline is therefore the key to developing our moral character. This notion of a structure for choice finds expression in the Kantian idea of autonomy as self-imposed law. The categorical imperative furnishes us with a system and acts as a check on our immediate inclinations and desires by enabling us to reflect critically upon them. It therefore provides us with a basis to assess and evaluate the options available to us. Finally, Prometheans are preoccupied with the idea of acting rationally. In this context Pometheans are concerned with consistency and the absence of compulsiveness. The central role rationality plays in Kant's conception of moral autonomy need hardly be emphasized. The categorical imperative ensures that all fundamental principles of action are internally consistent, and checks compulsive behaviour.

As this Promethean characterization of Kant's conception of freedom suggests, for Kant freedom is first and foremost a quality internal to the individual, fostered by education, culture and above all personal endeavour. Freedom here become a question of self-control and self-development. Kant's notion of freedom focuses on how man is, his character and virtues. Consequently, on a Promethean reading Kant's lack of interest in questions of civil freedom is no longer puzzling,[44] but can be perceived as the logical outcome of his conception of freedom. His emphasis in 'What is Enlightenment?' on intellectual rather than civil freedom reflects the Promethean preoccupation with the development of one's character through education.

Man's virtue or moral character therefore plays a central role in Kant's conception of morality. However, while so far I have focused exclusively on the role virtue plays in Kant's philosophy, I do not wish to suggest that his philosophy should be regarded as pure virtue ethics. His emphasis on morality as obedience to moral law and his conception of 'legality' as the outward conformity of an action to the moral law suggest that rules and conformity to them play an important role in his ethics. With regard to the actions of others we will frequently be in a position where we can do no more than assess their 'legality' or outward conformity to moral law. However, for Kant this does not imply that as actors we have no duty to cultivate the virtues. Rather than being easily characterized in terms of either 'virtue' or 'right', Kantian ethics offers a rich and complex conception of morality which allows us to question both an agent's acts and his character. Again, this can be seen as indicative of the extent to which his philosophy draws upon both teleological and deontological elements.

KANT'S ENLIGHTENMENT

To many critics the dominant contemporary conception of morality, with its emphasis on the prioritization of the right and obedience to rules, is deeply impoverished. While within the confines of this paper I am not in a position to provide a systematic assessment of the strength of this charge, I have argued that attempts to trace this 'modern malaise' back to the philosophy of Kant are misdirected. If my analysis is correct, Kant's philosophy is not characterized by a simple prioritization of questions of right, but is sensitive to the need for moral community and the cultivation of virtues. Here Kant's philosophy combines teleological and deontological elements. Yet, given our standard conception of the Enlightenment, these are not qualities we would expect to find in the work of a philosopher frequently regarded as one of the arch-exponents of enlightenment. None the less, Kant's status as a key Enlightenment figure cannot be easily dismissed. To my mind this suggests that, at least for Kant, enlightenment is a richer and more complex phenomenon than we tend to acknowledge. Therefore, if modern conceptions of morality are truly impoverished, the root of this malaise may well be more recent than the Enlightenment. Our failure readily to perceive the complexity of the approach to ethics of an Enlightenment philosopher such as Kant may well reflect the limitations of our present position rather than a weakness in Kant's original argument. Consequently, rather than condemn the Enlightenment as the root cause of our present predicament, critics of contemporary conceptions of morality may find in the work of Enlightenment philosophers such as Kant important clues as to how to construct a richer conception of morality which none the less remains relevant and accessible in the face of modernity.

NOTES

1. Alasdair MacIntyre, *After Virtue* (Notre Dame, Ind.: University of Notre Dame Press, 1984), *Whose Justice? Which Rationality?* (London: Duckworth, 1988); Charles Taylor, *Sources of the Self* (Cambridge: Cambridge University Press, 1989), *The Ethics of Authenticity* (Cambridge, Mass.: Harvard University Press, 1991), *Multiculturalism and the Politics of Recognition* (Princeton: Priceton University Press, 1992); Michael Sandel, *Liberalism and the Limits of Justice* (Cambridge: Cambridge University Press, 1982).
2. For example, while MacIntyre rejects the values inherent in contemporary liberalism and expresses a deep nostalgia for the past, Taylor recognizes liberal values as potentially admirable. However, in Taylor's opinion contemporary liberalism distorts and obscures these values.
3. Taylor, *Sources of the Self,* p. 79.
4. MacIntyre and Taylor are by no means alone in bemoaning the consequences of this marginalization of the good. For example, in feminist discourse the concern with questions of care and compassion reflects a renewed interest in the role of the virtues. C. Calhoun, for instance, suggests

that the feminist concern with an ethics of care has been accompanied by a renewed interest in the virtues (see C. Chalhoun, 'Justice Care, Gender Bias', *Journal of Philosophy*, 85, 9, 1988, pp. 451–63).

5. In his best-selling book *The Closing of the American Mind* (New York: Simon and Schuster, 1987), Allan Bloom decries the rise among young, educated Americans of a superficial moral relativism, which rests on the idea that everyone is entitled to their own values and that it is impossible to challenge the values of others. To Bloom such moral relativism is symptomatic of the extent to which our intellectual climate has become distorted and impoverished.

6. MacIntyre, *After Virtue*, p. 39.

7. Sandel, *Liberalism*, p. 175.

8. MacIntyre, *After Virtue*, p. 219.

9. Sandel, *Liberalism*, p. 7.

10. For a defence of Kant against the classical charge of formalism and rigour see O. O'Neill, 'Kant after Virtue', in her *Constructions of Reason* (Cambridge: Cambridge University Press, 1990).

11. For a critique of MacIntyre's account of the Enlightenment see R. Wokler, 'Projecting the Enlightenment', in J. Horton and S. Mendus, *After MacIntyre* (Oxford: Polity Press, 1994).

12. Again see O'Neill, *Constructions of Reason*.

13. Kant, *Political Writings*, ed. Hans Reiss (Cambridge: Cambridge University Press, 1991), p. 55.

14. H.L. Dreyfus and P. Rabinow, 'What is Maturity? Habermas and Foucault on "What is Enlightenment?" in D.G. Hoy, *Foucault: a Critical Reader* (Oxford: Blackwell, 1986), p. 110.

15. G.R. Lucas, 'Agency after Virtue', *International Philosophical Quarterly*, 28, 1988, 293–311.

16. Ibid., p. 310.

17. O'Neill, 'Enlightenment as Autonomy: Kant's Vindication of Reason', in P. Hulme and L. Jordanova, eds, *The Enlightenment and its Shadow* (London: Routledge, 1990).

18. O'Neill, *Constructions of Reason*.

19. Kant, *Political Writings*, p. 54.

20. O'Neill, *Constructions of Reason*, p. 46. O'Neill notes that in the *Critique of Judgement and the Logic* Kant offers us a more extensive acccount of the maxims of communication. Here Kant speaks of our 'sensus communis', which O' Neill translates as 'public sense'. To exercise this faculty we need to adopt three further maxims. In the first instance we need to think of ourselves, secondly we need to take the standpoint of everyone else into account, and finally we need to think consistently. For a detailed discussion of these criteria see O'Neill, 'The Public Use of Reason' and 'Reason and Politics in the Kantian Enterprise' both in her *Constructions of Reason*.

21. These concerns are mirrored in Kant's critical writings. Thus Kant's *Critique of Pure Reason* can be read as a call to fellow workers to come to his aid in the task of reconstruction following the failure of rationalism. For such a reading see O'Neill, 'Reason and Politics in the Kantian Enterprise' in her *Constructions of Reason*.

22. MacIntyre, *Whose Justice?*

23. M. Nussbaum, 'Kant and Stoic Cosmopolitanism', *The Journal of Political Philosophy*, 5, 1, 1997, p. 2.
24. M. Nussbaum, 'Recoiling from Reason', *The New York Review of Books*, 7 Dec. 1989, pp. 36–41.
25. MacIntyre, *After Virtue*, p. 151.
26. Kant, *Political Writings*, p. 54.
27. M. Foucault, 'What is Enlightenment', in P. Rabinow, ed., *The Foucault Reader* (London: Penguin, 1984), p. 35.
28. R. Louden, 'Kant's Virtue Ethics', *Philosophy*, 61, 1968.
29. O'Neill, *Constructions of Reason*, p. 151.
30. Ibid., p. 152.
31. Louden, 'Kant's Virtue Ethics', p. 485, discusses Philippa Foot's distinction between acts of charity based on a sense of duty and charity as something we truly want.
32. S. Mendus, 'The Practical and the Pathological', *The Journal of Value Inquiry*, 19, 1985, pp. 235–43.
33. B. Herman, 'Integrity and Impartiality', *The Monist*, 66, 2, pp. 233–48.
34. In his *Lectures on Ethics* (New York: Harper and Row, 1963) Kant also argues that if we love others from obligation we will, over time, develop a taste for it. Consequently, love from obligation can become love from inclination. Kant therefore appears to propose a complex two-way relationship between pathological and practical love in which the two reinforce one another.
35. P. Riley, 'The Elements of Kant's Practical Philosophy', in R. Beiner and W.J. Booth, *Kant and Political Philosophy* (New Haven and London: Yale University Press, 1993).
36. Ibid., p. 23.
37. B. Herman, *The Practice of Moral Judgment* (Cambridge, Mass.: Harvard University Press, 1993).
38. Riley, 'Elements', p. 23.
39. Ibid., p. 28. Riley is by no means the only Kantian scholar to suggest that the deontological/teleological distinction is not helpful in analysing Kant's philosophy. Barbara Herman makes a similar observation in *The Practice of Moral Judgement*.
40. Kant, *Political Writings*, p. 59.
41. Classical examples of the view that there are serious discontinuities between Kant's political and ethical writings include R. Aries, *History of Political Thought in Germany 1789–1815* (London: Frank Cass and Co. Ltd, 1965) and M.R. Cohen, 'A Critique of Kant's Philosophy of Law', in G.T. Whitney, ed., *The Heritage of Kant* (New York: Russell and Russell, 1962).
42. B. Bosanquet, *The Philosophical Theory of the State* (London: Macmillan, 1958).
43. D.E. Cooper, 'The Free Man', in A.P. Griffiths, ed., *Of Liberty* (Cambridge: Cambridge University Press, 1983).
44. This is not to suggest that advocates of Promethean freedom are prepared to accept all possible arrangements. For example, Private Stoics are not committed to condoning tyranny and despotism. Since careful reason-based reflection is central to Promethean freedom, regimes which are based on

blind arbitrary terror are alien to a Promethean framework. Furthermore, Prometheans do not have to deny the value of a certain minimum amount of civil freedom. Given that the notion of *self*-improvement and *self*-control are central to Promethean freedom, a society which completely regulates its members' behaviour in all spheres of life would simply not be suited to the development of such freedom.

4 Kant, Property and the General Will

Hillel Steiner

For Kant, a particular practical judgement – 'that I shall visit Smith, who is ill in the Manchester Royal Infirmary, on Monday evening' – is a judgement which I *ought* to execute if it is a judgement of a *kind* which I will to be executed by others and by myself on other occasions. The first formulation of the Categorical Imperative (CI_1) reads:

> Act only according to that maxim by which you can at the same time will that it should become a universal law.[1]

The import of the word 'can' in this formulation is notoriously ambiguous, and its ambiguity is not diminished by Kant's ensuing exploration of CI_1's implications. Does it refer to logical or only to psychological possibility? Kant's discussion of suicide, beneficence, false promising and cultivating one's talents, as practices variously proscribed or required by CI_1, is couched in the coercive language of logical necessity and the avoidance of inconsistency.

But the substance of his argument does not bear out his claim that, say, false promising is an instance of contradictory willing. At best, he succeeds in showing only that, since promise-breaking is a practice which (as a matter of empirical fact) is unlikely to be indefinitely sustainable, anyone who counts on it as a permanent source of income would be rather unwise. And while it is certainly true that neither lack of wisdom nor lack of consistency is an especially desirable influence on the formation of practical judgements, it is equally clear that they constitute distinctly different kinds of deficiency. Here as elsewhere in his moral and political philosophy, we are confronted with the unedifying spectacle of Kant straining to erect a substantive principle into a necessary truth – in this case, by illicitly deriving it from the purely formal criterion registered in CI_1.[2]

Contrary to what is maintained by many Kant scholars, this same relation of non-implication also holds between CI_1 and the second formulation of the Categorical Imperative (CI_2). The second formulation reads:

> Act so that you treat humanity, whether in your own person or in that of another, always as an end and never as a means only.[3]

Wick argues forcefully, but in the end mistakenly, that 'the two formulas mutually imply each other, which makes them equivalent in content if not in expression'.[4]

> To treat someone as a mere means is to regard his purposes as if they did not count – as if he were just an object that entered into one's calculations as an instrument to be used or as an obstacle to be pushed aside. Now any *maxim* formulating such treatment entails, when it is universalized, that one be willing to be treated that way in return. But that is a contradiction, for it can be no one's purpose that his purpose count as nothing. It follows, then, according to the first formulation of the categorical imperative, that a violation of the second must be wrong, and therefore that everyone ought to be treated as an end in himself, subject to no one's arbitrary will.[5]

It is undeniably true that one cannot, without contradiction, have as one's purpose that one's purpose count as nothing. But it is not true that the maxim of an action which treats someone as a mere means entails having such a purpose nor, therefore, that a violation of CI_2 is a violation of CI_1.

For consider: I am desperately late for an appointment, and the only available means of transport is Jones's car which I proceed to commandeer at gunpoint due to her unwillingness to lend the needed assistance. The universalized maxim of my act is something along the lines of 'Be punctual'. I have no particular animus against Jones and the maxim of my act, thus formulated, keeps me out of trouble with the enforcers of CI_1. But I would be unduly optimistic to imagine that the enforcers of CI_2 will not presently issue a warrant for my arrest.

The reasons for this are not hard to see. These two groups of enforcers have quite distinct tasks. The enforcers of CI_1 are philosophers and they are charged with bringing to book people who contradict themselves. But the enforcers of CI_2 are (Kantian) policemen whose sworn duty it is to apprehend those who treat others merely as means to their own ends. These are two very different kinds of offence. And the basis of the distinction between them lies in the fact that, whereas CI_1 is an injunction directly governing the *maxims* of acts – and only indirectly and partially governing their consequences – CI_2 applies directly to acts' consequences and not at all to their maxims. That is, CI_1 tells us that an act is impermissible if its *intended* consequences – the consequences we foresee and *desire* – are ones which we are unwilling that others bring about. But CI_2 is an injunction prohibiting the bringing about of certain consequences: it rules out acts any of whose consequences are such as to involve treating others merely as means to our own ends, regardless of whether those consequences are ones intended by us.[6]

Wick is certainly correct to claim that the maxim of my act – *if* it were one to treat Jones as a means to my being punctual – could not consistently be universalized and would, as such, be contrary to CI_1 as well as CI_2. But the fact that my act does treat Jones in this manner does not entail that this is the maxim of that act. And since, in this case, it is *ex hypothesi* not the maxim of my act, I am a fugitive only from the police and not from the philosophers. CI_1 is a purely formal standard of intelligible moral judging. CI_2 is a substantive, albeit very broad, principle for conduct. Accepting the first in no way implies affirming the second.

So much, then, for what is and what is not logically compulsory in our practical reasoning, Kant notwithstanding. We come now to the matter of what *does* follow from our acceptance of a principle like CI_2. And here Kant is notably more persuasive. Let us begin by noticing the peculiarly – in my view, uniquely – compelling character of CI_2. It is almost impossible to formulate a substantive moral principle, the negation of which is strictly unintelligible. Take the principle 'One ought to perform acts of charity when it is within one's means to do so.' There is nothing the least bit unintelligible, though there is much that is misanthropic, about affirming 'One ought *not* to perform acts of charity … etc.' The same cannot, however, be said with respect to CI_2. For the adoption of its negation entails affirming that 'One ought to have, as one's end, the subordination of one's ends to the ends of others.' And this is strictly meaningless, as Wick correctly suggests. His error, and Kant's, lies in inferring from this that the logical impossibility of the proposition's negation implies the necessity of its affirmation – an inference which is invalid with respect to normative propositions, even if the Law of the Excluded Middle is not denied (since there are three normative modalities – prohibited, permissible, obligatory – whereas there are only two descriptive ones – true, false).

But this error aside, it becomes clearer as to why CI_2 is a particularly powerful principle and, thus, why at least one of its implications should have come to occupy a pivotal position in Kant's political philosophy. The non-affirmability of its negation entails that any act conforming to CI_2's injunction – and most especially, any act which prevents one person from treating another merely as a means – is uniquely defensible inasmuch as its justificatory principle enjoys an exclusive logical immunity from contradiction.

Different individuals characteristically entertain different principles and policies as deserving of implementation. Often these different principles are incompatible for contingent sorts of reason, such as scarcity of requisite types of resource. Sometimes, moreover, these incompatibilities are, so to speak, incompatibilities in principle: one person's principle is the simple negation of another's. In a social environment which is densely populated with such possibilities of normative conflict, assigning precedence to a non-negatable principle, as a guide to practical and political choice, must be deemed to be something more than an arbitrary imposition of merely one amongst a number of competing principles, each clamouring for enforcement over the rest. Placeholders for negatable principles, when stopped in their tracks by the people from CI_2, cannot so easily dismiss their obstructors – as they can one another – with remarks like 'Well, that's just your value judgement which I don't happen to share.' For while it is true that subscription to CI_2 is not logically compulsory, subscription to not-CI_2 is logically impossible, which is more than can be claimed for any other principle.

What, then, does CI_2 tell us to do? In what circumstances would we be prudent to look out for the Kantian police? Every day, and in almost every way, we are engaged in treating others as means to our own ends. Why are we not arrested? Some people answer: 'Because Kant is not the Director of Public Prosecutions.' I think this is not a bad answer though, as we shall see, not perhaps the best answer to this question. For the *Office of CI_2* enjoins us only to refrain from treating one another *merely* as means to our own ends. Treating one another partly but not wholly, as such means is not an indictable offence within the terms of the statute. Now, how can we do this? How can we ensure that, in our various actions as they affect others, there is always at least some exculpating fragment which rescues our apparently otherwise unbridled pursuit of our own ends from the charge of violating CI_2, good intentions being insufficient for this purpose?

The answer to this question is to be found in Kant's *Universal Principle of Justice* (*UPJ*):

> Every action is just [right] that in itself or in its maxim is such that the freedom of the will of each can coexist with the freedom of everyone in accordance with a universal law.[7]

For this principle *is* logically implied by CI_2. How? How does conforming our conduct to *UPJ* keep us from treating others merely as means to our ends? The means to our ends are clearly many and various, reflecting the multifariousness of those ends themselves. But among these diverse means, there is one which is common to all ends and a necessary condition of their achievement. This is what Kant calls 'external' or 'outer freedom' and what we call 'negative liberty'. Individuals are necessarily debarred from achieving an end if their overt physical behaviour in pursuit of it is obstructed by others.

Now it is plain that many persons, in pursuit of their ends, perform actions which have the mediate or immediate effect of obstructing others in the pursuit of their ends. Are those others supererogatorily self-denying if they fail to get on the phone to the Kantian police? Hobbes says 'yes'. But Kant says 'not necessarily'. For although the obstructors are treating the others as means – by denying them what is necessary to attain their ends in order to achieve their own ends – it is by no means clear that obstructing the obstructors will accomplish anything more than a reverse form of oppression, subordinating their ends to those of their putative victims. Somewhere *in between* these competing ends, there is a distribution of negative liberty which permits each person to pursue at least some ends and which prohibits each person from pursuing some ends. By leaving this distribution undisturbed, an otherwise entirely self-regarding individual escapes the charge of treating others merely as means.

What is this distribution? What sort of constraint on conduct is implied in the *UPJ* requirement that acts must be such as to allow the freedom of each to coexist with the freedom of all according to a universal law? Up to what point is obstructing others permissible, and beyond what point should obstructors be met with obstruction? The answers to these questions fall within the province of the concept of justice (*Recht*), and are quite distinct from the concerns of virtue (*Tugend*) as such. For whereas the latter pertain to the content of the will – to intentions – and are thus governed by CI_1,

> the concept of justice does not take into consideration the matter [content] of the will, that is, the end that a person intends to accomplish by means of the object that he wills … Instead, in applying the concept of justice we take into consideration only the form of the relationship between the wills insofar as they are regarded as free, and whether the action of one of them can be conjoined with the freedom of the other in accordance with a universal law … For anyone can still be free even though I am quite indifferent to his freedom or even though I might wish in my heart to infringe on his freedom, as long as I do not through an external action violate his freedom.[8]

This condition of strict justice is also described by Kant as one permitting the 'possibility of the conjunction of universal reciprocal coercion with the freedom of everyone'.[9] Elements of these descriptions are not lacking in opacity. And it will, perhaps, save us from some painful, protracted and semi-parenthetical exegesis at this point if we simply take it as read that what *UPJ* prescribes is that we allow the same liberty to others as we enjoy ourselves and, thus, that any further enforced restrictions on an individual's liberty must be ones which she has freely incurred.[10] Justice enjoins equal (original) liberty and a person who engrosses more liberty than she allows to others thereby violates *UPJ*, and CI_2 which implies it.

So justice furnishes each will with its own private sphere, its own field of action within whose limits it may roam freely.[11] Kantian police hover vigilantly around the perimeters of these fields and, should a will commit an act of trespass – an unjustly coercive act – the constabulary are authorized, indeed obligated, to reciprocate that coercion. How are these perimeters defined? How are they to be conceived? In what do individuals' rights to outer or external or negative liberty consist?

> For Kant, the term 'right' has its primary reference within the context of property, where one person's right to an object is a limitation on the moral title of others to use that object, or an obligation on their part to refrain from using it.[12]

> Law considered as a system of laws can be divided into natural Law, which rests on nothing but *a priori* principles, and positive (statutory) Law, which proceeds from the Will of a legislator ... The first of these is called private Law; the second, public Law. The state of nature is not opposed and contrasted to the state of society, but to the civil society, for within a state of nature there can indeed be a society, but there can be no civil society (that guarantees property through public law). Therefore, Law in the state of nature is called private Law ... jurisprudence [is essentially concerned] to know exactly (with mathematical precision) what the property of everyone is.[13]

Each person's innate right to freedom – to a freedom consistent with the same freedom for others – is a right to acquire property rights.

> The juridical postulate of practical reason [asserts that] it is possible to have any and every external object of my will as my property ... it is an *a priori* assumption of practical reason that any and every object of my will be viewed and treated as something that has the objective possibility of being yours or mine.[14]

All rights entail correlative obligations – obligations which, unlike purely ethical duties, are enforcible. That is, any right implies a restriction, not only on what persons (other than the right-holder) may permissibly do, but also on their liberty. Each person's inherent right to freedom immediately confers upon him a right to the exclusive possession of his own person. And this exclusive possession of one's person has somehow to be extended to objects of choice. The mere possibility of an external mine and thine is insufficient, as Gregor notes, to distinguish what is mine from what is thine.

In order to apply the notion of intelligible possession to objects of experience – in order, that is to say, to acquire a right to any particular object – we must presuppose the condition under which the choice of others will be in agreement with our own. If I appropriate a particular object and exclude others from the use of it, I am limiting their freedom of action; and if my prohibition upon the use of the object is to be consistent with freedom under universal law, they must be able to give their rational consent to my limitation of their freedom. This they can only do if they are assured that I, in turn, will agree to the limitation of my freedom involved in their appropriation of objects.[15]

It is through the conjunction of my entitlement to freedom with a particular act of choice – a choice made with respect to a particular object – that I acquire a right to the exclusive possession of that object. But my entitlement to freedom, being limited to a freedom similar to that of others, does not license all possible acts of choice but only some of them. It licenses only those acts of appropriative choice to which all others can give their rational consent.

We have finally reached the point at which Kant's conception of the *General Will* makes its first, albeit shadowy, appearance.

Taking possession of a secluded piece of land is an act of private will without being an arbitrary usurpation. The possessor bases his act on [the concept of] the innate common possession of the earth's surface and on the *a priori* general Will corresponding to it, which permits private possession of land ... Even if a piece of land is regarded as free or declared to be so, that is, open for everyone's use, one still cannot say that it is free by nature or free originally, prior to any juridical act ... Because a piece of land can be made free only through a contract, it must actually be in the possession of all those (united together) who mutually prohibit to themselves the use thereof or suspend such use. The original community of land and, along with the land, of the things on it (*communio fundi originaria*) is an Idea that has objective (juridicial-practical) reality.[16]

One has not long to wait, however, before Kant begins willing on behalf of the General Will. Thus the first occupant of a piece of land, of whatever extent, thereby acquires a right to it.

The First Acquisition of a Thing can only be that of the Soil ... Occupancy is the Acquisition of an external object by an individual act of Will. The original Acquisition of such an object as a limited portion of the Soil, can therefore only be accomplished by an act of Occupation ... It is a question as to how far the right of taking possession of the Soil extends? The answer is, so far as the capability of having it under one's power extends, that is, just as far as he who wills to appropriate it can defend it.[17]

The rightfulness of further and supplementary modes of acquisition is, apparently, equally a deliverance of *a priori* reasoning. *Usucapion* is one such mode:

> I may acquire the Property of another merely by *long possession* and use of it ... Any one who does not exercise a continuous *possessory activity* (*actus possessorius*) in relation to a Thing as his, is regarded with good Right as one who does not at all exist as its Possessor ... And it would contradict the Postulate of Juridically Practical Reason to maintain that one hitherto unknown as a Possessor, and whose possessory activity has at least been interrupted, whether by or without fault of his own, could always at any time re-acquire a Property; for this would be to make all Ownership uncertain (*Dominia rerum incerta facere*).[18]

Similarly, acquisition by inheritance. For although (as Kant notes) a right-conferring transfer cannot be accomplished by a unilateral act of will and requires a simultaneous and united act of will on the part of the donor and the recipient, the seemingly insuperable difficulty this requirement poses for Caius' posthumous endowment of Titius is overcome by the providential pronouncement of practical reason that

> Titius acquires *tacitly* a special Right to the Inheritance as a Real Right. This is constituted by the sole and exclusive Right to *accept* the Estate (*jus in re jacente*).[19]

Thus it is Kant's view that both *UPJ* and the General Will determinately authorize a set of acquisitive modes the conjunction of which constitutes bequeathable private property rights in land, whence all rights to other things derive through inviolable acts of choice on the part of their owners. It is not hard to see that, on such an account, the juridical postulate of practical reason can be invoked to validate virtually all legal titles current in any society at any particular time. The work of the Kantian police looks to be somewhat less demanding than might have been supposed.

What is correct and what is mistaken in this account? Let us retrace our steps a little, to the site of the General Will's initial appearance. Kant says, correctly, that

> By an individual act of my own Will I cannot oblige any other person to abstain from the use of a thing in respect of which he would otherwise be under no obligation; and, accordingly, such an Obligation can only arise from the collective Will of all united in a relation of common

possession ... The conception of such an original, common Possession of things is not derived from experience, nor is it dependent on conditions of time, as is the case with the imaginary and indemonstrable fiction of a *primaeval Community of possession* in actual history. Hence it is a practical conception of Reason.[20]

Original common possession of things is indeed a necessary presupposition, a 'practical conception of reason'. And it is so for precisely the reason Kant offers. My wish, that you not drive a tank across the field I am cultivating, is logically insufficient to imply an obligation on you so to forbear. Nor is this deficiency entirely made good by the premise that you in fact consented to such forbearance. For one person's actual consent cannot of itself create a right in another nor, therefore, a correlative obligation in the first.[21] You may well be subject to another obligation which, contingently, requires you not to forbear in this respect. For example, you may be obligated to return the tank to its owner as quickly as, and hence by the most direct route, possible: namely, across the field. In such a case, you cannot (in Kant's phrase) 'give your rational consent to my limitation of your freedom'.

The conditions necessary and sufficient to encumber you – and everyone else – with an obligation to me not to use this field are: (i) that I wish all of you not to use it; (ii) that all of you have consented not to use it; and (iii) that, prior to your so consenting, none of you was obligated either to use it or not to use it. In short, my acquisition of the right to exclusive possession of the field presupposes that, prior to it, all of us were in joint possession of the field – possession which each of you transferred to me by consent. Anyone who did not so consent is not subject to this obligation of forbearance. And the same holds true for every other particular instance of private acquisition.

But here we encounter a most profound problem. The General Will – universal consent – is a necessary presupposition of private property rights. The General Will is *constitutive* of the rightful spheres of action inhabited by private wills. Kantian police patrol the perimeters of these spheres, ever alert to the danger that some persons may default on their contractual undertakings and attempt a trespass. Occasionally, indeed frequently, an unlucky poacher is apprehended and arraigned before a Kantian magistrate who proceeds to berate him severely for his dereliction. In the face of this crushing chastisement, and of the utterly incontrovertible evidence of his transgression supplied by the police, one might be inclined to think that the poacher would hardly have the effrontery to enter a plea of 'not guilty'. Yet, shockingly, he does just that, as do many others in similar circumstances. And what is even more shocking is that a very large proportion of them are acquitted. Even citizens who entertain a fairly relaxed concern for the maintenance of law and order are scandalized, and demand to know how this is possible.

The answer, of course, is that the miscreant (who is not entirely lacking in common sense) has the sagacity to hire the services of a Kantian lawyer in his defence. Waiving his right of cross-examination of the prosecution's witnesses, allowing fact after damning fact to pile up uncontested against his client, the lawyer bides his time. Finally, when his turn comes, he astonishes the court by announcing that he intends to call only one witness to testify in behalf of the defence. And the court is still further amazed when the lawyer reveals that his sole witness is to be none other than the widely respected *Mr X*, who occupies the august position of *Secretary to the General Will*.

Dispensing with all formalities and preliminary niceties, the lawyer opens his examination by requesting Mr X to outline the genealogy of the title to the property right which his client is alleged to have violated. This Mr X does, with all the proficiency and meticulousness that have come to be expected of him. And he concludes his chronicle with a statement of the precise time and date of the General Will's decision to create the particular rights from which the property title in question devolved through a series of uncoerced acts of choice. Having thus convincingly validated the violated title – and not, in any case, being overly sympathetic to his interrogator's brief – the Secretary sits back in his chair, and beams. The judge beams. The police beam. Law-abiding citizens everywhere beam.

Undaunted, the lawyer proceeds to his next question. He asks Mr X to present the names of those persons who participated in the making of the aforementioned decision of the General Will. The Secretary rifles through his voluminous collection of minute-books, extracts the one covering the relevant period, and begins the onerous process of reading out the names of everyone who was a member of the society at that time. When at last he has finished, the lawyer observes that his client's name does not appear to have been mentioned. Unflappable, and scrupulously concerned that justice not only be done but be seen to be done, Mr X again consults his records and even obtains permission to call his office to enquire as to the cause of the omission. But it seems that there has been *no* omission – a fact which is rather decisively confirmed when the lawyer points out that the General Will decision in question was made over two hundred years ago, whereas his client is a mere stripling of twenty-one.

Not content with this demonstration that his client has incurred no obligation to forbear from using the property he is charged with violating, the lawyer decides to press his argument a bit further. (Whether, in so doing, he is motivated by an unquenchable desire for justice – or only by an acute sense of irritation with the endless succession of indictments which have no foundation in any juridical postulate of practical reason – is difficult to discern in his outward expression.) He informs the court that he wishes to refer it, and the Secretary, to *The Book of Rules* itself – the sacred text which sets out in a systematic form all of the most fundamental principles of the legal order, and which is otherwise entitled *The Philosophy of Law* by Immanuel Kant. And he particularly draws their attention to the passage (quoted above) where the author insists that the necessary presupposition of original common possession is *not* an historical claim and is *not* one dependent on conditions of time.[22]

'This can only mean,' the lawyer suggests, administering the *coup de grace*, 'that the juridical validity of original common possession, not being primaeval, must be timeless. My client, and everyone else who has reached or will reach the age of legal responsibility after the *then* General Will made the decision which issued in the property right he is improperly alleged to have violated, can be subject to no obligation to respect it unless he and they have incurred one under the same necessary and sufficient conditions that applied to their predecessors' obligations. If these conditions are satisfied, he is obligated. So long as they are not, he is not. Any particular property right is not a thing, a substance, an elementary particle, which enjoys an existence independent of human will. Such a right is simply the sum of all the obligations of forbearance undertaken by others in respect of the use of the object of that right. And these obligations must be ones which are undertaken, rather than merely imposed – they must be contractual – if they are to be consistent with the dictates of *UPJ*. Each person's innate right to a freedom similar to that of others implies that no person is subject to any such enforcible obligation to which he has not consented.

'The *Bureau of First Occupancies*, the *Usucapion Commission* and the *Office of Testamentary Dispositions* are not independent agencies empowered to issue licences to various acts of acquisition according to their own rules. Rather they are just so many conventionally established subdivisions within the *Ministry of UPJ* and are answerable to, and may be overruled by, its director. No doubt these agencies should be allowed some measure of autonomy if considerable social inefficiency is to be avoided. But social efficiency is not the chief concern of the Ministry which is vested, in the first instance, with the task of protecting each person's right to equal freedom. When the demands of expediency collide with those of justice, it is the Ministry's solemn duty – and the court's – to accord priority to the latter. To do otherwise is to risk receiving a dismissal notice from the Prime Minister's office (*Office of CI₂*). And that is why, in this society, many poachers will continue to flourish – aided and abetted by juries who take seriously the injunction to treat others as ends and never as means only.'

POSTSCRIPT: THE IDENTITY OF THE GENERAL WILL

In Book I, chapter VII of *The Social Contract*, Rousseau claims that the General Will cannot bind itself. Arguably it is this claim, rather than the view that the General Will is the necessary source of all private property rights, that exposes Rousseau's sovereign to the charge of arbitrary despotism. The claim is wrong and, therefore, the charge is correct. For there is no reason why the General Will, like any other will, cannot be held to be obligated by its undertakings. In a society of three persons, the General Will – the common will of A, B, C – can most assuredly bind A, B, C. If A, B, C, consent to relinquish their joint possession of a right, they are perfectly at liberty to do so and, in so doing, they obligate themselves to forbear exercising any of the liberties that right entails. Is D – a more recent member of that society – similarly obligated? Clearly not. Is the will of D, as a member of that society, a constitutive element of its General Will? Clearly so. Does the General Will which is the common will of A, B, C, bind the General Will which is the common will of A, B, C, D? Clearly not. For these are two different common wills and, therefore, two different General Wills. The will common to A, B, C, cannot be identified as the one common to A, B, C, D, for the same reason that it cannot be identified as the will common to X, Y, Z. The two sets of wills are non-identical. The General Will can indeed bind itself, but it cannot bind another General Will. If it could, Rousseau and Kant would be indistinguishable from Burke, which they are not. If the General Will could not bind itself, Kant would be indistinguishable from Rousseau, which he is not. The plurality of contemporaneous private wills is a necessary condition for the existence of a General Will. Correspondingly, the plurality of non-contemporaneous private wills is a sufficient condition for the sequential existence of a plurality of General Wills.[23]

NOTES

1. *Foundations of the Metaphysics of Morals*, ed. Lewis White Beck (Indianapolis: Bobbs Merrill, 1959), p. 39.
2. Cf. Robert Paul Wolff, *The Autonomy of Reason* (New York: Harper & Row, 1973), pp. 163–71.

3. Beck, ed., p. 47.

4. Warner Wick, in his introduction to Kant's *The Metaphysical Principles of Virtue* (Indianapolis: Bobbs Merrill, 1964), p. xx.

5. Ibid., p. xix, emphasis added.

6. Thus Jeffrie G. Murphy observes 'that, contrary to much traditional interpretation of Kant, some of the *unintended consequences* of one's actions are clearly of moral relevance in determining the rightness of those actions'; *Kant: the Philosophy of Right* (London: Macmillan, 1970), p. 104.

7. *The Metaphysical Elements of Justice*, ed. and trans. John Ladd (Indianapolis: Bobbs Merrill, 1965), p. 35. In an earlier and unabridged, though less felicitous, translation of the same work, this principle is rendered as 'Every Action is *right* which in itself, or in the maxim on which it proceeds, is such that it can co-exist along with the Freedom of the Will of each and all in action, according to a universal law'; *The Philosophy of Law*, ed. and trans. W. Hastie (Edinburgh: T. & T. Clark, 1887), p. 45. Two points are worth noting. First, the presence of the 'maxim criterion' in both translations of the principle is not consistent with what was previously shown about CI_2's difference from CI_1, not consistent with Kant's claim that justice takes no account of the *content* of the will (see next quotation), and not consistent with other central aspects of his legal philosophy (e.g. his doctrine of strict liability). Second, the use of the term 'right' (parenthesized in Ladd's translation) in both versions expresses Kant's apparent view that the justness of an action is a necessary condition of its moral permissibility – a view which would be correct if CI_1 and CI_2 were mutually implicative, which they are not.

8. Ladd, ed., pp. 34–5.

9. Ibid., p. 36.

10. Cf. H.L.A. Hart, 'Are There Any Natural Rights?', *Philosophical Review*, 64 (1955), 175–91; Hillel Steiner, *An Essay on Rights* (Oxford: Blackwell, 1994), ch. 6.

11. To say this is not to say that an agent's actions, so long as they are confined to this sphere, are morally permissible. Within the constraints of justice, individuals are also obliged to be virtuous, i.e. to keep out of trouble with the enforcers of CI_1.

12. Mary J. Gregor, *Laws of Freedom* (Oxford: Blackwell, 1963), p. 47; cf. Steiner, ch. 3.

13. Ladd, ed., pp. 39, 43, 48.

14. Ibid., pp. 52, 53.

15. Gregor, pp. 56–7.

16. Ladd, ed., pp. 57–8.

17. Hastie, ed., pp. 87, 89, 91; the Ladd edition omits the second chapter of Kant's analysis of Private Right, where he elaborates the principles and forms of acquiring external rights.

18. Ibid., pp. 133–5. Apart from the strictly conventional element introduced into the construction of this ostensibly *a priori* deducible right, by terms like 'long possession' and 'possessory activity', it is difficult to see how making ownership uncertain constitutes a *contradiction* of the juridical postulate of practical reason. At best, insecurity of title may be judged highly inexpedient – the argument advanced by John Stuart Mill to show that utilitarianism

is compatible with, indeed forms the basis of, the demands of justice; cf. 'Utilitarianism', ch. V. Whether the liability of owners to be divested – when they have been possessorily inactive for a long period of time due to no fault of their own – makes ownership less uncertain or more so, is itself a purely empirical question.

19. Ibid., p. 137. On this particular bit of casuistry, it need only be remarked that it fails in its attempt to provide an *a priori* deducible construction of the standard practice of bequest. For if Titius acquires such a 'special Right', Caius is thereby disabled from altering his testamentary disposition. Cf. Steiner, ch. 7 (C).
20. Ibid., pp. 86, 88; see also pp. 69–70, 81–2, 89–90, 94–6.
21. As so many newly-landed immigrants in America discovered to their cost, when confidence tricksters 'sold' the Brooklyn Bridge to one after another of them at an extremely reasonable price.
22. The set of private property rights derivable from the premiss of original common possession – understood as 'a [trans-generationally valid] practical conception of reason' – is explored in Steiner, chs 7 and 8, where its cosmopolitan distributive implications are also displayed; see also my 'Territorial Justice', in *National Rights, International Obligations*, eds Simon Caney, David George, Peter Jones, (Boulder: Westview Press, 1996), and *Justice Among Nations* (forthcoming).
23. This essay has benefited from the comments of Katrin Flikschuh, who still disagrees with much of it.

5 Can Enlightenment Morality be Justified Teleologically?

Ian Carter

In this article I aim to provide a teleological defence of some basic Enlightenment principles of political morality. More precisely, I want to show that these principles can be defended on teleological grounds in so far as teleological justifications of moral principles are valid at all. My adversary in this debate is Alasdair MacIntyre, whose well-known claim that the Enlightenment Project 'had to fail' is largely based on a negative answer to the question that forms my title.[1] My critique of MacIntyre will make some use of textual evidence, taken, above all, from Condorcet, and to a lesser extent from Kant and Rousseau. However, my general aim is to provide a plausible analysis and reconstruction of what MacIntyre calls the 'Enlightenment Project', rather than an accurate historical account of it.

According to MacIntyre, the rational justification of a moral position depends on the use of functional concepts, where a functional concept implicitly refers to a particular good to be aimed at. For example, a functional concept of a farmer tells us what a good farmer does and thus what someone who calls himself a farmer ought to aim to do. So too, a functional concept of man tells us what a good man does and thus what someone who sees himself as a man ought to aim to do.[2] The use of functional concepts in moral discourse is, in MacIntyre's view, what allows thinkers in the Aristotelian tradition to treat moral claims as factual and to engage in fruitful, rational discussions about their validity. Enlightenment thinkers, who rejected the idea of man as having a specific and essential function or purpose, ruled out any rational basis for the discussion of moral precepts. They noticed that man did not always follow what they took to be the correct moral precepts, and thus that 'man-as-he-is' was not identical to 'man-as-he-ought-to-be'. However, their notion of man-as-he-ought-to-be was not informed by an idea of man's *telos*, as it was in the tradition from which they had inherited their moral precepts, but was simply defined by the moral precepts. And so these thinkers lacked a basis on which to engage in rational discussions about the moral precepts themselves. Only an Aristotelian-style teleological justification could supply such a basis, and that was exactly what the Enlightenment thinkers had ruled out. Therefore, once such a justification was ruled out, the Enlightenment Project was doomed to failure.

The argumentative strategy of this article is above all a defensive one. I aim to show that the Enlightenment Project, as MacIntyre defines it, cannot be seen to 'fail' any more than can its counterpart 'Aristotelian Project'. In other words, I shall concede to MacIntyre, for the sake of argument, that the rational justification of moral principles depends on appeal to a human telos or human tele, and shall argue that any objections that can be levelled in this connection against the Enlightenment can also be levelled against Aristotle. To the extent that Aristotle succeeded in justifying moral principles teleologically, Enlightenment philosophers too can succeed. I leave aside entirely the question of whether non-teleological justifications of Enlightened moral principles are available, and whether, if so, they are more convincing. They may well be both of these things. My aim here, however, is to show that even if they are *not*, then the Enlightenment philosopher winds up no worse off than the Aristotelian in terms of the possession of justificatory tools. My aim, in this sense, is to confront MacIntyre on his own territory.

My point of departure will be the notions of perfectibility and progress which, crucially, MacIntyre leaves out of his account of Enlightenment thinking (section 1). I shall then go on to show how these notions can ground a broadly liberal commitment to freedom and equality (section 2). The links I shall make between perfectibility and freedom and equality will depend on a number of empirical assumptions. These assumptions are open to challenge, and I shall offer no proof here of their validity. My aim is not to provide true empirical claims as such, but simply to show that the structure of an argument among Enlightenment philosophers about the validity of moral principles can be the same as that of an argument among Aristotelian philosophers.

1   PERFECTIBILITY AND PROGRESS

It cannot be denied that human perfectibility plays an important role in Enlightenment thought. The idea is central to Condorcet's *Sketch for a Historical Picture of the Progress of the Human Mind*,[3] as it is to Kant's *Idea for a Universal History with a Cosmopolitan Purpose*.[4] Kant does not use the term 'perfectibility', but he does nevertheless talk of the progressive 'perfection' of man through 'the development of his faculties'. As Morris Ginsberg says, the 'moralization and rationalization of man' was for Kant 'the *telos* of history'.[5] The idea is also present in the writings of Rousseau,[6] who indeed introduced the word *perfectibilité*.[7] For all of these authors, the idea of human perfection indicates a *potential* in human beings, a facet of human nature that points in some way to our future. Moreover, given that it is normally interpreted as a value-laden concept, we should take it that an adequate account of perfectibility will provide us with a *prescription*; we should expect it to tell us something about what people *ought* to do.[8] So the notion of perfectibility appears to be an excellent candidate for filling the missing role in MacIntyre's picture of the Enlightenment Project – the role of describing 'man-as-he-could-be-if-he-realized-his-telos'.[9]

Before expanding on this idea, I should insert two caveats. The first concerns the so-called 'is–ought' question. In presenting an argument in which perfectibility fills the role that MacIntyre says is missing in Enlightenment thinking, one need not deny the logical distinction between 'is' and 'ought'. A moral claim can be factual – inasmuch as it either is or is not a fact that a certain moral principle helps 'to enable man to pass from his present state to his true end'[10] (in this case, as defined by reference to the idea of perfectibility) – without it being the case that any claims about man's 'true end' are themselves factual. On the other hand, our Enlightened teleologist might want to adopt the strategy of denying the logical gap between is and ought, and claim instead that perfectibility ought to be pursued because it is part of human nature to do so. In this case, our resultant theory will be on all fours with Aristotle's. We can easily construct an Enlightened teleological moral theory which commits the naturalistic fallacy, if that is what MacIntyre wants of us. And if a naturalistic theory is not what he wants of us, then he can hardly set up Aristotle's moral theory in contrast as a shining success.

Secondly, the argument set out below is independent of the belief, expressed by Condorcet and many other Enlightenment and post-Enlightenment thinkers, that progress towards perfection is 'inevitable'. We should distinguish between the belief in progress as an ideal and the belief in progress as a future outcome. Progress has certainly not been as smooth as many eighteenth-century philosophers hoped, despite many undeniable improvements in human circumstances as measured by reference to Enlightenment ideals. But the idea of inevitability is not necessary to a teleological justification of moral principles. Moreover, there is clearly a tension between the inevitabilism of Condorcet and Kant and their otherwise firm belief in human freedom. I follow Ginsberg in claiming that we can have a clear notion of progress without adopting Kant's view of history as a process that 'goes on over men's heads throughout';

it need have nothing to do with 'metaphysical or theological theories of the *telos* of history',[11] *if*, by 'the *telos* of history', we have in mind an *irresistible* telos. Though I shall refer below to an 'Enlightenment telos', that telos need not be seen as irresistible.

Neither need it be said, at the other extreme, that the Enlightenment view of progress is hopelessly utopian, in the sense of being unattainable. If we look at human history in terms of very broad tendencies exhibited over the centuries – in terms, as Kant said, of 'the free exercise of the human will *on a large scale*'[12] – it is still possible to see the Enlightenment view of progress as based on actual practice. Enlightenment thinkers derive their ideas about human potential from their observations of historical tendencies. (Nine of the ten parts of Condorcet's *Sketch* deal with the past rather than the future.) This remains true despite the degree to which those tendencies have been subverted at various times over the last two centuries, and is important in allowing us to retain something, however little, of the optimism of the eighteenth century.

1.1 Two Concepts of Perfectibility

Why is the Enlightenment notion of perfectibility ignored by MacIntyre? I suggest that the answer lies in the different degrees of *specificity of content* in the Aristotelian and Enlightenment notions of perfectibility. The Enlightenment notion seems to lack a specific content, and this, as I see it, must be MacIntyre's reason for believing that Enlightenment thinking allows for *no* telos. Thus, for example, MacIntyre complains that the Benthamite notion of the greatest happiness of the greatest number is a notion 'without any clear content at all'.[13] When we come to examine the Enlightenment notion of perfectibility, it is not at all clear which particular ends, in concrete terms, this notion implies. Despite first appearances, however, the lack of specificity of content in the Enlightenment notion of human perfectibility does not prevent it from grounding specific moral principles. Indeed, it is this very difference between the Aristotelian notion of man's telos and the Enlightenment notion of perfectibility – the difference in terms of the specificity of content – which can lead the Enlightenment thinker, unlike the Aristotelian, to endorse the liberal values of freedom and equality. Let us begin, then, by contrasting these two notions of perfectibility.

Human perfection in Condorcet's *Sketch* is indeterminate along two dimensions. To visualize these two dimensions, imagine a signpost pointing out the path to perfection. This is no ordinary signpost, for it tells us that perfection is indefinitely many miles away, and it points in innumerable directions. Regarding the *distance* to perfection, Condorcet talks approvingly of 'the doctrine of the *indefinite* perfectibility of the human race'.[14] The reason for man's perfectibility being 'truly indefinite'[15] lies partly in the fact that the human mind can never gain knowledge of all the facts of nature, and partly in the fact that 'the actual number of truths may always increase'.[16] Similarly, in connection with the *direction* in which our progress towards perfection will take us, Condorcet recognizes that the nature of progress is by definition something that cannot be specified substantively: 'It is impossible to pronounce about the likelihood of an event that will occur only when the human species will have necessarily acquired a degree of knowledge of which we can have no inkling'.[17] Robert Wokler also appears to detect these two dimensions of indeterminacy in Rousseau's notion of perfectibility. He points out, for example, that for Rousseau 'there was no way of defining the limits of our potential development', and that 'perfectibility in the *Discours* lacks a positive goal'.[18]

Man's telos in the Aristotelian tradition has neither of these indeterminacies. Or, to be precise, it has them to a much lesser extent. Thus, if we imagine a spectrum of degrees of specificity of man's telos (along the two dimensions mentioned above), we can say that the Enlightenment tradition falls at the less specific end of the spectrum, and the Aristotelian tradition at the more specific end. For Aristotle, man has a relatively specific end – one which we can at present know, and which we can describe in concrete terms, if only by means of general concepts. As MacIntyre says, for Aristotle the nature of humans 'is such that they have certain aims and goals, such that they move by nature towards a *specific* telos'.[19] Thus, the 'virtues are, on Aristotle's view, dispositions to act in specific ways for specific reasons'.[20] While Aristotle begins by defining the good life by means simply of the abstract term *eudaimonia*, he nevertheless goes on to suggest that this is better realized through a life of contemplation than through a life of action. And in his *Politics* we learn that we are each born into certain general roles – those of man, woman or slave, for example – and that some of these are naturally subordinate to others. Each of these roles, and each of the more specific roles we find ourselves best fitted to – those of carpenter, statesman or philosopher – has its natural function in the polis, its own specific telos, which we can discover by observing and contemplating the nature of the role itself. The more abstract notion of perfectibility of the Enlightenment does not involve taking these further steps towards specifying the content of the good life for individuals.

John Passmore distinguishes between the Aristotelian and post-Renaissance views of perfectibility by underlining the tendency of the latter 'to value the journey more than the arrival, the process of finding out more than the truth arrived at, the doing rather than the having'.[21] For Aristotle, in contrast, 'to perfect oneself ... is to *achieve* an end, a *specific* end'.[22] Here we can see how it is also possible to contrast the two notions of perfectibility in terms of the difference between the terminal and the non-terminal. As Horace Kallen says, the Enlightenment notion of progress contains no terminus *ad quem*. At most, it involves movement away from something, such as scarcity or ignorance – a terminus *a quo*. The idea of a goal is taken over by a

> sense of the road *opened*, of pursuit *unhindered*. ... This, in part, accounts for the illogic of 'infinite perfectibility'. The phrase embodies the Enlightenment's unexpressed feeling that *distance from*, not *distance to*, gives the span of Progress, that hence the going is the goal.[23]

Given the reasons set out above for this distinction between non-specific, non-terminal perfectibility and the specific, terminal kind, it is clear that we should also distinguish between the perfectibility of the individual human and the perfectibility of the human species. Each of the two kinds of perfectibility I have set out above can in theory be applied either to the individual or to the species. However, Aristotle's discussion of *eudaimonia* concentrates largely on the perfectibility of the individual, and this partly explains how he is able to conceive of man's progress in more specific terms. While it is true that he also gives a teleological justification of the organization of the polis, what he certainly lacks is that long-term vision of the progress of the species which the results of scientific progress inspired in Enlightenment thinkers, and which one would naturally expect to be a less determinate notion. We should bear in mind this distinction between the perfectibility of the individual and that of the species when we come later to look at the justifications of liberty and equality.[24]

1.2   Filling in the Enlightenment Notion of Perfectibility

I have said that my aim is to show how perfectibility can fill the justificatory role of the telos that MacIntyre says is lacking in Enlightenment moral thinking. Now, the obvious objection which we can imagine MacIntyre raising, and which I touched on above, is that on my characterization of it, the Enlightenment notion of perfectibility is completely indeterminate. It does not tell us where to aim, or how far we shall have to go. If our goal is non-specific in these senses, how can it provide a useful premise in an argument that is intended to justify a *specific* moral precept? Surely we cannot say, 'human progress could take us any distance and in any number of directions, of which we are currently unaware, therefore you should cultivate *this* virtue'. My point, however, is that liberals *can* say this, and can do so in a way that fits MacIntyre's model of a rational justification.

The first step towards showing how this is so consists in pointing out that the Enlightenment notion of human perfection is not in fact *totally* indeterminate. I have said that the difference in specificity is one of degree, and that the Enlightenment tradition stands at one end of the spectrum. Aristotle defines man's end more specifically, but not *wholly* specifically: he does not say exactly what thoughts the man of contemplation should think in order to achieve perfection, or at exactly which hours of the day he should think them, and indeed he stresses that there is no perfectly precise answer to the question of what the good life consists in. Conversely, while for Enlightenment thinkers human perfection is to be defined in such a way that our progress towards it continues indefinitely and such that we cannot specify its content, the notion is nevertheless defined by reference to a particular abstract condition. This abstract condition has been described in various ways, of which it is worth noting three: it has been described, first, as a condition of moral perfection, second, as one of increased happiness, well-being and harmony, and third, as one exemplifying the growth of reason and knowledge and of our ability to overcome natural obstacles. All of these notions of perfectibility are to be found in Condorcet's *Sketch*.[25] The relevant distinction is therefore more akin to John Rawls's distinction between having a 'full' theory of the good and having a 'thin' one,[26] than to that between having a theory of the good and not having one at all.

Now it might be said that there is a problem involved in including the idea of 'moral perfection' in our reconstruction of the Enlightenment telos, if we are interested in that reconstruction providing an answer to MacIntyre. The human telos is supposed to provide a justification of moral principles. To include the moral dimension of perfectibility in the telos would therefore appear to lead us into a circular argument. Surely we cannot claim that a set of moral precepts is rationally justified on the grounds that their observance will bring about progress towards the greater observance of those very same moral precepts.

One way of answering this objection is by pointing out that whatever its validity, it is not an objection to which MacIntyre can appeal. For Aristotle, to say that the exercise of the virtues is what enables man 'to pass from his present state to his true end' is not to say that those virtues can simply be *deduced from* the nature of that end. This is because the excercise of the virtues is in part *constitutive of* the end:

> Although it would not be incorrect to describe the exercise of virtues as a means to the end of achieving the good for man, that desciption is ambiguous. ... [W]hat constitutes the good for man is a complete human life lived at its best, and the exercise of the virtues is a necessary and central part of such a life, not a mere preparatory exercise.[27]

So if Condorcet is to be accused of circularity here, then Aristotle (and MacIntyre) must stand equally accused. This problem in Aristotle has indeed been noted by J.L. Ackrill: 'if good and wise action is what *eudaimonia* partly consists in, we cannot explain *why* a certain way of acting is good and wise by saying that it promotes *eudaimonia*'.[28]

But we can avoid the charge of circularity in any case, by 'demoralizing' the telos. Ackrill suggests as a possible solution to the circularity in Aristotle that we interpret him as having held that 'the very aim of morality is the promotion of *theoria* [or pure philosophical contemplation], that what makes a type of action count as good is precisely its tendency to promote *theoria*'.[29] Similarly, in the case of Condorcet, we can think of moral improvement simply as the tendency to act ever more in accordance with those moral precepts that are justified by reference to the other dimensions of perfectibility. Condorcet certainly conceives of progress as in part constituted by a greater awareness of 'principles of conduct or practical morality', and of 'the necessary and immutable laws of justice',[30] where to respect the laws of justice is to respect the natural rights of others to liberty and equality. However, he also suggests that respect for these principles of conduct is in fact no more than a means to 'the absolute perfection of the human race', which is a state of harmony and above all of happiness.[31] We can therefore say, without departing too far from Condorcet's picture of perfectibility, that it is the harmony and happiness of human lives that lies at the 'end' of the chain of events in which progress consists (although as we have seen, it is incorrect, strictly speaking, to see the chain as coming to an end). Progress, on the other hand, can be said to consist in movement towards perfection, and can encompass the greater awareness of moral principles, in so far as respect for those moral principles itself promotes perfectibility on this more narrow definition. Finally, to complete the picture we should say that the cognitive dimension of perfectibility fits into this causal chain after the moral principles, and in some sense before the attainment of happiness. I say 'in some sense', because it is a moot point how far happiness is created by the growth of knowledge and reason, and how far it is created by the mere pursuit of that growth. As we have seen, according to Passmore and Kallen, the latter is what counts for Enlightenment thinkers: 'the going is the goal'.

2   THE RATIONAL JUSTIFICATION OF MORAL PRINCIPLES

We are now in a position to see how our Enlightened teleological thinker can answer MacIntyre by supplying a teleological justification of Enlightened political morality. We have seen how, though defined by reference to the abstract concepts of knowledge, reason and happiness, we are necessarily ignorant of the form that the end of moral action (i.e., human perfection) will take as we progress towards it. What we have next to notice is that there is nevertheless something that we *can* know. What we can know is the nature of the *means* to achieving progress towards this under-specified end. One of these means, it can be argued, is liberty.

2.1   Justifying Liberty

How can we know the means, MacIntyre will say, when we do not have a full account of the nature of the end that it is the means *to*? An analogy may help to answer this question. Imagine we receive a wrapped present. We do not know the exact nature of the present, but we do have reason to believe that we will like it, as it was given to us by a good friend. Moreover, we have a way of finding out the nature of the present, and that is to remove the wrapping paper. Would MacIntyre say that we have no good reason to remove the wrapping paper until our friend tells us what's inside?

Our task as Enlightened teleologists is to show why the pursuit of liberty is like the unwrapping of the present. In order to do so, we shall need to show how liberty possesses a special kind of value – a kind of value which I have elsewhere called 'non-specific instrumental' value.[32] We do not yet know the direction or directions in which progress will take us. For 'who would take it upon himself to predict the condition to which the art of converting the elements to the use of man may in time be brought?'[33] How, then, are we to assure the progress of this art if we cannot predict its direction? The answer, it can be argued, lies in an empirical correlation between human progress on the one hand and individual freedom on the other. Individuals should be left 'to use their faculties, dispose of their wealth and provide for their needs in complete freedom'. For 'the common interest of any society, far from demanding that they should restrain such activity, on the contrary, forbids any interference with it'.[34] This point has been taken up with great effect in the last century by J.S. Mill and in this one by Karl Popper and Friedrich von Hayek. Popper criticizes what he calls the 'historicist' assumption that the future course of progress can be deduced from certain laws of human nature, and suggests that we should look instead to the *conditions* of progress, which include the freedom to experiment, to make mistakes, and to learn from them.[35] The basic thought here, which strongly echo's those found in Mill's *On Liberty*, is that reason grows through mutual criticism: 'the only way of "planning" its growth is to develop those institutions that safeguard the freedom of this criticism, that is to say, the freedom of thought'.[36] Furthermore, because we cannot know beforehand which particular kinds of liberty are to prove the most beneficial, 'we shall not achieve our ends if we confine liberty to the particular instances where we know it will do good'. Indeed,

> if we knew how freedom would be used, the case for it would largely disappear…Our faith in freedom does not rest on the foreseeable results of particular circumstances but on the belief that it will, on balance, release more forces for the good than for the bad.[37]

Accepting this point means attributing value to freedom *as such*, despite the fact that we know it to be no more than an instrumental good. To say that freedom is valuable as such is to say that it is valuable in a non-specific way. Specific freedoms have value independently of the value of the specific things they allow us to do, despite being no more than a means to doing those things. Freedom is instrumentally valuable, but non-specifically so, in the sense that we cannot say of any one specific freedom how valuable it is in terms of the degree of progress it might give rise to – that is, as a means to which it is instrumentally valuable. The only knowledge we have available is that expressed by an empirical generalization: a correlation between increases in freedom and subsequent progress.

This empirical generalization provides us with a rational justification for the moral principle that we should pursue liberty – a rational justification which, contrary to MacIntyre's picture of Enlightenment thought, appeals to a human telos in the form of perfectibility. Perfectibility on the Enlightenment view is, as we have seen, a telos of an indeterminate nature. But, as we have also seen, it is exactly this indeterminacy which gives freedom the unique value it has.

As I have already suggested, the causal link between the promotion of and respect for freedom on the one hand and the growth of knowledge and reason on the other need not go in one direction only. This suggestion can now be substantiated. The link between knowledge and 'moral progress' in terms of increased respect for freedom as such (and, as we shall see below, for some form of equality) need not be claimed to arise only through the growth of that 'moral science' by means of which we are to 'determine the necessary and immutable laws of justice'. We need see nothing mysterious or 'metaphysical' about such a 'moral science', as it may simply consist in the observation and verification of empirical generalizations like the one just hypothesized. However, there is also a more straightforward sense in which scientific and technological progress can be seen as helping to safeguard what freedom has already been won, and even to increase it. I do not mean here the simple fact that technology allows us to do many more things (though that is of course itself an important point); most negative libertarians would see this as having nothing directly to do with freedom. What I mean is that, arguably, technological progress can make government interference with certain kinds of action more difficult. Condorcet shows great vision in citing the example of printing. After the invention of printing and the greater diffusion of information that this facilitated,

> it would be vain for any despotism to invade the schools, vain for it to issue cruel edicts prescribing and dictating the errors with which men's minds were to be infected ... It is enough for there to exist one corner of free earth from which the press can scatter its leaves.[38]

The contemporary Enlightenment sympathizer knows of course that many such measures have subsequently been taken; but she might also want to claim that they have been vain in proportion as information technology has advanced. For contemporary examples, one has only to think of radio and television, and the unsuccessful attempts of the oppressive regimes of East Germany, Albania and Iraq to prevent people from receiving information from West Germany, Italy and Egypt respectively. And beyond these media there is internet. Despite George Orwell's forebodings, there are surely grounds for thinking that censorship has never been so unsuccessful as in the second half of the twentieth century. Perhaps Condorcet's belief in the certainty of progress was partly fuelled by this perception of a virtuous circle set up by the mutual aid of increased freedom and technological progress. The idea is that the securing of each new freedom itself provides part of the means by which that same freedom is to become entrenched, and that in this sense there can be 'no turning back'. While it is surely too strong to describe such a process as 'inevitable', the basic insight nevertheless retains a certain plausibility.

So far we have only considered the progress of the species. It is also worth considering the non-specific notion of perfectibility as a potential of individual lives, as here too we have a premise on which to base an argument for freedom. Though such an idea of individual perfectibility is more evident in post-Enlightenment than in Enlightenment thinking – in the romantic idea of 'individual flourishing' as expressed in the works of Humboldt, Mill, and a number of contemporary liberal thinkers – it is worth noticing how, here too, the indeterminacy of the modern idea of perfectibility makes freedom especially valuable. Here, the ultimate value is the many-sided development of the individual's faculties, whatever those faculties may turn out to be. The growth of such faculties is something which can only come from within, and whose direction cannot be foreseen even by the agent herself, who knows that her own beliefs about what constitutes the good life may change as her experience and powers of reason grow. If we are trying to perfect ourselves in directions which we cannot at present foresee, it is clearly rational for us to desire freedom. It is rational, that is, up to a point, always to prefer more freedom to less.[39] The modern individual does not value liberty merely as a means to pursuing a certain specific way of life, but rather, as a means to pursuing whatever the good life might be. Liberty is non-specifically instrumentally valuable for the modern individual because it is one of the necessary means by which she can pursue perfectibility (defined non-specifically).

Once again, the possibility of rationally justifying freedom seems to have escaped MacIntyre. In the case of individual perfectibility, just as in the case of the perfectibility of the species, MacIntyre appears to be unaware that the grounds for the justification of a specific moral precept need not necessarily be provided by a specific-terminus telos. In fact, a non-specific, non-terminal telos also points to specific virtues as efficient to its pursuit. In particular, it points to the virtue of enhancing and safeguarding individual freedom.

2.2 Justifying Equality

Let us turn now to the justification of equality. I shall begin by looking at the principle of equal liberty, in so far as this can be seen to follow from the above arguments. I shall then turn more briefly to the justification of equality by reference to more positive claims about its long-term empirical link to the perfectibility of the species.

Let us start by assuming a purely individual (non-specific) notion of perfectibility. We have said that it is rational for an individual to desire freedom as such. This, however, only requires us to adopt a personal point of view – one of individual prudence. As a result, MacIntyre might well want to raise the following objection. Questions of morality, he might say, arise when we consider interpersonal conduct. Therefore, what is at issue is not the rationality of desiring freedom for oneself but, rather, the rationality of preferring a certain *distribution* of freedom. If I have a great deal more freedom than you, what reasons can be given for my giving up a portion of my freedom in your favour? Is not the lack of any reason for assuming an impersonal point of view exactly the problem with Enlightenment thinking? This is the essence of MacIntyre's criticism of Bentham, whose utilitarian morality stands or falls, MacIntyre suggests, with his implausible belief that 'the pursuit of my happiness... and the pursuit of the greatest happiness of the greatest number do in point of fact coincide'.[40]

Once again, however, MacIntyre should be careful not to throw out baby Aristotle with the Enlightenment bathwater. How does Aristotle arrive at the impersonal point of view, so as to be able to say, for example, that like cases should be treated alike? Will Aristotle's life of contemplation not be more fulfilling if he has a copy of every philosophy book? Why should books be shared out among philosophers? We cannot build book-sharing into the telos of each and every philosopher, as that would simply be a blatant case of the circularity touched on earlier (even though this at times would seem to be exactly what MacIntyre's Aristotle would have us do[41]). MacIntyre will perhaps answer that from an Aristotelian perspective we need not be interested directly in people's relative quantities of goods, and that it is enough to say that justice consists in each person receiving her *due*, where her due is defined by her specific roles in the polis and the specific telos of each of those roles.[42] But what of cases where resources are scarce? Perhaps there simply are not enough books to satisfy all the budding Aristotles, even assuming that each has attained the virtuous happy medium (and is thus not excessive) in terms of acquisitiveness.[43] In such cases, reference to people's relative quantities of goods seems unavoidable. Therefore, what MacIntyre needs to do in order to derive distributive justice in a non-circular way is to appeal to a *collective* telos – that of the polis – which will contain the idea of a well-ordered society as one in which like cases are treated alike. We have seen that the Enlightenment, too, can supply a conception of a collective telos as well as that of an individual one. For we have seen that Enlightenment thinkers believe in the perfectibility of the species as well as in that of the individual. And so it would seem that here, as before, Aristotle's position leaves us no better off than that of the Enlightened teleologist.

So while it is true that the Enlightenment thinker cannot provide a justification of the equal liberty principle – or indeed of any distributive principle – by reference to a purely individual notion of perfectibility, it is no less true that Aristotle cannot justify *his* principle of equality on the basis of such a notion. Who indeed could? It is logically impossible to justify an interpersonal distributive principle merely on the basis of a personal telos. In the absence of a collective telos, the most that one can do is to claim that the distribution of the relevant good or goods is exhaustively determined by all the specific individuals' specific tele, taken together, where no particular telos is seen as conflicting with any other. But we have seen that even for Aristotle, in a world of scarcity this cannot be so. Therefore, if Aristotle's theory of justice can be rationally justified, MacIntyre's criticism of Bentham is unfair: his criticism, one could say, does not treat like cases alike.

Can the Enlightenment notion of the perfectibility of the species justify an equal distribution of freedom? Arguably, it can. Again, a necessary premise in such a justification is the *non-specific* nature of human perfectibility. If our notion of perfectibility is sufficiently indeterminate, then we shall have no reason for giving priority to one person's actual goals rather than to another's, in terms of the degree to which they lead to human perfection. We do not, and cannot know which particular uses of freedom will best promote the perfection of the species. We only know that promoting freedom in general is likely to do so. Hence, equality emerges as the only distributive principle for freedom that can be rationally pursued. The only alternative would appear to be a *random* distribution of freedom. But, as Hillel Steiner has recently argued, any principle of random distribution *presupposes* a principle of equal distribution. Either a principle of random distribution is wholly indeterminate, and thus not rationally pursuable, or else we must fix upon a particular random distribution by some particular means, such as a lottery, which will itself presuppose a prior distribution of entitlements to freedom. And since that prior distribution cannot itself be a random one (for otherwise, we should have an infinite regress), it must (on the basis of the above reasoning) be an equal one.[44] While 'there is no logical necessity to adopt the equal freedom rule', we have nevertheless seen that we *ought* to adopt *some* freedom rule, since we have seen that freedom ought to be pursued. And 'you can't consistently affirm a rule entitling persons to unequal freedom'.[45]

Why not maximize societal freedom, instead of equalizing it? And may not maximal societal freedom involve a sacrifice in the freedom of some for a greater freedom for others, even if our choice of which individuals to privilege must be an arbitrary one? Steiner would answer this objection by saying that there is no way of maximizing freedom within a society: the overall extent of freedom within a particular system is always constant, and so the distribution of freedom among individuals can be our only concern.[46] But the Enlightenment philosopher does not in any case need this controversial premise in order to deal with the maximizer's objection. For there are arguments, which I shall not rehearse here, to the effect that if freedom is not constant sum, the policy of maximizing freedom within a group will in any case tend towards that of equalizing freedom, or will at least not conflict with that of equalizing freedom.[47]

It might of course be claimed that since some people are so much better at pursuing human perfection than others in *any* of the directions in which perfection might lie, they ought to be accorded more freedom than others (even though freedom may *not* as a result be maximized overall), and indeed more of every kind of relevant resource, such as wealth and education. In answer to this objection, our Enlightenment philosopher will need to bring in an Enlightened conception of human nature – a conception of human nature that is *descriptively* egalitarian. An Enlightened teleological argument for equality requires, as far as I can see, *two* premises: the first is the non-specificity of the concept of perfection; the second is the idea that people are roughly equal in their capacities. The use of the term 'roughly' here is intended to convey the idea that each person has some sphere of activity in which he or she is capable of achieving worthwhile results, and that no one person's 'capacity set' is likely completely to dominate that of another. Furthermore, this belief in rough equality of capacities is extended to all members of the human race; not just to Greeks or Aryans or males. If we combine this diversity of capacities with a non-specific conception of perfectibility, we arrive at an endorsement of equality as a distributive principle for at least some of the all-purpose means in life, of which we have seen liberty to be one. Michael Walzer entertains the possibility of there being a person who excels in every sphere of activity, and admits that this would be fatal for egalitarians. In so doing, he underlines the fundamental empirical assumption egalitarians make about human nature. There being such people, he says,

> would certainly make for an inegalitarian society [if we apply the theory of 'complex equality'] but it would also suggest in the strongest way that a society of equals was not a lively possibility. I doubt that any egalitarian argument could survive in the face of such evidence.[48]

Aristotle, in the words of Hobbes, 'maketh men by Nature, some more worthy to Command, meaning the wiser sort (such as he thought himselfe to be for his Philosophy;) others to Serve, (meaning those that had strong bodies, but were not Philosophers as he;)'.[49] How far does this contradict the above egalitarian view of human nature? Yet again, we should be careful not to exaggerate our differences with Aristotle. Aristotle's own capacity set does not completely dominate that of his slaves, who are physically stronger than him. Given this, it seems plausible to say that the real key to our difference with Aristotle lies in the difference between the specific and non-specific conceptions of perfectibility, despite the fact that natural inequalities with respect to specific capacities are for Aristotle very great. This suggests that the assumption of 'rough equality of capacities' is less controversial than might at first appear. Such an assumption is, as MacIntyre would be quick to point out, not *sufficient* to ground egalitarian moral principles. We also need a conception of collective perfectibility for that purpose. And it needs to be a non-specific conception.

Finally, we should take note briefly of some of the other justifications of equality available to the Enlightened teleologist, and their links with the arguments already canvassed. Condorcet, in particular, puts forward several more positive, long-term hypotheses which link equality with the perfectibility of the species. Equality, for Condorcet, can be usefully divided into three kinds: equality of education, equality of wealth, and equality between nations. As regards education, the idea is that progress will be facilitated by a greater diffusion of ideas. Condorcet favours 'true equality in the use of reason and in the acquisition of necessary truths', because he is deeply suspicious of the idea that an elite can effectively pursue the progress of the species in isolation from the masses: 'if the progress of the masses of the human race had in this way been suspended, ultimately, as in the far East, the progress of the sciences themselves would have come to a stop'.[50] Where on the other hand we increase the number of educated people, there will be 'a proportionate increase in the number of men destined by their discoveries to extend the boundries of science'.[51] This fits in well with our combined premises of rough equality of capacities and ignorance over the usefulness of those capacities as a means to progress. Furthermore, Condorcet sets out a plausible case for saying that equality of education tends to promote equality of wealth and *vice versa* (in other words, that they feed off each other in a virtuous circle), and that each helps to increase liberty, which, as we have already seen, itself serves to promote knowledge and happiness: 'with greater equality of education there will be greater equality in industry and so in wealth; equality in wealth necessarily leads to equality in education'; and 'in societies where laws have brought about this equality, liberty, though subject to a regular constitution, will be more widespread, more complete than in the total independence of savage life'. Equality therefore aids the progress of the species by producing 'ampler sources of supply', 'more extensive education' and 'more complete liberty', the ultimate aim of all this being 'the perfection of the human race'.[52]

As regards equality between nations, the above arguments get extended spatially, so as to argue empirically that the progress of the species depends on a global principle of equality, and is hampered, rather than furthered, by what might be called the policy of 'equality in one country'. Much more controversially, Condorcet claims that it is in the *interests* of richer and more scientifically advanced nations to share their discoveries with poorer ones.[53] But this claim is not necessary in order for us to extend the scope of our egalitarian morality to the international sphere. If our interest is in the progress of the species – the collective Enlightenment telos – we are necessarily adopting an impersonal point of view, and it is therefore not appropriate to argue from individual interests (be these the interests of an individual human or an individual nation). And this reference to the interests of richer nations is indeed not Condorcet's central point. What matters, rather, is that 'these discoveries will have repaid *humanity* what they have cost it only when Europe [and now, more generally, the developed world] renounces her oppressive and avaricious system of monopoly'.[54]

3   DISAGREEMENTS AMONG LIBERALS

All of these arguments are, as I have said, debatable on empirical grounds. I have been concerned with their validity (in the logical sense), but not with their soundness. It is sufficient for my case that the arguments have a certain empirical plausibility: enough plausibility, that is, to give rise to a discussion. To the extent that one criticizes Condorcet's empirical arguments – to the extent, for example, that one sides with Orwell in seeing technology as more of a threat to liberty than as one of its guarantors; or with Mill in seeing the state enforcement of equality in education as a threat to the diversity that guarantees progress; or with Hayek in seeing inequality of wealth as a necessary means to economic development – one has implicitly accepted the validity of the argumentative *method* being employed. Although the non-specific nature of perfectibility may imply that the problems being discussed by the moderns are particularly *difficult*, this does not mean that the moderns lack a rational basis for discussion any more than the ancients did. To admit the difficulty of specifying the best means to a non-specific end is not to deny the existence either of such a best means or of such an end. Neither should this difficulty be allowed to obscure the general direction in which a non-specific telos undoubtedly points us: that of liberalism in some form or other.

MacIntyre suggests that we have to choose between Nietzsche and Aristotle: these are 'the two genuine theoretical alternatives confronting anyone trying to analyse the moral condition of our culture'. The latter allows for a rational justification of moral principles by reference to man's telos; the former puts moral claims 'to uses at the service of arbitrary will': 'there is no third alternative'.[55] We have seen that MacIntyre has exaggerated the differences between Aristotle and the thinkers of the Enlightenment. What differences remain, on the other hand, show us that there most certainly *is* a third alternative – one which, for the sake of symmetry, we might call that of Condorcet. MacIntyre is blinded to this alternative by his failure to see how an indeterminate end can nevertheless generate a reasonably determinate set of moral principles. This mistake perhaps helps us to understand both why non-liberals so often accuse liberals of being Nietzschean, and why this makes liberals so irate. What those non-liberals rightly perceive in liberals is the latter's recognition of the modern transformation of the end of humankind into something diverse, flexible and nonspecific. What they miss is the liberal morality which, at least insofar as it derives from that end, is independent of arbitrary will.

NOTES

This is a revised, more concise version of an article of the same title that was published as a MANCEPT working paper. I am grateful to Ian Holliday, Mario Ricciardi, Veronique Munoz Dardé and Robert Wokler for their comments.

1. Alasdair MacIntyre, *After Virtue: a Study in Moral Theory* (London: Duckworth, second edition, 1985), ch. 5.
2. In the interest of stylistic continuity, I follow MacIntyre in using the obsolescent term 'man' to refer to the whole of human kind.
3. Trans. J. Barraclough (Westport: Hyperion Press, 1955).
4. Kant, *Political Writings*, trans. H.B. Nisbet (Cambridge: Cambridge University Press, 1991), pp. 41–53.
5. Moriss Ginsberg, *Essays in Sociology and Social Philosophy, Vol. 3, Evolution and Progress* (London: Heinemann, 1961), p. 13.
6. For example, in Rousseau's *Discourse on the Origins and Foundations of Inequality among Men*, trans. M. Cranston, *A Discourse on Inequality* (Harmondsworth: Penguin, 1984).
7. Cf. John Passmore, *The Perfectibility of Man* (London: Duckworth, 1970), p. 179.
8. Rousseau's view of perfectibility is of course atypical in this respect, since for him the concept had strongly negative connotations, and did not therefore play a role in justifying his moral and political prescriptions.

9. A similar point is made by Robert Wokler in his historical critique of MacIntyre, 'Projecting the Enlightenment', in J. Horton and S. Mendus, eds, *After MacIntyre: Critical Perspectives on the Work of Alasdair MacIntyre* (Cambridge: Polity, 1994), p. 125.
10. MacIntyre, *After Virtue*, p. 54.
11. Ginsberg, *Evolution and Progress*, p. 48.
12. *Idea for a Universal History*, p. 41, emphasis in original.
13. MacIntyre, *After Virtue*, p. 64.
14. Condorcet, *Sketch*, p. 142, my emphasis. See also Kant's *Appendix from 'The Critique of Pure Reason'*, in his *Political Writings*, p. 191: 'no one can or ought to decide what the highest degree may be at which mankind may have to stop progressing'.
15. Condorcet, *Sketch*, p. 4.
16. Condorcet, *Sketch*, pp. 184–6.
17. Condorcet, *Sketch*, p. 188.
18. Wokler, 'Rousseau's Perfectibilian Libertarianism', in A. Ryan, ed., *The Idea of Freedom* (Oxford: Oxford University Press, 1979), pp. 251 and 237 respectively.
19. MacIntyre, *After Virtue*, p. 148, my emphasis.
20. MacIntyre, *Whose Justice? Which Rationality?* (London: Duckworth, 1988), p. 109.
21. Passmore, *The Perfectibility of Man*, p. 48.
22. Passmore, *The Perfectibility of Man*, p. 46, my emphasis.
23. Horace M. Kallen, *Patterns of Progress* (New York: Columbia University Press, 1950), p. 27, emphasis in original.
24. For Kant, we must consider progress as applicable to the species, given that individual lives are finite and so cannot each fully develop their rational faculties (*Idea for a Universal History*, p. 44). See also Rousseau's *Discourse on Inequality*, p. 88: 'the faculty of self-improvement ... is inherent in the species as much as in the individual'.
25. They are all also present in Kant's political writings, despite his denial that happiness can be an end of individual moral action.
26. Rawls, *A Theory of Justice* (Cambridge, Mass.: Harvard University Press, 1971), §60.
27. MacIntyre, *After Virtue*, pp. 148–9.
28. J.L. Ackrill, *Aristotle the Philosopher* (Oxford: Oxford University Press, 1981), p. 138.
29. Ackrill, *Aristotle the Philosopher*, p. 140.
30. Condorcet, *Sketch*, pp. 133–4.
31. Condorcet, *Sketch*, p. 184. The use of the word 'absolute' in the above quote seems to contradict the idea of perfectibility being 'indefinite'. However, Condorcet's references to perfectibility as indefinite are much more numerous.
32. 'The Independent Value of Freedom', *Ethics*, 105 (1995), pp. 819–45.
33. Condorcet, *Sketch*, p. 188.
34. Condorcet, *Sketch*, pp. 130–1, cf. pp. 138–9.
35. Karl Popper, *The Poverty of Historicism* (London: Routledge, 1957), p. 154.
36. Popper, *The Open Society and its Enemies*, Vol. II (London: Routledge, 1966), p. 227.

37. F.A. Hayek, *The Constitution of Liberty* (London: Routledge, 1960), p. 31.

38. Condorcet, *Sketch*, p. 102, cf. p. 140.

39. I have further analysed this claim, including the qualification it contains, in 'The Independent Value of Freedom'.

40. MacIntyre, *After Virtue*, p. 63.

41. MacIntyre, *Whose Justice? Which Rationality?*, ch. 7.

42. Cf., in particular, *Whose Justice? Which Rationality?*, pp. 111–13.

43. As Martha Nussbaum writes, for Aristotle the criterion for excellence in political arrangements is 'that the people involved should be enabled ... to choose to function well ... *in so far as the polity's material and natural circumstances permit*'. Nussbaum, 'Aristotelian Social Democracy', in R.B. Douglas, G.M. Mara and H.S. Richardson, *Liberalism and the Good* (London: Routledge, 1990), p. 208, my emphasis.

44. Hillel Steiner, *An Essay on Rights* (Oxford: Blackwell, 1994), p. 219.

45. Steiner, *An Essay on Rights*, p. 220. Steiner's own argument is not teleological. Rather, it is based on the premise that the different recipients of equal freedom have conflicting moral codes.

46. See section D of ch. 2 of *An Essay on Rights*.

47. Cf. Carter, *A Measure of Freedom* (Oxford: Oxford University Press, 1999), ch. 9.

48. Michael Walzer, *Spheres of Justice: a Defence of Pluralism and Equality* (Oxford: Blackwell, 1983), p. 20.

49. Thomas Hobbes, *Leviathan*, ch. 15 (Harmondsworth: Penguin, 1985), p. 211.

50. Condorcet, *Sketch*, p. 118.

51. Condorcet, *Sketch*, p. 186.

52. Condorcet, *Sketch*, pp. 183–4.

53. Condorcet, *Sketch*, p. 105.

54. Condorcet, *Sketch*, p. 105, my emphasis.

55. MacIntyre, *After Virtue*, pp. 110–18.

6 Ganging A'gley

Alistair Edwards

Enlightenment political thought deals with the same basic problems of order tackled by earlier writers. The principal shift, most notable in the Scottish Enlightenment, is from artificial and imposed order to more natural and spontaneous forms; Hobbes and Locke to Hume and Smith. Alongside this shift there is a move away from explicitly normative concerns towards a more empirically focused form of inquiry. Many eighteenth-century writers are more interested in analysing the nature and source of moral beliefs than in laying down a specific standard by which conduct must be judged. Thus we learn from Hume the 'measures of allegiance' whereas Hobbes provides us with a proper theory of 'political obligation'.

Emerging from these two changes in perspective is a theme that many have identified as the Enlightenment's key contribution to social explanation: that social order is an unintended product of individual actions and that the institutions comprising that order are, to borrow Hayek's phrase 'the results of human action but not of human design' (Hayek 1967a, 96–105). Emphasis is thus placed on the move from imposed to spontaneous order, at the expense of the artificial/natural distinction. The new emphasis is held to lend greater clarity to the identification of this central achievement (Hayek 1967a, 96–7).

Those most ready to hail this achievement generally identify it with only one strand of Enlightenment thought. Mandeville, Hume, Smith and Ferguson are the true standard-bearers for a properly modern social scientific inquiry. With the important and influential exception of Montesquieu, French thought remains underdeveloped, fails to incorporate the insights of the Scots, and continues to pursue a 'rationalist constructivism' in clear opposition to the more modern, more explanatory, and more correct idea of the unintended consequences of action (Hayek 1960, 54–70; 1967, 99; 1982, 8–34).

In simple and commonsense terms, this division has some real existence: Hume loses few opportunities to stress the 'frivolous', accidental or contingent factors that are implicated in the growth of social institutions; Rousseau founds his model of legitimate order on enlightened general *will*. The argument to be developed here will seek to raise doubts about this simple and commonsense judgement. These doubts will be expressed at a number of levels: the historical, questioning the interpretations that point to the division referred to above; the conceptual, questioning the claim that reference to unintended consequences provides a distinctive form of explanation, frequently encountered in the work of the Scottish Enlightenment; the ideological, where the validity of claims at these first two levels has had some bearing on recent political debate. It will be argued that attitudes to constructivism operate independently from speculative historical accounts and from the abstract identification of causal mechanisms generating social order.

SPONTANEOUS ORDER VERSUS RATIONALIST CONSTRUCTIVISM?

Hayek's view rests upon a sharp distinction and opposition between 'spontaneous order' and 'rationalist constructivism'. I will examine the question of the distinction between the two ideas in the next section. Here I want to subject their alleged opposition to scrutiny.

A clear opposition between these ideas is difficult to sustain, if only because both may be encountered in the work of the same author. Marx provides a striking example. If anyone deserves the label 'rationalist constructivist', then surely it is Marx. Even if not a utopian blueprint, the idea of the dictatorship of the proletariat is a clear case of rational transformation and reconstruction of the social order as willed by a specific class. Yet, at the same time, Marx's historical analysis deals extensively in unintended consequences. History is not only made under conditions unchosen by its actors. It is made behind their backs through mechanisms that are largely unknown to those actors. The example of Marx is particularly apposite since Hayek himself accepts Marx's dual position, taking issue only with the claim that Marx was the *first* writer to build his social analysis around unintended consequences (Hayek 1967a, 100n). But examples can also be identified in the work of key figures of the Enlightenment.

The chief culprit among French Enlightenment constructivists, Rousseau, produced one of the earliest general and systematic stories of unintended consequences. In *A Discourse on the Origin of Inequality*, Rousseau repeatedly explains how attempts to deal with an immediate problem or opportunity led to consequences unsought and unforeseen by the actors (Rousseau 1973, 82–8). The need for shelter was first met by the construction of crude huts, giving rise to 'a kind of property, in itself the source of a thousand quarrels and conflicts'. As skills became more developed, the skills themselves and their products became the objects of both esteem and envy. The individual's need to dominate nature had paved the way for a system of social domination and dependence. Only when concluding the sorry tale with an analysis of the introduction of strict laws of property and justice does Rousseau attribute the development to rational foresight. And even here, foresight is only enjoyed by a small section of society.

> Destitute of valid reasons to justify and sufficient strength to defend himself, ... the rich man, thus urged by necessity, conceived at length the profoundest plan that ever entered the mind of man ... let us institute rules of justice and peace, to which all without exception may be obliged to conform ... All ran headlong to their chains, in hopes of securing their liberty; for they had just wit enough to perceive the advantages of political institutions, without experience enough to enable them to foresee the dangers. (Rousseau 1973, 88–9)

Rousseau's prescriptive attitude is, of course, rather different. A legitimate social order must be based on the enlightened intentions of individuals who enact general principles, the consequences of which must be relatively transparent. But in his analysis of the origin and development of central features and institutions of society he is, with the one partial exception cited above, dealing with the unintended and unanticipated consequences of action. In contrast, Hume, one of the supposed apostles of spontaneous order, accounted for the origins of social institutions like justice, property and government in much more rationalist and constructivist fashion.

Although the *sentiment* of justice arises only after experience of property relations, the laws of justice *themselves* arise from perceptions of mutual interest in stable private property, free exchange, and consequent recognition of their value. These perceptions produce conventional (that is, intentional but not properly contractual) adjustments to behaviour such that adherence to the laws of justice becomes general (Hume 1978, 487–541). Problems emerge in these merely conventional arrangements requiring new motives to be sought for cooperation in the form of the recognition of political authority and the right of government to enforce obedience.

Although Hume by no means presents the transition from conventional to governed society as a single enlightened step, the erecting of government itself exhibits just such deliberate and intentional action. The need for authoritative command in war is the first step on the road to government. But the experience of military leadership is not, in itself, a simple solution to the problem of order. It provides a lesson that must first be learned and then put into practice. The society does not continue to obey the military leader simply out of habit. The military leader does not carry his new status into civil life; it is lost at the end of hostilities. Rather, the whole society carries back into civil life the experience of authority, making possible a new kind of relationship to be applied in other contexts. The genesis of civil authority lies not in the continuation of individual rule, from war into peace. It lies in the continuation of 'the same kind of authority' which 'naturally takes place in the civil government, which succeeds the military'. 'Camps are the true mothers of cities' (Hume 1978, 540–1), but they are so by the will of men, rather than through an insensible acceptance of prolonged generalship. *Not only* does Hume's account deal centrally in conscious and rational will, a *promise* to obey must be supposed as the *normal* basis for the emergence of political authority (Hume 1978, 541–6).

Whereas promising was not an available device at the birth of conventional society, being a result of that birth (Hume 1978, 516–25), it would be an obvious and commonly used security in a society seeking to institute government. So although conventional property is not *promise-based* (Hume 1978, 490), and although government is established to maintain conventional promising and other laws of justice, government itself is first formed by a promise of obedience to magistrates (Hume 1978, 537).

Justice, government and society itself arise from perceptions of a common interest in their institution, and from acts intended to satisfy that interest. This is not the usual reading of Hume. His work is generally held to portray the social fabric as neither generated nor maintained by the artifices of an individual or group. Social order and its constitutive rules emerge spontaneously from day-to-day interaction (Haakonssen 1981, 4–39; Hayek 1960, 54–70; Hayek 1967b). I think it is hard to maintain this as a reading of Hume's *Treatise*, although it is certainly worth considering as an aspect of Hume's later work.

Hume's later position, expressed in the *Essays*, appears to move away from the language of will and consent towards a more spontaneous form of order: much more is made of the gradual transformation of military to civil authority (Hume 1985, 39–40 and 467–70); force, habit and acquiescence replace universal consent (Hume 1985, 40). Yet this shift is not so significant as it might first appear.

The real change in the later accounts is not from will to spontaneous order. It is from the general embrace of an enlightened solution to the problems of social and political order towards a solution that is imposed by one group upon another (Hume 1985, 33 and 38–9). Here the motives of the superior or governing group are crucial. If the motives for imposing order are quite separate from the outcome Hume is trying to explain, if the political reinforcement of legitimate rules of justice is not the end sought in imposing order, then we may have evidence of a move towards unintended consequences and spontaneous order. But there are grounds, at least, for doubting this.

John Stewart has argued that Hume's later view

> emphasises increasingly the extent to which the actualization of the principles of governance comes about, not by human insight and design, but rather, accidentally, as an unanticipated consequence of less worthy human strivings. (Stewart 1963, 158)

This is fair up to a point. But if we focus more closely on Hume's account we will see that this obscures the extent to which insight, design and worthy strivings remain aspects of the *Essays*. Hume's instigators and intentional supporters of political authority are, in the terms chosen by Hume, not at all like Rousseau's self-interested confidence tricksters. They are 'partizans and all men of probity', the 'peaceable and well-disposed'. And the subjects of their attentions are not the bulk of society insensibly rushing headlong to their chains. They are the 'refractory and disobedient' (Hume 1985, 38–9).

However, it is not this difference in detail with which I am here concerned. It is rather the more general similarity. Within the terms of their own characterizations of the outcomes, Hume's account in the *Essays* and Rousseau's final stage in the *Discourse* are remarkably similar. In both cases the more powerful section succeeds in imposing its will over the less powerful. In both cases the outcome is foreseen, intended and achieved by the more powerful group. What is different is the outcome itself. For Hume, the outcome is the solution to a problem. For Rousseau, the outcome is itself a problem. It is this difference that underlies their use of a common language of intention and design to quite different purposes. Crudely, 'Hume's solution' is presented as the result of probity and benevolent intention, 'Rousseau's problem' is presented as the product of self-interest and malign motive.

We may conclude that there is no very sharp line to be drawn between some of the key figures of the Enlightenment on these matters. Explanations in terms of unintended consequences are combined with more rationalist constructivist accounts.[1] The key difference lies not, I think, in the type of *explanation* offered for the development of basic social and political institutions but directly in the normative attitudes taken to the existing order.

THE POINT OF INTENTIONS

Hayek attributed much confusion in European social thought to 'the mis-leading division of all phenomena into those which are "natural" and those which are "artificial"'. This is misleading partly because the terms can be used to describe two quite different distinctions:

> either the contrast between something which was independent of human action and something which was the result of human action, or ... the contrast between something which had come about without, and some-thing which had come about as a result of, human design. (Hayek 1967, 96–7)

Hayek may well be right in pointing out the confusion generated by vari-ous natural/artificial distinctions. But he may be mistaken in thinking that similar confusion can be avoided by introducing notions like 'unintended consequences', 'spontaneous order' and the 'invisible hand'. These by no means constitute a *distinct* group.

Exactly what constitutes an explanation in terms of unintended conse-quences? What features might we require and value in identifying this form of explanation? Most of the difficulties here centre on the nature and role of 'intention'.

It is far from obvious what meaning should be given to 'intention' when attempting to specify an unintended consequence explanation. There are two main alternatives. We might require that 'intention' be identified with the deliberate end motivating the act such that only outcomes purposely sought may be explained by the intentions of the actor and, conversely, that all other outcomes must be explained as unintended consequences of action. Alternatively, we might define 'intention' more broadly to include outcomes knowingly brought about by the act: the anticipated results of deliberate action. Here the notion of *unintended* consequences becomes identical to *unanticipated* consequences. (See Merton 1936.)

Variations are possible within these broad alternatives. Specific knowl-edge and purpose might be required as either a necessary or a sufficient condition for action. The category of anticipated consequences may be adjusted to include only those favourable to, though not necessarily directly sought by, the actor. Various requirements can be imposed concerning the degree of conscious purpose or explicit knowledge. The requirement for explicit knowledge may be replaced altogether by some notion of what an actor might reasonably have been expected to know.

It will be difficult to offer any very compelling argument for selecting one set of criteria rather than another. From an operational point of view the exercise may be fruitless since cases clearly displaying the required criteria may be all too rare (Giddens 1976, 82–5). But even conceptually, the exercise will be impossible without some idea of the intended point of the explanation. What interest might we have in providing an explanation within this general form?

If our concern is primarily normative, particularly where our interest is in exercising moral or legal judgement, the more precise requirements will be determined by the conditions for fixing moral or legal responsibility in relation to both motive and knowledge. From an ideological point of view our interest may be in placing as much or as little as possible within or without human control; typically, the conservative may impose very strict and narrow ideas of intention while the radical operates with broader notions. From a purely explanatory or social scientific perspective, it is not easy to identify any reasons for either broad or narrow definitions. If we are just trying to explain the mechanisms generating certain outcomes then there seems little point in insisting on one or another definition. A full explanation must, in any case, try to identify the nature and role of both purpose and knowledge. Were we to agree with Nozick's claim that invisible hand explanations are somehow more fundamental than those of design and intention (Nozick 1974, 18–19), we might be able to proceed further. If 'fundamental' can be taken to track 'unexpected' and 'deeply hidden', then the narrower definitions should yield the better explanations. But the claim seems mistaken. Assuming that events just do sometimes unfold in accordance with our wills or expectations, and sometimes not, I think it more reasonable to look for empirical fit than to privilege one particular form of explanation.

This need for *explanation* must be emphasized. Many references to outcomes that are unintended by actors provide no real explanation for the outcome, beyond eliminating the intentional candidate. Even specifying the background conditions that may explain the frustration of intentions does not, of itself, explain the specific outcome. To the extent that the operative causal mechanism remains unspecified, the outcome itself must remain mysterious. For instance, I may set out to establish a successful catering business and achieve only bankruptcy. Subsequent enquiry by the Official Receiver reveals my total ignorance of all matters commercial and culinary. We may suppose that some knowledge and experience is necessary for success and accordingly sketch a rough explanation for the failure of my intention. But we have no idea of the specific mechanism that produced the outcome. Only as we fill in the detail of this do we produce an unintended consequence which serves as an *explanation*.

The Official Receiver may have no interest in providing such an explanation. After all, it is not his business to educate me either in business
skills or the culinary arts. He will be more concerned to fix responsibility
for my indebtedness and, more specifically, whether my ignorance can be
counted negligent. Social science generally displays broader interests and
will be concerned to uncover more detail of the mechanisms positively
involved. It will generally not be informed by the central concern for
intentions that legal officials and moral philosophers most clearly display.
If it seeks to locate explanation by reference to some specific notion of
'intention', this remains to be uncovered in particular cases.

There are different members of the same rough grouping of explanations, satisfying different cognitive interests. Different degrees of explanation may be sought. I shall examine some familiar examples to illustrate
this variety and to prepare the way for questioning some of the conclusions commonly drawn from them by arguing that this range of different
types of explanation is present in the work of the Scottish Enlightenment;
and that some sense of intention and design are more common features of
the social world, and of the Scottish Enlightenment's view of that world,
than is generally supposed.

I have already outlined the reasons for my reluctance to accept that
much in the way of unintended consequence explanations can be found in
Hume's work. Even where he is not describing the deliberate invention
of social institutions, no mechanism distinct from the intentions of the
individual actors is uncovered. When two people act justly towards one
another they do so because they have recognized the mutual advantages of
justice. They may not intend to create or contribute to the creation of a
full-scale *institution* of justice; they may not even anticipate that outcome.
But the wider social institution comprises only the aggregated actions of
similarly motivated individuals.

In the work of Adam Smith the picture is more mixed. In his *Theory of
Moral Sentiments* he claimed that the rich

> are led by an invisible hand to make nearly the same distribution of the
> necessaries of life, which would have been made, had the earth been
> divided into equal portions among all its inhabitants, and thus without
> intending it, without knowing it, advance the interest of the species, and
> afford means to the multiplication of the species. (Smith 1976a, 184–5)

By pretty well all of the criteria and on all of the counts listed above, this
must count as an unintended (and unanticipated) consequence explanation.
If we allow that Smith has provided an adequate account of the mechanisms involved, there can be no doubt that these mechanisms are quite

separate from the intentions of the individuals themselves. There is a definite and specific *pattern* of need satisfaction that is created without knowledge and therefore without any of the senses of purpose or intention. Nothing like the same can be said of two other examples to be found in Smith's *Wealth of Nations*. There Smith famously remarked that 'it is not from the benevolence of the butcher, the brewer, or the baker, that we expect our dinner, but from their regard to their own interest' (Smith 1976b, 26–7). And that when 'by preferring the support of domestick to that of foreign industry, he intends only his own security ... (but) ... he is in this, as in many other cases, led by an invisible hand to promote an end that was no part of his intention' (Smith 1976b, 456).

These passages are problematic in their status as unintended consequence explanations. As might be expected from the analysis offered above, there are a number of different reasons that may be offered for this claim.

Consistent with his general account, Smith began his description of the relation between butcher and consumer in different terms:

> Give me that which I want, and you shall have this that you want ... it is in this manner that we obtain from one another the far greater part of those good offices which we stand in need of. (Smith 1976b, 26)

Here it is clear that both parties are agreeing on action that will satisfy each of their needs. They know this. They intend it. And the exchange is exactly according to their mutual designs. No specific pattern of need satisfaction is created by other mechanisms. Only by employing a very strict notion of 'intention' does an unintended consequence explanation appear. It is not the butcher's *end* to satisfy his customers' needs. That is merely instrumental to the satisfaction of his own self-interest. Smith draws our attention to this by counterfactually proposing an alternative altruistic motive.

The domestic preference case is slightly different since, aside from explicit reference to the invisible hand, three parties (producer, consumer and public) are now involved. Whereas the butcher must give some attention to his customers' needs, the supporter of domestic preference may have no thought of public security. But here the outcome, enhancing the public interest, is a simple aggregation of private interests, enhanced individual security. In other words, while the end was not part of his intention his intention *was* part of the end.

In neither case is any identified mechanism at work beyond the broad intentions and knowledge of the actors. In the first case the outcome is designed and anticipated by all concerned. In the second the outcome is a simple aggregate of individual intentions where the aggregation may or may not be recognized by the actors.

Finally, no proper explanation is offered by *any* of these passages. This may seem an odd claim. After all, Smith does elsewhere specify the market mechanisms that produce the cited outcomes just as Hume explains the processes by which justice and political authority arise. What I mean to emphasize here is that the explanation offered and its explicit identification as an unintended consequence explanation are quite separate. Smith explains the working of the invisible hand and then points out that its product does not flow directly from the benevolence or public interest of the actor. Unintended consequence explanations have two components: the positive, which sets out, as any explanation must, the mechanisms that produce the outcome; and the negative, which draws attention to some alternative means by which the outcome might have been generated. In order fully to understand the account we need to know the reason for the choice of alternative, and to be able to accept this reason as salient. If Smith had told us that the provision of our dinner was not due simply to the intrinsic nature of meat, beer and bread we would be rather puzzled. Why should Smith bother to inform us of this? The information lacks salience since we would never have supposed that these commodities could, of themselves, have found their way to our table. The negative aspect of the explanation must refer to some commonly and plausibly held alternative account (see Ullman-Margalit 1978).

So why is Smith telling us this? Why is the positive economic analysis suddenly turned towards a view of what does *not* lie behind the outcomes? Is Smith claiming that he has provided a new approach to social explanation? I think not and I have argued here that, were those his intentions, he largely failed. Smith was not seeking to disabuse his readers of the notion that their dinner is provided by the benevolence of the butcher. His readers have sufficient knowledge of butchers to work that out for themselves and Smith is counting on that knowledge. Rather he is pointing out rhetorically that we need not suppose that virtue and public spirit are, in all areas of life, the necessary preconditions for social stability and well-being. His intended targets are not rationalist constructivists who hold primitive beliefs about the origins and nature of social institutions. It is more likely that the targets are orthodox christians and classical republicans whose beliefs about the role of virtue in the nature and ends of man and society might lead to misplaced concern about commercialization.

There is a close parallel to be drawn here with Hume. I have argued that Hume's critique of contract theory fails to offer an account that is markedly different, at the level of mutual expectations and intentions, from its apparent target. His account of conventional society is very similar to a contractarian account, remarkably so for one apparently concerned to demolish contract theory. His analysis of the origins of government includes the notions of promise or consent. And although Locke's version of contract theory appears to be one of Hume's main targets, his critique seems to bite very weakly on Locke, if at all (Thompson 1977; Miller 1981, 85; Parry 1978, 150). The problem here, I think, is that Hume is not concerned with the broadly rationalist and intentionalist elements of contract theory. His quarrel is instead with the primary role accorded to promising, in the sense that a divine sanction is being introduced as the basis for obligation. The primary aim of the argument is to show that the promise itself arises artificially and conventionally, that its obligation derives from perceived human and secular interests (Forbes 1975, 66–83).

Just as Hume is seeking to remove God and the divine sanction attached to promises from the picture, Smith is seeking, for slightly different though related reasons, to supplant the place of virtue. Neither writer is concerned to provide new and distinctive forms of social explanation; their intentions and their achievements are more narrowly focused.

The various 'explanations' set out here form a distinct group only in their negative aspect, in contrast with explanations in terms of the successful attainment of consciously sought ends by individuals or groups. This is a more or less empty category. No such explanations are seriously offered or are worthy of serious consideration. The closest candidate is probably the social contract tradition. But most examples of this are self-consciously abstract and hypothetical. They are not intended to operate as full and detailed empirical explanations.

The same may be said of the analysis provided by Hume and Smith. This is modestly offered in the form of speculative sketches and its 'unintentional' aspects are offered with limited and negative intent. Most examples of unintended consequence explanations tell us plainly that some factors are *not* responsible for a given outcome but indicate the actual mechanisms much more abstractly.

INTENTIONS, IGNORANCE AND PRACTICE

Unintended consequence explanations are frequently accompanied by a definite political message: if social institutions deliver goods independent of any design of the constitutive actors, then constructive design will impede the delivery of goods. In order to avoid an obvious logical mistake we must add the linking assumption: the nature of social interaction is such that design must prevent delivery.

This link is very hard to sustain. No very definite and interesting practical message can be derived from the narrowest versions of unintended consequence explanations. If the likely outcome of action *can* be foreseen by the actors, then it *can* be deliberately produced. The fact that other motives frequently prompt the action is neither here nor there from the perspective of constructive planning. Of course, the policy-maker must plan on the basis of accurate information about the motives that are likely to prompt other actors. But the precise nature of those motives has no bearing on the possibility of successful planning. What *does* have bearing is the knowledge available of mechanisms and likely outcomes within the system. We must therefore deal with the broader notion of unanticipated consequences.

Humourists are fond of developing 'laws' to catch the frequent frustrations of human endeavour. Many of these laws fall under the general description 'something always goes wrong'. This is clearly not an explanation. It indicates that whatever the outcome is, it is unlikely to realize the aims of the actors. It does not provide any explanation of the outcome itself and we might therefore regard it as an unintended consequence non-explanation. If an *explanation* can be provided, then the mechanisms generating the outcome can be known and, in principle, the actors could have adjusted their actions accordingly. There may be cases when, in practice, this adjustment is impossible and there may be cases when the mechanisms can only be identified after the event, but these have scant bearing on the present argument. If we have an explanation for a type of outcome then, even if it runs counter to our original intuitions, we can adjust our actions accordingly.

Hirschman has noted cases of this sort. If we think that 'safer' cars may produce reckless driving and more deaths, or more deaths of innocent victims, then we may save some innocent victims by making cars less 'safe' (Hirschman 1991, 35–42). Unanticipated consequence explanations depend on the contingent existence of ignorance and, in explaining, provide their own correction. They do not prohibit or discourage rationalist constructivism. They license it.

Hirschman cites a further example of interest. His earlier work, *Exit, Voice and Loyalty*, was apparently inspired by a single observation. Subjecting the Nigerian railway system to more competition from roads did not result in its increased efficiency. It resulted in its collapse. The more users exited, the less they pressed for a better railway system. Its operators were thus able to display even greater disregard for its efficient operation than before (Hirschman 1970, 44–5).

In terms of the events themselves, rather than the decision precipitating them, the consequences may or may not have been anticipated. But no very mysterious mechanism beyond human ken was operating. Disregard for efficiency is likely to produce exit. Exit withdraws revenue and voice. In so far as, *ceteris paribus*, this will have some deleterious effects, these may be reasonably anticipated by the actors. The only information simply not available to the actors is the exact volume of exits and the point at which further moves trigger total breakdown. The general tendency to which their deliberate acts are contributing is pretty transparent. With regard to the policy-makers, unintended consequences may be involved. If the policy-makers were working with the general rule 'competition will increase the efficiency of the railways', then the consequences were certainly unintended. But this is purely contingent. It is not a necessary feature of all similar situations that mistaken knowledge be applied. Ignorance, not the working of any invisible hand, constitutes the core of the explanation.

Any support offered by an unintended consequence *explanation* to an anti-interventionist stance derives not from the role of intentions but from the presence of ignorance. To the extent that ignorance is identified as a necessary feature of all similar situations (not just as a contingent characteristic of some actors), explanatory force is progressively reduced. The strongest argument against intervention is to be gained from a position of complete scepticism, where it is claimed that no consequences can conceivably be anticipated since the interactions are so complex that no definite or stable pattern can possibly be discerned. But in claiming this we cannot also claim to provide an unintended consequence *explanation*. All we can provide is a rough sketch of the reasons for an explanatory void. This may remain our position. As Hahn has noted of various 'invisible hands': 'Our knowledge of the actual movements of the hand is rudimentary and vastly incomplete' (Hahn 1982, 20).

CONCLUSION

I have suggested that the role of unintended consequences and spontaneous order has been overstated in some interpretations of the Scottish Enlightenment, and that its role elsewhere has been ignored. One of the reasons for this may be the failure to identify the proper context for eighteenth-century references to intention and design. But a more straightforward reason can be offered. A one-sided reading of the Scottish Enlightenment has clear ideological implications.

We are led to believe that the genius of Hume and Smith lay in their ability to penetrate the surface of social order and to show that it was produced by something other than individual intentions. The harmonious elements of order are not produced by a harmony of intentions. Social structures, including ideas like 'justice', are unintended consequences of action. A complex, civilized society cannot be entrusted to the rational judgement and will of the populace. Only the insensible threads of tradition, woven into the fabric of society over centuries of unconstrained interaction, can bind society together and satisfy individual interests.

Read in this way, writers like Hume and Smith could be appropriated for the purposes of the New Right. A nice blend of conservatism and liberalism emerges. To detach social outcomes from intentions is to protect the existing order by casting doubt on our ability, rationally or wilfully, to improve it. Any change must seek to allow market mechanisms to operate at all levels, free from any imposed constraints.

There can be no strong objection to this general exercise in appropriation. Everybody engages in it; and there is ample material in the Scottish Enlightenment to support these particular views. My objection is rather that the wrong material has been appropriated and that this misappropriation has exposed us to the danger of extending the identification of 'spontaneous order' in the service of 'rationalist constructivism'.

The claims of the New Right repeat the errors of constructivism. Its members claim to have discovered a form of *explanation* and a specific set of mechanisms which can be used to deliver the publicly desired and valued goods. They have done no such thing. They have acutely identified the source of our ignorance of the detailed mechanisms of social order. They have then proceeded to recommend policy as if that ignorance had been abolished by its identification. With a nice irony, the Nigerian policymakers who provided Hirschman with his inspiration, were as plausibly operating from new right assumptions as from constructivism.

Hayek and others have conflated two elements in the Scottish Enlightenment. One is the modesty and scepticism its leading members display in ample proportion. This element, taken alone, would offer support to a (modest) New Right position. The other element is the discovery of 'spontaneous order' and explanations in the form of unintended and unanticipated consequences. This latter element must be distinguished from the former, occurs in a wider variety of forms, and has less substance than its proponents allege.

NOTE

1.   Stewart's later work on Hume accepts this. Contrasting Mandeville with Hume, he notes that 'Hume is not content to rely on spontaneity alone; the

discovery of the principles of justice and governance makes it possible to correct policies and improve institutions' (Stewart 1992, 216n).

REFERENCES

Forbes, Duncan (1975) *Hume's Philosophical Politics*, Cambridge: Cambridge University Press.

Giddens, Anthony (1976) *New Rules of Sociological Method*, London: Hutchinson.

Haakonssen, Knud (1981) *The Science of a Legislator*, Cambridge: Cambridge University Press.

Hahn, Frank (1982) 'Reflections on the Invisible Hand', *Lloyds Bank Review*, 144, 1–21.

Hayek, F.A. (1960) *The Constitution of Liberty*, London: Routledge & Kegan Paul.

Hayek, F.A. (1967a) 'The Results of Human Action but not of Human Design', *Studies in Philosophy, Politics and Economics*, London: Routledge & Kegan Paul.

Hayek, F.A. (1967b) 'The Legal and Political Philosophy of David Hume', *Studies in Philosophy, Politics and Economics*, London: Routledge & Kegan Paul.

Hayek, F.A. (1982) *Law, Legislation and Liberty*, London, Routledge & Kegan Paul.

Hirschman, Albert O. (1970) *Exit, Voice, and Loyalty*, Cambridge, Mass.: Harvard University Press.

Hirschman, Albert O. (1991) *The Rhetoric of Reaction*, Cambridge, Mass.: Harvard University Press.

Hume, David (1978) *A Treatise of Human Nature*, 2nd edn, ed. L.A. Selby-Bigge, Oxford: Oxford University Press.

Hume, David (1985) *Essays: Moral, Political, and Literary*, ed. Eugene F. Miller, Indianapolis: Liberty Press.

Merton, Robert K. (1936) 'The Unanticipated Consequences of Purposive Social Action', *American Sociological Review*, 1, 894–904.

Miller, David (1981) *Philosophy and Ideology in Hume's Political Thought*, Oxford: Oxford University Press.

Nozick, Robert (1974) *Anarchy, State, and Utopia*, Oxford: Blackwell.

Parry, Geraint (1978) *John Locke*, London: George Allen & Unwin.

Rousseau, Jean-Jacques (1973), *The Social Contract and Discourses*, London: Dent.

Smith, Adam (1976a) *The Theory of Moral Sentiments*, eds A.L. Macfie and R.R. Raphael, Oxford: Oxford University Press.

Smith, Adam (1976b) *An Inquiry into the Nature and Causes of the Wealth of Nations*, eds R.H. Campbell and A.S. Skinner, Oxford: Oxford University Press.

Stewart, J.B. (1963) *The Moral and Political Philosophy of David Hume*, New York: Columbia University Press.

Stewart, J.B. (1992) *Opinion and Reform in Hume's Political Philosophy*, Princeton: Princeton University Press.

Thompson, Martyn P. (1977) 'Hume's Critique of Locke and the "Original Contract"', *Il Pensiero Politico*, X, 189–201.

Ullman-Margalit, Edna (1978) 'Invisible-Hand Explanations', *Synthèse*, 39, 263–91.

Part II
Assessing the Enlightenment Roots of Modernity

7 English Conservatism and Enlightenment Rationalism
Ian Holliday

Conflict between English conservatism and Enlightenment rationalism has been well advertised ever since Edmund Burke published his *Reflections on the Revolution in France*. For Burke, the revolution was at least in part an authentic product of the rationalistic speculations of Enlightenment philosophers. 'I am certain,' he wrote, 'that the writings of Rousseau lead directly to this kind of shameful evil' (Nisbet, 1986: 8). In attacking the political practice of the French revolutionaries (and their would-be English imitators), Burke also sought to undermine the political theory of Enlightenment rationalists.

In subsequent years, many conservatives have joined Burke in making Enlightenment rationalism a prime target for criticism. In the nineteenth century, Benthamism replaced Jacobinism as the focal point of attack, and was roundly condemned by English conservatives. The Panopticon, which Bentham thought appropriate not only to prisons but also to schools, hospitals, asylums and factories, was dismissed by Disraeli as 'the unlovable issue of a marriage between reason and inhumanity' (Nisbet, 1986: 17). Lesser utilitarian minds and projects were of course also brought within conservative range. In the twentieth century, Marxism in turn replaced Benthamism as the rationalist project which chiefly exercised conservative thinkers. For Michael Oakeshott (1991: 31), it was 'the most stupendous of our political rationalisms', a judgement from which few conservatives have sought to dissent. To the present day, conservatives have found instances of Enlightenment rationalism to criticize.

Yet conflict has not invariably characterized relations between English conservatism and Enlightenment rationalism. One of the most important points made by Oakeshott in his 1947 essay 'Rationalism in Politics' was that in the post-war era rationalism had come to infect a wide spectrum of political activity. This, he thought, was the 'main significance' of Hayek's *Road to Serfdom*, published just three years previously: 'A plan to resist all planning may be better than its opposite, but it belongs to the same style of politics' (Oakeshott, 1991: 26). More relevant to this discussion, for Hayek was neither English nor in any straightforward sense conservative (Hayek, 1960), is the fact that Oakeshott made a similar point in reviewing Quintin Hogg's *The Case for Conservatism*, also published in 1947, stating that it provided clear evidence of the rationalistic disposition of contemporary Conservatism. In case there should be any doubt about the matter, Oakeshott included in a list of projects which were 'alike the progeny of Rationalism' both the Beveridge Report of 1942, which the Conservative Party endorsed, and the Education Act 1944, which one of its leading figures enacted (Oakeshott, 1991: 11). His summary judgement was emphatic: 'almost all politics today have become Rationalist or near-Rationalist' (Oakeshott, 1991: 5).

During the course of the past two centuries, English conservatism has, then, had changing relations with Enlightenment rationalism. The deeply critical and strongly oppositional strand launched by Burke in the late eighteenth century has been sustained into the late twentieth century. However, since Burke's time conservative accommodation with Enlightenment rationalism has also taken place. This chapter analyses the changing relations between English conservatism and Enlightenment rationalism, beginning by stating what it takes the term 'Enlightenment rationalism' to mean.

ENLIGHTENMENT RATIONALISM

The term is, of course, controversial, because to many the Enlightenment was not a particularly rationalistic movement or age. From the very start a distinction was drawn between seventeenth-century rationalism and eighteenth-century empiricism (Cassirer, 1951), and in years since that distinction has been reinforced by a wealth of studies dedicated to documenting the empiricism of Enlightenment thought and the substantial sensitivity to local circumstance which characterized the age. The vogue for travel and travel writing surveyed by Ursula Vogel's chapter in this collection was one element of the Enlightenment's empiricist temper, and was both cause and consequence of the relativist thinking of the age. But empiricism was revealed by many other aspects of eighteenth-century thought. Its sheer extent prompted Peter Gay (1970: 189) to state that 'the Enlightenment was not an age of reason but a revolt against rationalism'. The point could not be made more clearly.

To talk of Enlightenment rationalism would thus seem mistaken. Yet it is not entirely so, and has certainly not been seen as folly by a number of English conservative writers. For the fact is that in the political, if not in the philosophical, sphere, Enlightenment rationalism was substantially seeking, as a matter of urgency, to subject all institutions and practices to rationalist scrutiny, or, as Condorcet put it, 'to bring every authority before the bar of Reason' (Gay, 1973: 801). In the eighteenth century, this element drew on natural law rhetoric, often duly secularized. In the nineteenth and twentieth, its inspiration has been chiefly utilitarian. Throughout, it has generated a belief that no social or political institution or practice can be accorded legitimacy until it has been provided with a rational defence.

The position has been refined and extended, but this has always been core. Diderot wrote a classic statement of it into the *Encyclopaedia*: 'All things must be examined, debated, investigated without exception and without regard for anyone's feelings...We must ride roughshod over all these ancient puerilities, overturn the barriers that reason never erected, give back to the arts and sciences the liberty that is so precious to them' (Gay, 1973: 289). In liberating the arts and sciences, reason was of course also to be set free. Voltaire made a more succinct statement of Enlightenment rationalism when he declared, in an echo of Plato, that the only way to have good laws is to burn all existing laws and start afresh (Oakeshott, 1991: 9). Enlightenment rationalism may also be found in the political practice of the late eighteenth century. According to Oakeshott, but not Burke, it was present during the revolution in America. 'The Declaration of Independence,' wrote Oakeshott (1991: 33), 'is a characteristic product of the *saeculum rationalisticum*.' According to both men, it featured in the revolution in France. As was decreed by the Committee on Public Safety, 'You must entirely refashion a people whom you wish to make free, to destroy its prejudices, alter its habits, limit its necessities, root up its vices, purify its desires' (Nisbet, 1986: 10).

The rationalism of the Enlightenment which is analysed here may not then be the same as that which had characterized the previous century. Indeed, in terms of method a shift undoubtedly did take place. Yet in the political sphere the difference was that the eighteenth century was more rationalistic than had been the seventeenth. The 'recovery of nerve' which Gay (1970: 6) states took place in the eighteenth century encompassed a novel confidence in human ability to refashion human institutions according to the dictates of reason. Alongside the empiricist sensitivities of the age may thus be found the belief that universal standards are discoverable by reason, and may appropriately be applied to existing human societies and arrangements. In the political sphere the Enlightenment placed a premium on reason and on strict deduction of the kind found in geometry. It was, moreover, unusual to its point in history in the extent to which it believed political reform to be possible. One of its lasting legacies has been a faith in human ability to recast social and political institutions on a more rational footing. The 'spirit of innovation', or idle worship of change for its own sake, which appalled Burke is in essence the rationalism which Oakeshott held to be a pervasive feature of twentieth-century politics.

ENGLISH CONSERVATISM

Why English conservatism has been selected as the perspective from which to view Enlightenment rationalism should also be explained. It is, after all, merely one of a series of possible perspectives, and even of possible critiques. Within the conservative tradition, the increasingly authoritarian French and often romantic German responses to Enlightenment rationalism are alternatives. Outside the tradition, a wide range of responses has been witnessed, possibly the closest to conservatism in its many guises being the authoritarianism and fascism which can plausibly trace their roots to conservative writers.

The focus on English conservatism has two main justifications. The first is that it was within this tradition that the first great response to Enlightenment rationalism, that of Burke, was articulated. Burke's writings have remained a reference point for many subsequent thinkers and are often central to debate of this kind. The second is that a fairly continuous 'conversation' about Enlightenment rationalism has been a feature of the English conservative tradition for the past 200 years. That said, it must be acknowledged that the conversation has not been entirely self-contained, and has not even had unanimously agreed terms of debate. Many English conservatives, notably Coleridge, Carlyle and a number of English idealists, have drawn inspiration from Germany. Some have even sought to distance themselves, at least in part, from the Burkean heritage. Oakeshott is one of these, having stated in a rare explicit reference to Burke that conservatives probably have more to learn from Hume. In much of his own work he was of course most influenced by Hobbes and Hegel. Yet despite each of these qualifications, the English conservative conversation about Enlightenment rationalism has been sustained and vibrant. These are the principal reasons for its selection.

THE CONSERVATIVE CRITIQUE

The English conservative critique of Enlightenment rationalism has had a number of dimensions and many proponents. Only two dimensions and two proponents are analysed here. The two dimensions are the most significant to have been developed by conservatives. The first is epistemological, and seeks to demonstrate that Enlightenment rationalism is poor theory.

The second is sociological, and attempts to show that it is poor practice. Of the two, the second has generally been more important to conservatives, who tend to rank political practice above political theory. The two proponents are Burke and Oakeshott, the most sophisticated analysts of Enlightenment rationalism to have been produced by the English conservative tradition, and proponents of distinct critiques.

Burke's epistemological critique depends upon careful delineation of the proper province and most reliable sources of knowledge. In determining its proper province, Burke in no sense holds reason to be irrelevant to practical politics. He does, however, maintain that any grand attempt to subject human arrangements to rational scrutiny through application of the deductive method is doomed to failure. 'The science of constructing a commonwealth, or renovating it, or reforming it, is, like every other experimental science, not to be taught *a priori*' (Burke, 1968: 152). The explanation for this failure relates chiefly to Burke's estimation of the most reliable sources of knowledge: not the 'sophisters, calculators, and economists' who undertake the rational scrutiny, however sharp they may be, but the institutions themselves. He argues that the accumulated wisdom embodied in established institutions simply cannot be matched by any individual or committee. In the middle of the present century, Hayek and the Austrian school of economists made a similar point about the market order. Burke, at the end of the eighteenth century, did not live to see rationalistic control of the market become a serious possibility, and was more concerned to place limits on feasible scrutiny of established social and political institutions. His case, in essence, was that as a matter of empirical fact the locus of knowledge in society prevents really radical or revolutionary change from succeeding. Moreover, no society is in such a bad state of repair as to be unreformable on the basis of existing institutions. Even the *ancien régime*, frequently derided in England prior to the revolution, was held by Burke after it to have 'the elements of a constitution almost as good as could be desired' (Cobban, 1960: 11).

For Burke, this state of affairs was merely an aspect of 'the nature of things', immutable and inescapable. 'For, gentleman, it is not your fond desires or mine that can alter the nature of things; by contending against which, what have we got, or shall ever get, but defeat and shame?' (Freeman, 1980: 16). Burke's advice was that reformers and, indeed, ordinary men and women take advantage of the wisdom embodied in prejudice: 'We are afraid to put men to live and trade each on his own private stock of reason; because we suspect that the stock in each man is small, and that the individuals would do well to avail themselves of the general bank and capital of nations, and of ages' (Burke, 1968: 183).

Burke's argument that the political rationalism of the Enlightenment operates on less knowledge than it might, and is therefore irrational, has been largely accepted by subsequent conservative writers, or at least by those who have taken an interest in this aspect of debate. One key individual who at least partially disagreed with Burke was, however, Oakeshott. His critique of Enlightenment rationalism is both theoretically more substantial and empirically less incisive than was Burke's.

Oakeshott's starting point is similar to Burke's, and indeed to that adopted by other mid-twentieth-century thinkers, such as Ryle and Polanyi. Human activity draws on a social fund of experience. However, for Oakeshott this is the case to such an extent that 'Mind as we know it is the offspring of knowledge and activity' (Oakeshott, 1991: 109), and in a strict sense does not exist in absence of experience. The result is that the world described by Oakeshott is at least as heavily structured as that described by Burke. Human activities, for Oakeshott, are based on patterns. Those patterns have no extrinsic source, and no clear rationale. They are instead intrinsic to activities themselves. By providing human activity with coherence, they serve to integrate the individual into society and to establish standards of right and wrong. Oakeshott is, then, deeply conscious of the texture and quality of shared human practices which, he believes, are among the greatest of human achievements. Practices provide the context within which individual autonomy and self-expression take place. They are conditions of human freedom.

In a more analytical way than Burke's, Oakeshott describes the nature of the human social condition. He also moves a step further than Burke in denying that the practices which structure that condition can ever be significantly undermined. For Oakeshott, social practices are themselves part of what Burke called 'the nature of things', and whilst isolated practices can fall into disrepair or even in some cases disuse, as a body social practices can never be wholly destroyed. The difference might be thought to be one of degree, and to some extent it is. However, Burke's concern that French schemes of 'geometrical symmetry' in the state might actually succeed in substantially refashioning human institutions is dismissed by Oakeshott, for whom rationalistic change is a logical impossibility. His radical claim is that even the rationalist is trapped by tradition, and cannot significantly amend or distort it.

In Oakeshott's work, then, the Burkean contention that Enlightenment rationalism is irrational because it operates on less knowledge than it might is rejected. As even Enlightenment rationalists are prisoners of their social context, they are forced when seeking to engineer political change to make use of the vernacular knowledge accumulated through the ages.

It is merely in failing to realize that this is the case that rationalists are irrational. This analysis informs Oakeshott's celebrated notion of the 'pursuit of intimations', which is advanced by him not as a statement of desirability but as a point of fact. 'In political activity, then, men sail a boundless and bottomless sea; there is neither harbour for shelter nor floor for anchorage, neither starting-point nor appointed destination. The enterprise is to keep afloat on an even keel' (Oakeshott, 1991: 60). Entirely appropriately, Oakeshott (1991: 66) in the essay which develops these themes borrows F.H. Bradley's sardonic reworking of Leibniz's aphorism: 'The world is the best of all possible worlds, and *everything* in it is a necessary evil.'

As might be expected, differences between Burke and Oakeshott at the level of epistemology have consequences for their sociologies. Burke's key prediction in the *Reflections*, proved by the course of events to be highly accurate, was that the revolution in France would descend first into anarchy and secondly into tyranny. His contention is that rationalistic success in stripping away the bonds of society must mean that only force can restore order. Once the 'inns and resting-places', the 'little platoons' and the 'neighbourhoods and provincial connections' on which we habitually rely have been destroyed, the outcome can only be to 'confound all citizens ... into one homogenous mass'. As others were later to put it, the annihilation of internal social structures, integrating tradition and shared moral values creates the possibility of totalitarianism, for once social structures have been eliminated the very possibility of politics, as opposed to mere exercise of force, is denied. To prevent such a calamitous state of affairs from being reached, Burke maintained, it is necessary for an 'unsuspecting confidence' in existing institutions to prevail. The state, he wrote, 'is to be looked on with other reverence ... It is a partnership in all science; a partnership in all art; a partnership in every virtue, and in all perfection' (1968: 194).

It is important to get Burke right at this point. He did not believe, as did his French contemporary de Maistre, that the ordinary person was a tiger on a leash who could be kept in place only by explicit manifestation of the authority of the state, best represented by the hangman. Instead, Burke felt most individuals – or at least most of those about whom he claimed to know something, such as the English and the French – to be nicely adjusted to their condition. They tended to rub along pretty well, and to be largely satisfied with their stations and their duties. In consequence (and notwithstanding the blame he attached to Rousseau), Burke did not believe, as de Maistre did, that 'books did it all' in 1789. Despite the romanticized account of the *ancien régime* presented in the *Reflections*,

Burke was certainly prepared to acknowledge that the revolution had real social and political origins, and that it was not merely the product of philosophical speculation (Freeman, 1980: ch. 10). Nevertheless, he also felt that it was not sensible to sanction too much institutional inquiry. 'It is always to be lamented,' he wrote, 'when men are driven to search into the foundations of commonwealth.' Indeed, in 1791 he became very alarmed at the expression of radical opinions in the *Morning Chronicle* and other newspapers, and in 1792 he opposed the Unitarians' petition on the grounds that this was not merely a theological sect requesting toleration, but a political faction harbouring designs against church and state. For Burke, proposals for political change should properly be handled at elite level and kept from the masses. As Plamenatz (1992: 102) put it, 'innocence is safer than curiosity, at least for most people'. Underlying Burke's entire sociological analysis was a pre-Marxian understanding of class which did not posit the harmony sometimes read into his notion of an organic society, but which held that proper and often jealous defence of class rights and privileges is actually desirable in functional terms. In this sense, Burke was essentially a classicist of the Machiavellian kind, believing that classes ought to be able and ready to stick up for their traditional advantages. Such a conception did not readily stretch to a right to revolution, for it presumed a settled and stable institutional framework.

Burke, then, treats the classic conservative issue of order with extreme concern. 'Good order,' he wrote, 'is the foundation of all good things' (Freeman, 1980: 21). His concern is not shared by Oakeshott, for whom the question of order is comparatively uninteresting. This, of course, is the counterpart of his contention that no one can significantly disrupt a set of social practices. For Oakeshott, the French and all other revolutions were not genuinely revolutionary at all. The terms we have coined are merely shorthand for the more complex phenomena at issue. There is, he argues, 'little to support the view that even the most serious political upheaval carries us outside [the] understanding of politics [as the pursuit of intimations]' (Oakeshott, 1991: 59). Because he views rationalistic change as a logical impossibility, Oakeshott thus tends to the view that a structured and ordered social whole is largely inevitable. So substantial is his conception of the textured nature of human societies that he virtually dismisses the possibility of destruction. In consequence, the problem of order is not particularly pressing for him. The Oakeshottian universe is a rather well-mannered place where failures to live up to the best tend to be criticized merely as impolite.

Burke and Oakeshott articulated the two classic critiques of Enlightenment rationalism from within the English conservative tradition.

Burke's was increasingly characterized by the aggression, and sometimes despondency and gloom, displayed in the final decade of his life. Oakeshott's, by contrast, was marked by the comparative equanimity and detachment with which he viewed the rationalistic endeavours of the modern age. These two critiques do not, however, exhaust the range of possible conservative dealings with Enlightenment rationalism. In a rather schematic way, those dealings are surveyed in the next section of this chapter.

ENGLISH CONSERVATIVE DEALINGS WITH ENLIGHTENMENT RATIONALISM

The factor which has done most to complicate those dealings has also been the central problem faced by English conservatism in the past two centuries (and more). This is the social and economic change which has driven much political radicalism. Even as Burke bemoaned the demise of the tolerant Christianity which he rather romantically saw as a source of unity in the Europe of an age earlier than his own, and celebrated as one of its major achievements, substantial social fragmentation and dislocation were already taking place, prompted less by the French than by the industrial revolution. Fragmentation and dislocation have continued throughout the two centuries which have followed Burke's angry condemnations of the 1790s, culminating in the divided societies we now inhabit. In these circumstances, the challenge to conservatism has extended far beyond the theory of change propounded by Enlightenment rationalists. Indeed, were Enlightenment rationalism the limit of their difficulties, at least some English conservatives would have slept a lot more soundly in their beds. Instead, they have had to respond to something much larger, and in so doing have engaged in a series of distinct dealings with the Enlightenment's political rationalism.

As such, English conservatism has moved beyond the concern for the civilization of Christendom which marked its initial reaction to the changes of which the French Revolution was the most evident political manifestation (O'Sullivan, 1976: 32). Then Burke in England was joined by de Maistre in France and by Novalis in Germany in attempting to recapture the alleged unity of the pre-1789 European order (even though it had already experienced substantial secular decline prior to this date). In the longer term, however, conservative concerns altered. With time it became clear that the critical problem generated by the French Revolution was not that it had produced something unwelcome, but that it had produced nothing. France had not moved into the New Era promised by revolutionary leaders, but into a moral void. The death of Mirabeau had left only Napoleon (Culler, 1986: 153). As a result, the key conservative question shifted. In the nineteenth and twentieth centuries it increasingly became how to maintain and promote order in societies in which consensus on fundamental values has been replaced by profound ideological divisions on first-order issues. Indeed, the question often took a still sharper form, focusing on whether order is in fact possible in the absence of an underlying consensus of opinion upon fundamental values amongst the members of a modern state.

In seeking to develop answers to this question, English conservatism adopted strategies which had relations with Enlightenment rationalism stretching from outright rejection to substantial accommodation. Six main lines of thought are identified here: conservative romanticism, heroicism, resignation, materialism, legalism and organicism.

Conservative Romanticism

One early conservative response to the 'world turned upside-down' of the 1790s was highly nostalgic and sought, essentially, to pretend that neither Enlightenment rationalism nor social and economic change posed a real threat. The vogue for merrie England which continued well into the nineteenth century, and the obsession with rural life which has always been an aspect of modern conservative thought, are prime examples of it. In this vein too were nineteenth-century critiques of capitalism of the 'dark, satanic mill' variety, which came from many sources. Coleridge wrote of the 'tearing, rending, and shattering' impact of commerce and industry on social ties. Carlyle (1869: 320) held that 'Men are grown mechanical in head and heart, as well as in hand'. Disraeli expressed his hatred of 'a sort of spinning-jenny, machine kind of nation' (Nisbet, 1986: 65). In the twentieth century, rural nostalgia has been found in the speeches of Conservative Party leaders such as Stanley Baldwin and John Major, even though both men were a good deal more than mere conservative romantics. As we move into the twenty-first century, much Euroscepticism is rooted in this aspect of the conservative tradition.

It is rare for conservative romanticism to issue in reform proposals, the whole point being that the world was a much better place before reformism took hold of it. This, in essence, is an evasive and escapist strand of conservatism. When it has done so, however, it has tended to seek to create or recreate unity and a common identity in either church or state. Roger Scruton's contemporary brand of conservatism could plausibly be cited as an example. However, at this point conservative romanticism frequently shades into some form of conservative heroicism.

Conservative Heroicism

Within the conservative tradition, a tendency to seek strong, and preferably charismatic, leadership in difficult times has been a persistent theme (O'Sullivan, 1976: 93). As many of the past 200 years have been difficult, conservative heroicism has been a regular feature of the tradition. However, it perhaps reached its peak in the middle decades of the nineteenth century, when it was promoted subtly by Samuel Taylor Coleridge, polemically by Thomas Carlyle, and pragmatically by Benjamin Disraeli. Conservative heroicism is distinct from conservative romanticism in that it acknowledges that change is taking place and possibly even that rationalist schemes for addressing it are on the political agenda. It sets up the heroic individual as an alternative agent of change to the Enlightenment rationalist.

Coleridge was one of the first English conservatives to seek not simply to resist political change but instead to understand it. In so doing, he became convinced of the need for, and indeed inevitability of, reform. The stable and organic social order described by Burke no longer existed, and could not simply be recovered. Instead, a new political settlement was needed, by means of which a new organic social condition could be created. It could, Coleridge argued in *On the Constitution of the Church and State*, only be generated by a new spiritual elite organized into a national – not Christian – church. Although this also made Coleridge one of the first English conservatives to advocate a positive role for the state, he mainly saw change in spiritual rather than political terms. He was led by the logic of his argument to seek a species of charismatic leadership to promote change.

This element of mid-nineteenth-century conservative thought was taken a good deal further by Carlyle who, like Coleridge, believed regeneration of society to be dependent on individual conversion, not legislation. 'To reform a world, to reform a nation, no wise man will undertake; and all but foolish men know, that the only solid, though a far slower reformation, is what each begins and perfects on *himself*' (Carlyle, 1869: 342). Carlyle too, therefore, tended to look to a church for salvation, taking as his model in *Past and Present* the medieval monastic order, characterized by an ordered fellowship of souls. However, with the passage of time Carlyle became increasingly concerned, and indeed agitated, about the signs of irremediable disorganization which he thought were beginning to engulf contemporary society. From the *Latter-Day Pamphlets* it is clear that

'Carlyle's reality, his vision of England of 1850, was truly one of social and psychological chaos' (Seigel, 1976: 173). To counter systemic disorder, he therefore increasingly turned his attention to open adulation of the strong hero, identified by him as the 'missionary of order'. What had started as a passionate desire to rebuild shattered human communities became an anxious demand for authority and order. Still Carlyle claimed heroicism to be no more than a temporary expedient necessary to rescue individuals from the anarchy which characterizes a transitional period and to lead them to the genuine freedom which can only exist in an organic period. Yet in its growing polemicism Carlyle's work became an increasingly pure form of conservative heroicism, sought less in the traditional aristocracy than in the emergent commercial elite. 'The Leaders of Industry, if Industry is ever to be led, are virtually the Captains of the World; if there be nobleness in them, there will never be an Aristocracy more' (Carlyle, 1843: 335).

In practice, conservative heroicism was most successfully advanced by Disraeli. Disraeli believed that underpinning what he described in *Sybil* as the 'two nations; between whom there is no intercourse and no sympathy' (Disraeli, 1895: 74) there was in fact a basically organic society with a uniform character. Indeed, one of the main charges he levelled at utilitarianism was precisely that it was ignorant of this underlying unity. 'Nations,' he stated, 'have characters, and national character is precisely the quality which the new set of statesmen in their schemes and speculations either deny or overlook' (Nisbet, 1986: 26). His own view envisaged the statesman creating a national ideology and uniting the nation around the key institutions of Church, Monarchy and People. This was a weaker conception of leadership than that held by Carlyle and even Coleridge, but it drew on a similar understanding of contemporary politics. It was largely instituted in the Conservative Party which Disraeli helped to reform following passage of the second Reform Act of 1867, and was sustained by the myths of class (represented by Whigs and Liberals in the nineteenth century, and by Labour in the twentieth) and nation (represented by Tories throughout) which he helped to create. It was strongly reinforced by the imperialism which Disraeli introduced to Conservative ideology in his Crystal Palace speech of 1872 (O'Sullivan, 1976: 102).

In one form or another, then, heroicism has been an important aspect of practical conservative responses to the challenges of the past 200 years. It is by no means stretching a point to identify it in the Thatcherite Conservatism of the 1980s. The relationship between conservative heroicism and Enlightenment rationalism has usually been conflictual: the heroic individual stands as an alternative to the rationalist in judging existing institutions and proposing ways forward. However, this conflict does not have to be intense, and it would be quite possible for the heroic individual to engage in rationalist speculation and reform.

Conservative Resignation

Before leaving the nineteenth century, one further brand of conservative response to the problem of managing change may be noted: resignation. Underpinning the entire conservative tradition has always been a certain bleakness about the human condition: rarely is the Hobbesian state of war of all against all far away. O'Sullivan (1976: 43–4) shows that resignation as a response to the modern world is most profoundly displayed in the work of the French liberal conservative, Benjamin Constant. Here modern man is shown to be doomed to suffer inner self-division, inescapable loneliness and ultimate solitude to a degree not exceeded in the eighteenth-century writings of Rousseau or the twentieth-century writings of Beckett. Yet resignation also characterized the thoughts of other conservative writers, notably in the English tradition Lord Salisbury and his immediate circle. 'I confess much doubt,' wrote Hicks Beach, chief secretary for Ireland, to Salisbury, prime minister, in 1886, 'whether the country *can* be governed nowadays by persons holding opinions, which you and I should call even moderately conservative' (Gilmour, 1977: 11). Salisbury himself published his own thoughts – anonymously – in a *Quarterly Review* article entitled 'Disintegration'. Whilst accepting that nothing could be done to reverse many recent political changes – notably Disraeli's disastrous Reform Act of 1867 – Salisbury was determined to develop some means of disciplining a popular government which to his mind was moving ever further out of control. He had, however, no illusions about the kind of success that could be hoped for. Stalling was the most that could be achieved. 'Delay is life' (Marsh, 1978: 325).

This strand of conservatism is really the first of the six surveyed here to make some accommodation with political rationalism of the Enlightenment variety. Although its adherents have no faith in rationalistic endeavour, they have no plausible alternative to it either and end up going along with it whilst bemoaning their fates. This, too, is a theme which has persisted into the twentieth century. It tends to be partnered by a retreat into the private sphere, where a simple attempt to maintain personal integrity in the face of a hostile world is made.

Conservative Materialism

English conservatism did not, however, lose its nerve and succumb entirely to resignation in the twentieth century. Instead, in the middle decades of the century it developed a materialism which brought it into close accommodation with the rationalism in politics derided by Oakeshott in the late 1940s. This strand of conservative thought may be traced to James FitzJames Stephen's *Liberty, Equality and Fraternity*, published in 1873 (O'Sullivan, 1976: 112–15). It was most developed, however, by the so-called technocratic Tories who took some inspiration from Harold Macmillan's *The Middle Way*, published in 1939, but whose most prominent contributions to party policy were the industrial and other charters produced by R.A. Butler and others in the late 1940s, and the various neo-corporatist initiatives taken under Edward Heath in the early 1970s. At the core of this strand of conservatism lies an attempt to secure legitimacy and social order through material advance for all. In consequence, politics tends to be subordinated to administration, and some form of corporatism may emerge.

The accommodation made by this strand with Enlightenment modes of thinking is its willingness to subscribe to rationalist projects as a means of securing the material advance it seeks. The most evident recent example of this kind of accommodation is Conservative promotion of British membership of the EEC by Macmillan and Heath in the 1960s, and by Heath and his supporters in subsequent years. Based on a prominent materialist foundation, this policy has been anathema to many Conservatives precisely because it is viewed as too destructive of British practices and traditions. The post-war period has, however, witnessed many other instances of rationalist Conservative reform undertaken for materialist ends.

Conservative Legalism

Setting itself in opposition to conservative materialism has been a more legalistic brand of contemporary conservatism. Prompted in large part by what was held to be excessive accommodation with fundamentally non-conservative values and indeed approaches to politics, a group of conservative writers emerged in the 1960s and 1970s to promote a conservative rule of law ideal. It comprised the likes of Enoch Powell, Sir Keith Joseph and Nevil Johnson. Arguably, Oakeshott, Shirley Robin Letwin and John Gray have also contributed to this line of thought. For this group, the organicism and intermediary institutions held by Burke (and others) to be necessary to social order are in many ways irrelevant. There is, they tend to argue, no need for specific agreement on substantive values. What is required is only that all acknowledge the authority of law in the conduct of their lives. Indeed, this form of conservatism often positively rejects organicist ideals. Respect for rules is the key reference point for good and bad behaviour. Other attempts to promote legitimacy are likely to distract from it. Social justice is, then, dismissed by rule-of-law conservatives because it places citizens' political obligation outside the state and thereby disrupts institution of uniform rules (Devigne, 1994: 118).

This strand of conservatism currently poses a substantial challenge to the materialism which has dominated English conservative thought for much of the twentieth century. Its central objection is that by focusing political debate on material satisfaction conservative materialism risks losing sight of liberty and could thereby undermine it (Aughey, Jones and Riches, 1992: 166). Clearly, Thatcherism can plausibly be brought within this strand of conservatism (Letwin, 1992). The important point to be made here, however, is that this strand is in many ways as rationalist as the conservative materialism with which it contends. Its focus on the rule of law as the central aspect of a political order distances it substantially from anti-rationalist conservatism.

Conservative Organicism

Confronting both materialistic and legalistic strands of the tradition have been proponents of the notion that conservatism is organic or it is nothing. Among the leading individuals here are Gray (in a distinct persona from that already mentioned) and, in slightly different senses, Jonathan Clark and Alan Macfarlane. Gray, in his communitarian phase, explicitly rejects conservative romanticism and nostalgia – 'Once the cake of custom is broken, we must do our best with what is left. It cannot be baked anew' (Gray, 1991: 10) – and seeks to foster new forms of social cohesion, aiming 'to infuse an irreducibly pluralist and self-critical society with the conservative virtues of coherence, self-confidence and stability' (Gray, 1991: 10). The 'common culture' to which Gray appeals is a shared commitment to liberty and responsibility, bolstered by the intermediate institutions which structure contemporary society, and reinforced by a positive role for the state to limit pluralism when necessary. To those who argue that the shared commitments and intermediate institutions required by this vision are increasingly absent from contemporary society, and that this indeed is the key problem, Gray has no clear or precise answer. In many ways more interesting are, therefore, Clark and Macfarlane, whose reading of the British tradition holds that its organicism has never been particularly thick. Instead, since at least the thirteenth century England certainly and other parts of Britain possibly have been individualist societies characterized by the free economy and strong state themes into which Thatcherism was later to tap (Gamble, 1988). Authoritarian individualism is in fact organic to Britain, and was properly recreated in the 1980s (Clark, 1990).

This strand challenges conservative materialism by holding that what Carlyle famously dubbed the 'cash nexus' is never likely to be enough to hold society together. It challenges conservative legalism by maintaining that a rule of law ideal is too thin for even British (or English) society to cohere around. It challenges both strands on anti-rationalist grounds. They, in response, may well argue that organicism is now little more than a pipe dream.

CONCLUSION

English conservative dealings with Enlightenment rationalism have therefore been many and varied. The plausibility of the conservative critiques developed by Burke and Oakeshott turns on matters of degree. Extreme rationalism is now widely recognized to be impractical for many of the reasons forcefully advanced by Burke and in some ways restated by Oakeshott. Moderate or pragmatic rationalism is less readily denied. Debate between the conservative strands which have sought, in their distinct ways, to deal with Enlightenment rationalism turns largely on sociological issues. Conservatives at the end of the eighteenth century placed in opposition to Enlightenment rationalism what they considered to be the reality of organic or 'thick' societies, the disruption of which could only lead to catastrophe. What Salisbury termed 'disintegration' has nevertheless taken place, what Maitland called 'pulverizing and macadamizing' forces (Nisbet, 1986: 22) have destroyed many of the institutions which used to lie between the individual and the state, and conservatives are now required to consider how to promote the order they habitually seek in fragmented or 'thin' societies.

Burke wrote that 'We fear God; we look up with awe to kings; with affection to parliaments; with duty to magistrates; with reverence to priests; and with respect to nobility' (Freeman, 1980: 23). The challenge which faces conservatism is what to do when we no longer do all, or even any, of these things, and when the many elements which structured Burkean society – religion, class, hierarchy, conformity, tradition – no longer have much purchase. Contemporary polities tend not to generate traditions sufficient to sustain themselves. Norms and conventions that instil political and social discipline are now lacking. Civil traditions, a shared morality and conventional sources of authority have all been undermined. Where, in these circumstances, does the conservative turn?

The answer to this question is by no means clear. For many of the past 200 years, conservatives have responded by seeking ways of recreating some form of organicism. In this century, however, new brands of English conservatism have emerged to suggest there may be something in political rationalism after all. In so doing, they have contributed to a situation in which British politics is, as Oakeshott saw, largely dominated by political rationalism, and traditional conservative objections to it are only rarely heard.

REFERENCES

Aughey, Arthur, Greta Jones and W.T.M. Riches (1992) *The Conservative Political Tradition in Britain and the United States* (London: Pinter).

Burke, Edmund (1968) *Reflections on the Revolution in France; and on the Proceedings in Certain Societies in London Relative to that Event*, ed. with an introduction by Conor Cruise O'Brien (Harmondsworth: Penguin).

Carlyle, Thomas (1843) *Past and Present* (London: Chapman and Hall), Book 4.

Carlyle, Thomas (1869) 'Signs of the Times', in *Critical and Miscellaneous Essays: Collected and Republished* (London: Chapman and Hall), Vol. II, 313–42.

Cassirer, Ernst (1951) *The Philosophy of the Enlightenment*, trans. Fritz C.A. Koelln and James P. Pettegrove (Princeton: Princeton University Press).

Clark, Jonathan (1990) 'Introduction', in J. Clark (ed.), *Ideas and Politics in Modern Britain* (Basingstoke: Macmillan), 1–9.

Cobban, Alfred (ed.) (1960) *The Debate on the French Revolution 1789–1800*, 2nd edn (London: Adam and Charles Black).

Culler, A. Dwight (1986) 'Mill, Carlyle and the Spirit of the Age', in Harold Bloom (ed.), *Thomas Carlyle* (New York: Chelsea House), 127–60.

Devigne, Robert (1994) *Recasting Conservatism: Oakeshott, Strauss, and the Response to Postmodernism* (New Haven: Yale University Press).

Disraeli, Benjamin (1895) *Sybil, or The Two Nations* (London: Macmillan).

Freeman, Michael (1980) *Edmund Burke and the Critique of Political Radicalism* (Oxford: Blackwell).

Gamble, Andrew (1988) *The Free Economy and the Strong State: the Politics of Thatcherism* (Basingstoke: Macmillan).

Gay, Peter (1970) *The Enlightenment: an Interpretation: the Science of Freedom* (London: Weidenfeld and Nicolson).

Gay, Peter (ed.) (1973) *The Enlightenment: a Comprehensive Anthology* (New York: Simon and Schuster).

Gilmour, Ian (1977) *Inside Right: a Study of Conservatism* (London: Hutchinson).

Gray, John (1991) *A Conservative Disposition: Individualism, the Free Market and the Common Life* (London: Centre for Policy Studies).

Hayek, F.A. (1960) 'Why I Am Not a Conservative', in *The Constitution of Liberty* (London: Routledge & Kegan Paul).

Letwin, Shirley (1992) *The Anatomy of Thatcherism* (London: Fontana).

Nisbet, Robert (1986) *Conservatism: Dream and Reality* (Milton Keynes: Open University Press).

Oakeshott, Michael (1991) *Rationalism in Politics and Other Essays* (Indianapolis: Liberty Press).

O'Sullivan, Noël (1976) *Conservatism* (London: J.M. Dent and Sons).

Plamenatz, John (1992) *Man and Society: Political and Social Theories from Machiavelli to Marx*, Vol. 2, *From Montesquieu to the Early Socialists* (London: Longman).

Seigel, Jules P. (1976) '*Latter-Day Pamphlets*: The Near Failure of Form and Vision', in K.J. Fielding and Rodger L. Tarr (eds), *Carlyle Past and Present: a Collection of New Essays* (London: Vision Press), 155–76.

8 Four Assumptions About Human Nature
Norman Geras

In his last book Ralph Miliband identifies as one of a number of crucial problems socialists need to address – putting in question the credibility of the socialist project itself – the massive evidence we have of atrocious human cruelty, murderous division and conflict, the seeming aptitude of our species for large-scale organized blood-letting. The sceptical question as to whether with such 'human material' a radical re-ordering of society toward cooperative harmony is not merely a utopian illusion has, Miliband suggests, to be confronted seriously. He urges us, nevertheless, against the pessimistic answer to that question, judging it 'a counsel of despair to say ... that evil on a huge scale is part of the human condition, that its conquest is impossible'.[1] In this essay, I support Miliband's standpoint, but by way of examining more closely some of the assumptions about human nature that he reviews or deploys in articulating it.

The challenge posed by history, Miliband writes, is to 'the fundamental optimism about human capabilities which pervades the socialist enterprise – a belief, inherited from the Enlightenment, in the infinite per-fectibility of human beings'. I take this as one distinctive view of human nature and shall identify it as assumption (1). Having so expressed it, Miliband then goes on to put it, as he says, 'in more contemporary terms', as if only expressing the same thing in another way. In fact, however, he presents in the reformulation a second, different view. For he speaks now just of 'the belief that human beings are perfectly capable of organizing themselves into cooperative, democratic, egalitarian and self-governing communities, in which all conflict would certainly not have been elimi-nated, but where it would become less and less frequent and acute.' I shall call this assumption (2), and I differentiate it from (1) on the grounds that where (1) asserts that human beings are perfectible, (2) requires no such ambitious claim. It requires only that, whatever imperfections human beings may have, these are not so great as to exclude the possibility of creating communities with the specified characteristics, communities of a socialist kind. And (2) even permits, via the reference to continuing although rarer and more moderate conflicts, the inference that there might be enduring human faults: tendencies perhaps to selfishness, to

135

indifference toward the misfortunes of others, to undue pride or vanity, needless aggression or whatever else. Along with the run of better human qualities, such tendencies would also be, on this assumption, a permanent part of the constitution of humankind.

In any case, whether on the grounds of the more or of the less ambitious claim, because human beings are perfectible or because the weaknesses in their nature are not so vitiating as to be bound always to defeat the collective efforts conceivable from their virtues, 'socialism's essential point of departure', Miliband says, 'is – has to be – that there is no implacable curse which dooms humankind to perpetual division and strife.' By negating this last proposition we will get the source of the original sceptical question; we will get a view of human nature according to which there *is* such an implacable curse. Let us call this assumption (3). It is the assumption, as we have already seen it expressed, 'that evil on a huge scale is part of the human condition'. It is the assumption that 'humanity ... cannot escape from the slaughterhouse, and is doomed to add, generation upon generation to the end of time, to the catalogue of collective cruelty.' It is the assumption that, as to the many smaller-scale 'individual acts of cruelty perpetrated by men and women upon each other, or upon children, or for that matter upon animals', these too 'are to be explained by traits ineradicably embedded in human nature'.

One further passage will complete the set of views I want to distinguish from one another for consideration. Miliband for his part asserts that more plausible than this last pessimistic view is the idea that:

> such acts [of cruelty] ... are mainly produced by the insecurities, frustrations, anxieties and alienations that form an intrinsic part of class societies based on domination and exploitation. The 'injuries of class', allied to injuries of race, gender, religion and many others, readily lend themselves to pathological and morbid deformations which deeply and adversely affect human relations. This can only be effectively tackled in societies where conditions are created which foster solidarity, cooperation, security and respect, and where these values are given substance by a variety of grassroots institutions in all areas of life. It is these conditions which socialism seeks to advance.

Now, I take the precaution of saying that, so far as Miliband's own intended meaning is concerned, his argument here, of a kind common in socialist and other radical discourses, probably does not yield a further and quite separate view of human nature. This argument is construable, in particular, as being consistent with assumption (2). For the notion we have seen to be contained in (2) that human beings are characterized by a combination of virtues and vices, or (otherwise expressed) that human nature embodies different and even opposed kinds of inner potentiality or tendency, is perfectly compatible with the idea that it is the social conditions in which people live that, loosely speaking, shape those people, bringing out some qualities, blocking or frustrating others, and so on. There are aspects of Miliband's text which indicate just such a line of thought. I shall come back to this.

I propose to wring another meaning from the passage just quoted all the same. This meaning is that the social conditions people inhabit do not merely bring out or frustrate, encourage or deform, the various qualities generally present within human beings; rather, they create them. Or, formulated differently: the social conditions, or relations or institutions, fully determine the traits borne by any given group of social agents. Human nature, in other words, is neither like this nor like that, for there is no human nature. There are just socially, culturally, historically produced specificities and differences. I call that assumption (4) and I permit myself forcibly to extract it from what Miliband says for two reasons. One is that it remains a standard position upon this general terrain of problems and so needs some consideration here. The other is that though Miliband's views do not, strictly speaking, entail it, there are nevertheless aspects of his text also – so I shall later argue – that evince a certain over-socializing or over-historicizing tendency on his part. It seems reasonable therefore as a procedure of discussion to include the limit position of this tendency for the sake of greater comprehensiveness.

I now collect up and re-order the four different views I have elicited, giving each one a brief and standardized formula.

From (3) > (a) Human nature is intrinsically evil.
From (1) > (b) Human nature is intrinsically good.
From (4) > (c) Human nature is intrinsically blank.
From (2) > (d) Human nature is intrinsically mixed.

This formulaic listing is for convenience only, and is consciously made at the cost of two over-simplifications which I at once try to undo.

The pessimistic assumption, (a), need not require that people are by nature wholly, or even that they are all inordinately, evil. It could just take the form that impulses towards evil are sufficiently strong and extensive in humankind that they can never be lastingly pacified, and must continue to produce horrors on both a small and a large scale. Equally, the optimistic assumption, (b), that human beings are intrinsically good does not have to exclude that these beings are capable of nastiness, even of a serious kind. Indeed the derivation of assumption (b) from a formula of perfectibility implies that human beings precisely are so capable. It is just that, under (b), this capability is to be seen as less typical of, or less powerful within, the species, as adventitious and removable, as due possibly to the corrupting influence of bad circumstances or inadequate education; where the potentiality for good is more integral, more deeply laid. Both (a) and (b), in other words, can be construed in ways allowing that human nature is, as I have put it in formula (d), mixed. However, (a) and (b) take a position on the weight of, respectively, evil and good within the 'mixture', so as especially to insist on the long-range centrality of one of them. My simplified formula in each case merely accentuates the viewpoint in order to distinguish it sharply from (d), in which the balance between good and evil within humankind is left more open.

It is perhaps prudent also to point out that the view of human nature as expressed in (c), human nature as a blank, is not so much simplified in that formula as purified. By which I mean that this view is hardly ever held by anybody in pure form, but rather in conjunction with other propositions with which it is inconsistent. There is no good reason for taking it other than freed of the inconsistencies. In any event, (c) shares with (b) a belief that human evil is eradicable; but the belief is differently based in the two cases. Proponents of (b) think that evil is not intrinsic in human nature because good is; whereas proponents of (c) think that evil is not intrinsic in human nature because nothing is.

Finally (d) is to be entertained here in a form that makes it genuinely, and not only apparently, distinct from (a) and (b). This is to say that, with the balance between potentialities for good and potentialities for evil being taken as more open than in those formulas, neither kind of potentiality is held to bulk so large as to be overwhelming or to render the other inconsequential or null. Base or egregious human impulses, under assumption (d), are not so all-consuming as to make pervasive and enormous evil forever inevitable, but nor are they so weak or insignificant that they might be conceived as entirely eliminable, as one day gone, as even now 'really' something else than they appear, not human impulses after all, but alienated, capitalist, class-oppressive or class-oppressed, patriarchal, corrupted ones. Conversely, benign and admirable tendencies, under assumption (d), are not so dominant as to make the possibility of serious human evil only a temporary, albeit long, historical phase which may one day pass, nor so feeble or so sparsely distributed as to make attempts to limit and counteract that baleful possibility a pointless quest. Both sorts of impulse or tendency are conceived under (d) as being permanent features of our nature, realities to be negotiated, lived with, if possible understood – and if possible tilted toward the more benign and admirable, and tilted as far that way as possible.

In completing my clarification of the four assumptions, I anticipate the argument that follows. The socialist enterprise, along with other ideas of radical human progress, generally presupposes, as Miliband says, rejecting assumption (a). I want to argue that seriously confronting even so, as he suggests we must, the sceptical question which is raised by the sponsors of assumption (a) amounts to this: that socialists henceforth should not allow themselves the easy convenience of assumption (b) or assumption (c). To adopt either of these is precisely not to take the mass of evidence to which Miliband alludes *seriously*. It is to make light of it. The hope of socialism has to be sustained on the basis of assumption (d). The goal of a much better and a more just society is to be fought for not because human beings are by nature overwhelmingly or essentially good, nor because they do not have an intrinsic nature; but because and in spite of the combination in their nature of bad impulses with good ones. Because of the bad impulses, this struggle is necessary. In spite of them, it is to be hoped, a socialist society may yet be possible.

Socialist advocacy is too often and too much informed by the kind of thinking I encapsulate in assumptions (b) and (c). Now, I repeat, the two assumptions are not the same in the way they ground an optimistic outlook: to the suggested permanence of great evil the first opposes the claim that there are deep, massively preponderant tendencies towards good inherent in humankind, whereas the second just opposes the notion of an infinite human plasticity. This difference is not immaterial. The first view has the significant advantage of being willing to deal in *some* conception of a common human nature, such as the second view for its part rejects. And I call this an advantage, because the claim that there is no human nature at all is at best a thoughtless exaggeration, one that it is impossible to uphold with any genuine lucidity of mind.[2]

However, I shall concentrate on what I perceive to be the shared weakness of viewpoints (b) and (c). This is their common unwillingness to accept, as significant realities in their own right with some independent explanatory weight in human affairs, dispositions in the make-up of human beings that are less than beneficent – whether of selfishness and envy, malicious glee, the enjoyment of power or advantage over others, a certain passion to exclude, cruelty, destructiveness, and a good number of other things. So far as some such dispositions may appear to leave a rather large mark on the historical record, these are always really (so the suggestion is) a product or expression of something *else*. Rendered in one conception overwhelmingly benign, and in the other entirely empty of fixed content, human nature does not autonomously contribute anything of its own to how things can go badly, the apparent human capacity for evil becoming mere epiphenomenon *par excellence*. Can this way of thinking withstand a sober look at how grim the historical record in fact is?

Let us bring into relation with the more easily optimistic assumptions about human nature to be found in the arguments of many socialists, some views about it emerging from an experience *in* that record: of all the events of the twentieth century mentioned in the present connection by Miliband himself, the one that has perhaps done most to instil a general melancholy about future human possibilities. The Holocaust has come to occupy a prominent place in contemporary consciousness. It has given rise to an extensive literature, coming from survivors, historians and theologians, most kinds of social scientist, and from psychoanalysts, novelists, poets, dramatists, literary critics. But it has not left much of a mark on the moral and political philosophy of socialism, and this reflects a broader state of affairs in which the Holocaust has not figured very conspicuously amongst the concerns of moral or political philosophers in general.

It was a human catastrophe which may be thought, for all that, to pose some troubling questions for anyone committed to progressive change, and it is certainly not a good reason for ignoring these questions that troubling is what they are. The words of the Polish sociologist Anna Pawelczynska, herself a former prisoner at Auschwitz, are to the point here:

> People living within the orbit of European civilisation today defend themselves from the naturalistic eloquence of facts which have no analogy in their experience by a failure of the imagination ... Such people, as members of that same human species to which the murderers and their victims belong, resist identifying with either murderer or victim ... [They] protect their view of the world, their optimistic philosophy of life, from the consequences of understanding the concentration camp as a dimension of the evil man can do and of the depth of contempt to which he can sink.[3]

A socialist philosophy worthy of being taken seriously cannot afford such a 'protected' optimism, shut off against the brutal realities beyond just by virtue of declining to look at them.

In 'The Visit' by Tadeusz Borowski – a survivor of Auschwitz who transmuted his experiences there into a series of unflinching, terrible stories, before later taking his own life – the narrator details some of the wretched human sights he has witnessed in the camp, and goes on:

> And every one of the people who, because of eczema, phlegmon or typhoid fever, or simply because they were too emaciated, were taken to

the gas chamber, begged the orderlies loading them into the cremato-
rium trucks to remember what they saw. And to tell the truth about
mankind to those who do not know it.[4]

Irene W., another survivor, speaking of how she has had over the years
to attend to the needs of daily life without allowing her memories to
overwhelm her and prevent her from functioning normally, reports:

> Yet it's always there; it's more a view of the world, a total world-
> view ... of extreme pessimism, of sort of one feels ... of really knowing
> the truth about people, human nature, about death, of really knowing
> the truth in a way that other people don't know it.[5]

The 'truth about mankind' and 'the truth about people, human nature'
is what they call it; a truth, they both say, that others do not know. What
is this truth?

There are doubtless different facets of it, but in the more theoretical
literature on the Holocaust it looks, with some writers, rather like our
assumption (a). Thus, according to the theologian Richard Rubenstein,
'just as depth psychology was able to expose the ineradicable dark side
of human personality', so the world of the death camps has shown it to be
'an error to imagine that civilisation and savage cruelty are antitheses ...
Mankind never emerged out of savagery into civilisation'.[6] Another
theologian, Arthur Cohen – for whom the Holocaust is *tremendum*, a kind
of unfathomable abyss of evil, 'orgiastic celebration of death' – has
written in like vein:

> Liberalism (and in its radicalisation, Marxism) may well be the fallen
> messianism of the Jews, the familiar secular inversion of Jewish utopian
> hope, but liberalism is predicated upon assumptions regarding the
> nature of man and his educable potentiality which the *tremendum*
> destroyed ... In the holocaust is a configuration of evil; it writes large
> what should have been recognised all along – that the oppository,
> destructive character of evil drains of credibility every notion of an
> ongoing teleology of the good that was required by the rational opti-
> misms ... of the nineteenth century.[7]

Something similar can be expressed more indirectly, and I take as a
case of this one of the few well-known contemporary political philosophers to have addressed himself, albeit briefly, to the subject of the
Holocaust, namely Robert Nozick. Nozick lists the multiple and wanton
barbarities, to read the details of which, as he puts it, 'staggers and numbs

the mind'. He goes on to suggest that the Holocaust is an event 'that radically and drastically alters the situation and status of humanity'. He explains the suggestion so:

> I do not claim to understand the full significance of this, but here is one piece, I think: It now would not be a *special* tragedy if humankind ended, if the human species were destroyed in atomic warfare or the earth passed through some cloud that made it impossible for the species to continue reproducing itself... Imagine beings from another galaxy looking at our history. It would not seem unfitting to them, I think, if that story came to an end, if the species they see with that history ended, destroying itself in nuclear warfare or otherwise failing to be able to continue.

Nozick, it is true, also qualifies his suggestion in a number of ways. He does not mean that human beings deserve this to happen; it would involve much suffering and individual loss; it would be wrong for anyone actually to bring it about. Nor does he overlook other, earlier cruelties and calamities. Perhaps it is just the case, he says, 'that the Holocaust *sealed* the situation, and made it patently clear'. He wonders, too, whether we might be able to redeem ourselves as a species, were people to begin to take the suffering of others upon themselves by suffering whenever they did. However, despite these various qualifications, the judgement which they qualify already concludes a balance sheet between the actual past of humankind and its possible futures. If 'its loss would now be no *special* loss above and beyond the losses to the individuals involved', if humanity has forfeited 'its claim to continue', as Nozick thinks it has, and if this is so the talk even of an effort of redemption notwithstanding, does that not amount to fixing the nature of the species by the enormities of evil in its past, to the discount of any better possible futures? More than by whatever good we might still hope to bring about, not to speak of the good already done, we are characterized by the atrocities and iniquities that have been perpetrated, in a judgement of metaphysical resignation and despair.[8]

Looking into the depths of the experience on which Nozick here reflects, it can be hard not to share something of the same mood. What Elie Wiesel has to say in a related connection is apposite. 'Examine them', he writes – with reference, this, to 'snapshots' of the Holocaust, photographs of murder in progress which we have by courtesy of the murderers themselves or of the numerous spectators to murder – 'and you will forget who you are... Nothing will be important any more. You will have glimpsed an abyss you would rather not have uncovered. Too late.'[9]

The person is perhaps unfortunate who does not know a like response to horrors of this magnitude. A mood of resignation or despair in the face of them is to be resisted, all the same, by those who can. We ought to resist the cosmic pessimism of Nozick's judgement; resist any unilateral definition of human nature in terms only or principally of its worst excesses; resist the identification we have seen made above, between the Nazi universe of death and *the* truth about humankind. So I shall eventually get around to arguing.

We need, in resisting it, however, to respect what is *a* truth here and not just casually dismiss this as some would-be irrelevance to socialism and other utopian projects. I have in mind the sort of dismissal which is involved in claiming that an event like the Holocaust discloses nothing about the inner or natural propensities of human beings, because the behaviour patterns and personality traits it reveals to us are to be put down, wholly or largely, to the historically determinate social and situational conditions of the event. Such a claim, it may even be thought, has a certain plausibility on account of the very extremity of the case. Why judge human nature, it could be asked, on the basis of conditions of life and death that were exceptional, on the basis of a hellish and in no way typical human situation?

An initial answer to this seemingly plausible question is that we are in possession of some considerable wisdom from and about that particular hell which emphasizes to us, warns us, that the actions, reactions, postures and personalities constitutive of it, exceptional and shocking in many ways as they obviously were, were also continuous with ones familiar in and to ordinary human beings in more ordinary circumstances. This was a world populated not by monsters and brutes – or not only by monsters and brutes, for in some necessary and still usable moral meaning there were more than enough of these – but by beings who were precisely human beings, with characteristics that are all too recognizable, human vices and weaknesses amongst them, common faults and frailties.

Most easily recognizable in that regard are the bystanders: those who, not directly active in the process of mass murder, did nothing to try to stop it either. These are the people who affect not to know, or who do not care to know and so do not find out; or who do know but do not care anyway, who are indifferent; or who are afraid, for themselves or for others, or who feel powerless; or who are weighed down, distracted or just occupied (as most of us) in pursuing the aims of their own lives. Such people formed the background to the tragedy of the European Jews and they continue everywhere to provide an enabling condition for other tragedies large and small, and for great but avoidable suffering. The ubiquity of the bystander surely testifies to a remarkable capacity in members of our species to live comfortably with the enormous sufferings of others.

It is not only the bystanders, however, who are recognizable here. It is also the perpetrators. The theme is a difficult one and must be treated with some care, since it comes otherwise to promote a glib and corrosive moral cynicism, actually encouraging what it purports only to observe. There is a need to understand; but without being too understanding. Yet the theme itself is inescapable. If amongst the perpetrators is to be found an ample complement of sadists and thugs, there is now a large literature documenting for the more general run of them – that is, the camp personnel, the members of execution squads, the civilian users of slave labour, the planners and the bureaucrats and the doctors of death – that these bearers of Nazi genocide fell well within the range of psychological normality. They were not, for the most part, psychopaths. They were ordinary people.

And the same literature makes available to us a wide-ranging exploration of the mechanisms, psychological and social, by which such ordinary people could bring themselves, or be induced by others, to contribute their share to the evil. These mechanisms are many and I can only gesture towards them here: the fears and resentments focused on people who are different, and the feelings of self-enhancement or even elation at the disaster brought upon them; the thought of being authorized to act by a legitimate higher source, or the thought that this, one's own 'segment' of the overall process is only one of a very large number and not the decisive one morally speaking; the idea of its being an impersonal role, a job, and thus not due in any strong sense to the particular individual filling it; self-serving, careerist motives; a simple bending to social pressures, not wanting not to conform with the opinions of one's peers. And being implicated gradually, incrementally; accustoming oneself, as to anything in the way of a routine; for many, not being able to *see* what finally happens to the victims of the process; regarding them as insignificant morally; dehumanizing them, first in thought, then by social and symbolic practices, in the end by physically demeaning and brutalizing ones. By a combination of these means the line is crossed.[10]

It is as necessary to insist upon what is not being said here as to emphasize what is. This is not offered in that style of knowing and satisfied pessimism which assures us that deep down we are all so badly flawed as to become, just given the appropriate circumstances, instigators of or accomplices in any moral crime. It is not true. There are always those who refuse and those who resist. There are people who risk everything, and others who, though they cannot find the strength to do this, still do what they feel they can to oppose or mitigate the consequences of the crime in question. To explore the motivational pathways toward participation in or compliance with great iniquity is not to say that these must inevitably be taken. Nor is it to deny the reality of the choice there is, restricted or dangerous as it can sometimes be: the choice to act *against* the habits of thought and the impulses just rehearsed, upon other motives, for better reasons.

The point, therefore, is not a cynical, but it is a realist one. It is that even this (as it is sometimes said) utterly demonic of twentieth-century horrors was the work of human beings such as we are acquainted with. It was compounded of well-known sorts of prejudice, ambition, temptation, taste of power, evasion, moral failure. When they are not doing philosophy or talking theoretical politics, socialists and other radicals know as well as anyone the motivational range here, comprising, with all the admirable qualities and the excellences, also elements which are less than admirable, and indeed some of them downright repugnant. This range is simply part of the stuff of ordinary existence. It is a form of practical experience taken from every area of life: every family, circle of friends and acquaintances, every neighbourhood; every milieu, social stratum, vocation, organization. It is an experience – again, together with what is generous, loving, courageous and so on – of jealousies and vanities, petty unkindnesses and hatreds, wilful deceits, self-importance and self-promotion. It yields to us a knowledge complementary to the one we have from the Holocaust itself: a knowledge of the ordinary raw materials of great evil, those common vices and human failings which can become, in another setting or combination, suddenly exorbitant.

Lastly in this connection, there is the victim group to be considered as well. With a share of the same common vices and failings distributed unevenly across it, it too becomes stained by the crimes of the perpetrators. Another difficult theme. To write about this from the outside, however carefully, runs the risk of appearing to proffer a judgement on others, of which everyone *from* the outside ought to be cautious. 'It is a judgement,' as Primo Levi has put it, 'that we would like to entrust only to those who found themselves in similar circumstances, and had the possibility to test on themselves what it means to act in a state of coercion.'[11] I shall let Levi himself represent what is a rather more general message from survivors of the Nazi camps.

In some reflections on what he has called the 'grey zone', Levi for his part firmly casts aside any levelling cynicism in this matter, writing:

I do not know, and it does not much interest me to know, whether in my depths there lurks a murderer, but I do know that I was a guiltless victim and I was not a murderer...and that to confuse [the murderers] with their victims is a moral disease or an aesthetic affectation or a sinister sign of complicity ...[12]

But Levi asserts, all the same, that '[i]t is naive, absurd, and historically false to believe that an infernal system such as National Socialism was, sanctifies its victims; on the contrary it degrades them'. The grey zone is one feature of what he has in mind. He refers by this to 'the space which separates (and not only in Nazi Lagers) the victims from the persecutors'.

> Only a schematic rhetoric can claim that that space is empty: it never is; it is studded with obscene or pathetic figures (sometimes they possess both qualities simultaneously), whom it is indispensable to know if we want to know the human species, if we want to know how to defend our souls when a similar test should once more loom before us, or even if we only want to understand what takes place in a big industrial factory.[13]

The grey zone, Levi says, has 'ill-defined outlines which both separate and join the two camps of masters and servants'. If it is never empty, that is because 'in the Lager and outside, there exist grey, ambiguous persons ready to compromise.'[14]

It needs to be emphasized that Primo Levi was not well disposed towards the too facile equation of the Nazi camps with other sites of hierarchical power: 'the comparison,' he has said, 'arouses revulsion in us, those of us who have been "marked", "tattooed" ... There's no gas chamber at Fiat.' The more notable therefore is his repeated allusion, in these reflections just quoted, to the existence of some similar elements 'in the Lager and outside'. The Nazi camps were not for him a microcosm or the mere 'condensation' of the world beyond them; but he was willing to describe them as being 'a distorting mirror' of that world none the less.[15]

It is a not uncommon observation amongst the survivors. Levi again: 'the prisoner who gets ahead on the backs of his comrades exists everywhere'. Hanna Lévy-Hass (in a diary written while she was imprisoned at Belsen): 'I shall keep firmly in my mind everything that I have seen, everything that I have experienced and learnt, everything that human nature has revealed to me ... I shall judge each man according to the way he has behaved, or could have behaved, in these conditions that surround us.' Viktor Frankl: 'Is it surprising that in those depths we again found only human qualities which in their very nature were a mixture of good and evil?' 'In the concentration camps ... we watched and witnessed some of our comrades behave like swine while others behaved like saints. Man has both potentialities within himself ...'[16]

On the basis of her conversations with survivors of the death camps, Gitta Sereny has spoken of the 'fatalistic lack of vehemence of those who have come to terms with the inevitability of human failings in everyone, themselves included'.[17] In the attitude she thereby identifies is joined an ancient, indeed a commonsense knowledge with the wisdom brought back – and at what a cost – from the places of Nazi barbarity.

Now, a standard riposte exists to being presented with considerations of this kind. It would disqualify them at a stroke from being accepted as genuine wisdom. Common sense, it is often said, is a form of ideology; and, likewise, so-called practical experience is a bounded experience only. Both are the product of particular social forms, historically specific worlds. As such, neither common sense nor practical experience can be a reliable guide to the patterns of behaviour we may expect with other social forms, in future possible worlds. Whether inside the camps or beyond them, what we have knowledge of are people who grew up in a deforming social environment. Even if it is the case that the Holocaust universe is recognizable as having been populated by ordinary human beings, these were human beings who had been moulded by capitalism, class, patriarchy and the rest, by gross inequalities and differentials in power, with the profoundly limiting and corrupting effects upon their attitudes that all that must entail. Anything vouchsafed to us, consequently, out of the experience of the Holocaust is relevant only for the type of society which gave birth to, or accommodated, it. It is not relevant to the prospects of a future society which has been transformed.

As much weight as is bound to be given to arguments of this general kind by those of us who entertain the possibility of progressive change, in such blanket form they are inadequate – in face both of the terrible enormities and of the more run-of-the-mill individual failings they purport to respond to, and with which the human story is so crowded. I shall now go on to offer three reasons why trying thus to 'neutralize' the negative features of this story, by just ascribing them to societal defects of a historically specific and remediable sort, is unconvincing. It is a poor basis for the hope of human progress.

First, one may bring to this domain an argument of Marxian pedigree but which ought to carry force also more widely, with anyone sceptical of grand projects of a speculative nature. This is the argument that the better society of the future is to be thought of, and fought for, as emerging out of real tendencies within the present, and not counterposed to the latter as a merely abstract ideal unanchored in existing empirical forces or in any proper grasp of them. That argument, much used (and not only by Marxists) in relation, for example, to what sort of political or economic goals are foreseeably feasible, and to the question of who are likely to be the agents for achieving them, is rather less often invoked by socialists in relation to the topic under discussion. When it comes to what kind of beings human beings are and might one day become, and more particularly to what limitations they have and how these might constrain the feasible shapes of an alternative future, it is not uncommon for socialist advocacy to be couched in terms of a quite remarkable leap. This can take us from people as we know and have known them to beings wonderfully freed of the familiar human faults and vices, or saved at any rate from ever having to let these reveal their unpleasant outward effects; to people improved, in the well-known phrase, beyond recognition.

It seems, however, as appropriate to this area of reflection as to any other to hold that we have to start from where we are, therefore from the realities of human motivation, of moral weakness as much as moral strength, with which we are familiar, and not simply fly forward towards a speculative ideal. The least that one can say is that it ill befits socialists, whether of Marxist formation or of some other more or less realist cast of mind, to find easy refuge in such an insubstantial ideal.

But I want to take it further than this. For some will be tempted to minimize the weight of the point by treating it as a *merely* political one: intended, that is, to give some hope of proximate practical success, but having no deeper theoretical significance, no implication for the degree of changeability or fixedness in the human personality over the longer term. This temptation should be resisted. The point, I will maintain, does go deeper. It comes down to the need to show a proper regard for the continuities and the resistances of human history in the framing of any emancipatory project. This history certainly encompasses continuities as well as discontinuities, some of the continuities are long ones, and some of these long continuities are long precisely because they are due to nature, both external and human nature.

Let us take a range of common human emotions, say, anger, desire, love, fear, pride, shame, melancholy, disgust; and some familiar dispositions too, say, submissiveness and dominance – whether in a sexual context or outside it – and community, spontaneity, constancy, self-regard. Like the more basic human needs and the most common human capacities, such emotions and dispositions plainly have a general, transhistorical basis. Whatever cultural variation their forms might display, it would not be plausible to propose that they are all wholly social constructs, and the idea of some future society in which they would be no more gives meaning, well and truly, to the phrase 'beyond recognition'. This is a world virtually unimaginable by us. It is hard to say whether it would be, for the new kind of 'people' within it, a utopia, but it scarcely looks desirable from here.

Let us now take in turn – and as is not the same thing – a range of some of the less attractive human qualities and tendencies: say (in a list loosely paralleling the one just given), hatred or vengefulness, greed, covetousness and envy, overbearing attachment, moral cowardice, vanity, self-abasement, destructiveness; and then servility, love of power, cruelty; and ethnic prejudice, lawlessness, fanaticism, uncaring privilege. We should like to believe in the possibility of a world with much less of this sort of thing, much less of it, especially, that is accorded public space and the means of advancement or growth through hierarchies of great privilege, sites of tyrannical power, bouts of collective violence, and so on. But how much more plausible or imaginable is a world, even, from which these uglier human attributes have disappeared? They seem generally to bear connections of one kind and another to the common emotions and dispositions by way of which I came to them: as exaggerated or aggravated forms of those, fixations of them, deteriorations, imbalances. It suggests that they too have, in some sort, a durable natural foundation, capable as they are of being brought out by a very wide variety of interpersonal circumstances and relationships – such as there is also bound always to be in any society of more or less equitably distributed freedoms. It seems more realistic to reckon that humankind will have to go on living with these less salutary human attributes in some proportion. If socialism, at any rate, will still be a society of human beings, much about them will be recognizably the same. We have nothing at present but the emptiest of speculations to tell us that the common faults and vices might disappear or all but disappear; that everything that is productive of grave mischief belongs with the discontinuities of history, with the societally generated, and nothing of it with our underlying human nature.

This brings me directly to the second of my three reasons. For there is in any case an odd feature, rarely remarked upon, of arguments of this sociologizing type which assert that nothing or very little is to be attributed to human nature. It is an assumption of, so to say, fixed explanatory quantity, such that the relation between (for short) sociological and naturalist explanation of human behaviour must vary inversely: if human behaviour has much to do with social conditions, it has little to do with natural traits; if very much, then very little; and so on. Or, expressed in qualitative terms, if the social is very important in explaining human behaviour, then human nature is very unimportant. This is not the only way of thinking about the issue, however, and it is not the most persuasive way. One might observe, instead, that whatever the explanatory weight here – undeniably immense – of social structure and cultural mores, there is, as well, a weight that is due to our natural make-up and of its own considerable magnitude. There is, because as much as the particularities of society and culture may influence the forms of conduct and the run of inclinations and values within human populations, such particularities can only work, to put this baldly, on what it is *in* people to do or be. They can only work on the potentialities, and within certain limits, that are set by the nature of our species.

You can train a horse, and you can accustom a cat, to various things. But you cannot teach a horse to read or get a cat to live on vegetables, and you will not get either to be forever stationary, like an object. There are, by the same token, natural limits to what human beings can do and sustain, and there are material needs, capacities and impulses which will find expression in one social form or another. Nothing about the rich diversity of social forms, or about the irrepressible freedom of the human will and creativity of the imagination, subtracts by so much as a single scintilla from the contribution to human affairs which is made by natural determinants of that kind.

I want to explore the relevance of this point to our subject by coming back to Ralph Miliband's reflections. There are aspects of these, I earlier said, that can be read as affirming a hope in progress on the basis of assumption (d): the assumption of a mixed human nature, with potentialities for both good and evil. I noted his formulation envisaging socialism together with some persisting, albeit much diminished, human conflict. This formulation would allow the possibility of some continued wrongdoing also, though it does not itself necessarily entail it. In fact, Miliband writes in the same connection of a situation 'where collective and individual *misdeeds* can be turned into increasingly marginal phenomena'. And he writes, as well, of 'a context in which collective cruelty would be … made impossible by the resistance which it would evoke'.[18] Both anticipations suggest a continuing space of potential evil.

For what has been pressed back to the margins of social life still has its place *at* the margins, and presumably therefore also its living sources; and we know well enough how the marginal can often find its way, whether creeping or irrupting, towards the centre. Likewise, a thing (collective cruelty) made impossible by the resistance 'it would evoke', sounds to have some impulses sustaining it still, to be a live capacity and not merely a historical memory of what was there once but is no longer, having been eradicated or smoothed away. I propose, in the light of these inferences, one kind of interpretation of the long passage I earlier quoted from Miliband, referring to 'conditions … which foster solidarity, cooperation, security and respect, and where these values are given substance by a variety of grassroots institutions in all areas of life'.[19] It is an interpretation in which the said conditions and institutions are conceived as being, at least in part, externally blocking or obstructing, and simultaneously accommodating and facilitating. That is to say, they put up barriers against certain types of human tendency or impulse, while at the same time leaving room to certain other types. Such a conception of them precisely concedes the existence of what I have just called a space of potential evil. It does so in the metaphor of blocking, which presupposes something there needing to be blocked, troublesome tendencies and impulses of a durable sort, not entirely removable by education, acculturation or whatever.

A competing conception would make the human person, or else the miscreant human person, more entirely the product of the conditions and institutions which envelop it. It is a conception of these conditions and institutions as 'possessing' the innermost core of the individual self, or as disfiguring it; so that, once given a good social environment, we would have only good individuals, without significant residue of ill-will or viciousness. Now, of course, any adequate notion of the person will need some pretty large element of this latter kind of conception. For social structure and culture do certainly 'enter' the make-up of the person, shaping its very identity, as much as they can be thought of also as external barriers, or channels, against and along which the human-natural dispositions of individuals have to make their way. The overall balance of any viewpoint is therefore everything here. Some other aspects of Miliband's reflections than those I have focused upon so far situate him closer, I believe, to the extreme limit of this possessing or disfiguring conception of social conditions than is warranted.

One indication is his use of the metaphor of pathology. Adverting again to the long passage quoted towards the beginning of this essay, we find Miliband referring there to the 'injuries' of class, race, gender and religion – as though acts of cruelty or other misdeeds were the result of damage from without and not inner possibilities of the normal organism. Equally, his talk in the same place of 'pathological and morbid deformations' may evoke an image of diseases foreign to the healthy body, so of external provenance once more. It is true that in thus counter-posing as he does explanation of cruelty in terms of the psychological by-products of 'societies based on exploitation and domination' to expla-nation of it in terms of 'traits ineradicably embedded in human nature', Miliband speaks of cruelty as being produced 'mainly' by the former.[20] However, this is a unilateral and misleading formula. How does one adjudicate what is 'main' in this context? It might be replied that, since we can imagine other social conditions in which human beings would behave cruelly very much less than they do now or perhaps hardly at all, this suffices to validate the judgement that cruelty is principally due to adverse social conditions. But one could imagine, too, other *beings*: beings who, even in adverse conditions, would not be provoked to the amount and to the extremes of cruelty, oppression, venality, violence and so forth, of which human beings have shown themselves to be so richly capable. The point is that adverse social conditions have the effects that they do only upon a certain configuration of naturally delimited potentialities and dispositions; and, this being the case, those potentialities and dispositions merit the distinction, for their part also, of being accounted 'main'.

The issue may be further elucidated by considering another aspect of Miliband's argument. Self-consciously and explicitly, to 'the attribution of guilt to human nature' he opposes what he sees as 'the crucially significant fact that it was from above that have almost always come the initiation and the organisation of mass killings'. The 'mass of "ordinary people"', he says, have seldom been responsible for the decisions producing wholesale slaughter. 'Most such collective actions have been initiated and organised by people of power in pursuit of whatever purposes and fantasies moved them.' Miliband does at once go on to qualify any too easy optimism over this fact by adding that ordinary people have nevertheless often enough acquiesced to, cheered on or participated in the episodes of blood-letting initiated by people of power.[21] But the qualification does not go far enough. For it needs to be stated clearly also that these people of power are not from elsewhere, they are from amongst us. They are members of our species, a species in which there have ever been candidates aplenty, not just for being acquiescent and obedient to the powerful, but for occupying places of power and privilege themselves. Human beings have shown themselves very available for this and rather good at it, and it is a vain recourse to believe that it has nothing whatever to do with their intrinsic nature that they have.

A would-be Marxist (or just sociological) argument generally comes in here to say that our nature is the effect of class, power, privilege and so on, and not any of these the effect of our nature. But a different Marxism (and sociology) is possible in response. It says that human beings would not have been open, open so long and so geographically universally – and not only open, but so *very* available – to the class option of social organization and the benefits of power and privilege, if these things did not meet any impulse in their make-up. Why have they not, unanimously or in large enough numbers to be effective, simply refused the chance of enjoying huge power or advantage over others – as being intolerable to them, humanly unliveable? It is as if a single individual, having been presented over a lifetime with many opportunities to behave badly, and having taken them, betraying people, profiting unjustly at their expense, openly harming them, losing no sleep over any of it, were then to plead that this reflected nothing at all about his inner character, but was the result of external circumstances only. How widely would he be believed? Even allowing for there having been other, neglected possibilities in his nature which could have produced a different kind of life, one would be unwise to let them obscure the traits of character which he had actually seen fit to give free rein.

By way of another observation on this ill-doing individual, I come now to the third reason for thinking it unconvincing to try to ascribe all bad features of the human story to the influence of defective but remediable social conditions. There is a charitable impulse that explains why we are often reluctant to see wickedness as in a person's character. We give her the benefit of her moral freedom: that she might be able, even with a record behind her of misdeeds, to prevail over whatever it was that led her to them, by making different and better choices from now on. Envisaging this possibility, we treat the ill of which we know she has been capable as being something extraneous to her actual character, in a sort of wager that she may prove it to be so. The strong desire evident in progressive political discourses and the social sciences and humanities more generally – and formalized earlier in what I designated assumptions (b) and (c) – to deny any malignity intrinsic to human nature itself might perhaps be seen, then, as a methodological generalization of this generous impulse. It represents a wager on the good character of humanity within the more favourable enveloping conditions and institutions of a future utopia.

There is no question but that this does describe something of the nature of the socialist hypothesis, taken *by and large*. Unless, in a different institutional and cultural setting, humankind in its generality can prove itself of very much better character (to speak in such terms) than it has shown itself hitherto, the hope of socialism would have to be reckoned a delusion. Taken, however, as anything more than this broad expectation of improvement, taken as the hope of a world all but free from significant human nastiness, the suggestion is self-defeating. For if it is asked in the spirit of this suggestion why people enfolded, raised, in good and supportive conditions, and leading lives as unthreatened by the more frightening or debilitating of social ills as can be envisaged, and reinforced in all their attitudes by cultures of a humane and tolerant kind, why they still might, some of them, find it in themselves to perpetrate continued mischiefs – the simple answer to this question is that they might because they can. Like the opportunity of better patterns of behaviour, the mischiefs are just a possible product of their freedom.

It is, indeed, an anomaly of one common way of thinking about a socialist future to see this future as populated by beings with a freedom enormously expanded and enhanced, and simultaneously to envisage those beings as so much the creatures of their now benign social conditions that they could not be the authors of any evil choice. They could be. It is an implication of their freedom, *ex hypothesi* greater than ever before, that they would not be exhaustively delimited by the conditions that surround them. And this is more especially the case when one considers what the range and variety of interpersonal relationships must continue to be. Of mothers and fathers to children, brothers to sisters, lovers to each other and to possible or actual other lovers; of friends, neighbours, collaborators, colleagues, workmates, passing strangers and acquaintances of every degree; of carers to cared for, doctors to patients, public officers to members of the public; of the bold to the cautious, the orderly to the chaotic, the exuberant to the pensive or the weary; of those agreeing to those dissenting, 'insiders' to 'outsiders'; and then with a multitude of differences within every imaginable category – it would be an endlessly shifting picture of human contacts and situations. Within this multiplicity of forms, a freedom of putatively unprecedented scope renders the image of the socialist person as mere benign 'effect' (effect, that is, of *generally* benign circumstances) an unpersuasive one.

A shadow stretches across the vision at the heart of the socialist project. It reaches there from what may seem to be the remotest distance, from the very depths of the concentrationary universe. Socialism is often thought of as a world of almost infinite potentiality. With good reason is it, since who could now foresee or estimate the further wealth of creativity that would be opened up by extending to everyone on the planet the chances of even a moderately secure existence. If that wealth could be but glimpsed, it would astonish any person living. We touch here on an idea of unlimited human possibility. Over and again, however, those who have survived incarceration at Auschwitz and the other sites of Nazi murder and enslavement articulate something learned there in exactly such terms. 'Normal men do not know,' David Rousset has written, 'that everything is possible. Even if the evidence forces their intelligence to admit it, their muscles do not believe it. The concentrationees do know ...' Livia E. Bitton Jackson has written, similarly, of the time 'before [she] knew that there are no limits to human cruelty'. And Charlotte Delbo also: 'Did you know that suffering is limitless/that horror cannot be circumscribed.' And Primo Levi: 'I know that in the Lager, and more generally on the human stage, everything happens...' And Elie Wiesel: 'Evil, more than good, suggests infinity.'[22]

Can it be an accident how many who say this present it, confidently but not in accents of dogmatism, with that lack of vehemence referred to by Gitta Sereny, in the mode of what is *known*? They tell in any event of a particle which the vision of socialism shares with the experience of the Holocaust. It is, to be sure, a 'small' particle only, since we compare here a hope of the best for humankind with the very worst, the most infernal product of the human spirit. But small as it is, it is highly fertile: the capacity for imagination and choice, for reaching beyond the given, whether time, circumstance or boundary. It may be a mistake to expect that great evil could not continue to threaten once there was no longer any great (social) cause of it. It could come, like acts of great goodness, like any masterpiece, from a concatenation of small causes magnified or transmuted in the medium of the imagination and the will.

****

It has become a common theme in discussion of the Holocaust that this tragedy now puts in serious question what have been, over the last two centuries, some cherished assumptions of Western civilization and modernity. As Henry Friedlander has written, 'Since the eighteenth century we have largely accepted the ideas of the Enlightenment, including the idea of progress... [A] serious consideration of the Holocaust would necessitate a re-evaluation.' Or as it has been expressed more recently by another writer, 'Auschwitz decisively closed the Enlightenment era of faith in the coordinated growth of reason, moral betterment, and happiness.'[23] I conclude the present essay by agreeing that some re-evaluation in this matter is indeed called for and faith in human progress not appropriate; but by arguing that *hope* in human progress, and more particularly in the possibility of socialism, is tenable and necessary nevertheless, and the alternative to this hope extremely unappealing.

In so far as they were haunted by assumptions of teleology, inevitability, perfection or paradise, the notions of progress that have characterized socialist and, more generally, democratic and radical political traditions certainly need to be moderated. There is no necessity at all of steady forward movement without possibility of regression and catastrophe, and even 'modest' utopia, never mind perfection or paradise, is not only not the pre-written truth or destiny of humankind, it is not even its prevailing tendency. All it is (we have to hope) is one of its possibilities, and this forever shadowed from within by other darker possibilities. Democrats, liberals and socialists of the last century would not have anticipated the horrifying and, as it has now proved, endless killing grounds of this one. That in itself is testimony to what their shared ideas about progress lacked, the shadow of potential disaster, the threat of forms of evil which challenge the best resources of our understanding.

Neither as beckoning truth or end-point nor as linear, uninterrupted forward advance should we think about human progress today. We have to think about it simply as an enduring battle, an open process, to try to create societies from which the gravest social and political evils familiar to us have been removed; and to try to prevent, drive back or put right any resurgence of these evils where or once they have been removed, any fresh emergence of unmerited inequalities and privileges, episodes of persecution, sporadic or not so sporadic injustices, tyrannies large and small, crimes by some persons against others, hitherto unrecognized forms of wrong. We would do well to substitute for every image of progress as a course being travelled, a road, a journey, or as an unfolding, a line of development, the spirit of it being rather a struggle without end;[24] which is what it is for all practical purposes anyway.

In the light of what has gone before, I think we would do well also to substitute a working hypothesis of, precisely, modest or minimum utopia for all visions more ambitious, whether an end to alienation, unpoliced social harmony, the elimination of serious wrong-doing, the absence of new political menaces or of old but renewable ones. By modest or minimum utopia I mean a form of society which could generally provide for its members the material and social bases of a tolerably contented existence or, as I have already put this, from which the gravest social and political evils familiar to us have been removed. The point of this substitution is not, as such, to reject more ambitious visions: universal and all-round individual development, perpetual peace, ubiquitous altruism, and so on. It is only to highlight the following: we do not need to know, and in fact we do not know, that any of these visions is a real possibility for humankind in order to know that it is a matter of crying need that certain ills, for their part all too well-known, should be finally remedied if *this* at least is possible.

We surely require no ideal of perfection, near perfection or even breathtaking excellence – and whether as an outward state of affairs or as the inner character of the human being – to recognize the need for radical institutional change. It is enough that without such change relations of injustice, sometimes terrible injustice, and conditions of life of a wretched and awful kind, are allowed to persist. Let these be attended to and the more maximalist dreams of socialist utopia may take care of themselves.

Or they may not. Or they may await another day. It is of less moment. I have myself offered a speculation as to the likely creative consequences of extending to everyone on the planet just a moderately secure existence. The case for doing this, however, is quite strong enough irrespective of what may be thought of the strength of the speculation.

I support, then, a limited notion of progress and of socialist utopia. Two other points need, briefly, to be made about this. First, limited, modest or minimal as the proposed conception is, it is not to be confused with the idea that the objectives in view are attainable through merely small modifications to the prevailing economic and social order, the order of world capitalism. The conception is modest or minimal only *vis-à-vis* some of those more far-reaching aspirations typically associated with notions of utopia. *Vis-à-vis* the world we actually inhabit, the programme of providing everyone with the material and social bases of a tolerably contented existence, of trying to get rid of the gravest social and political evils familiar to us, remains revolutionary through and through. It is incompatible with the extremes of wealth and need, the patterns of effort and reward, the structures of economic power and social powerlessness, which capitalism goes on reproducing.

It is the more necessary, perhaps, to insist on this first point in view of the second one here: which is that it follows from the argument I have put forward above about the 'mixed' potentialities in human nature that a limited socialist utopia would have to be limited as well in the specific sense of being a *liberal* political order. Opposing the idea of perfectibility or intrinsic goodness, accepting the threat of evil as a permanent human possibility, we cannot entertain any confidence in some would-be universal benevolence and harmony, or in the prospect of an end to the rule of law. On the contrary, in the light of what human beings can do and have done to one another, we have every reason to want to continue setting limits around the more harmful and menacing types of human potentiality. All the paraphernalia of the rule of law – of secure, enforceable individual rights, democratically based legislation, checks on power, independent judicial processes, the means of redressing injustice, the means of defending the polity and the community against attack, and so on – follow. The realm of freedom is restricted, then, not only on account of the unpassable boundaries of the realm of material necessity. It is restricted also on account of another, inner limitation; one that we have, by now, more than enough grounds for not taking too lightly.

Still, when all this has been said, we cannot give up on socialist utopian hope and on the hope of progress. To advise resigned acceptance of the world as it is – life-and-death inequalities, universal exploitation, widespread political oppression, festering communal hatreds, genocide, recurring war – as well as being, as Miliband says, 'a counsel of despair', is to eschew a naive, optimistic teleology, only to speak the script of another, grimmer one. It is to risk making oneself, in a certain manner, the willing voice of ugly moral forces.

Some sense of situational perspective may not come amiss here. Even in the depths, in the most notorious of the humanly-created hells of our century, there were many who did not give up hope. Plenty of others did, of course, and they cannot be blamed for it. But many did not. It is a theme that I will not go into here other than to say that these many fought as they could to survive, and to preserve what they could of dignity and value in conditions of the most appalling barbarity.[25] What part do the better situated have to make themselves the sponsors of discourses of human defeat?

If continued hope in the better possibilities of human nature can come, as it sometimes did 'down there', from an extra piece of bread, a small gratuitous act of kindness or solidarity, the recollection of a few words of poetry, then who can now say what might reasonably be hoped for if the great social and institutional causes of inequity and suffering, the great economic barriers to a more fulfilling existence for millions of people, could be levelled or lowered? To be sure, caution is today in order on the question of whether and how that objective can be achieved, as on the question of just what we could expect from its achievement in the way of the 'moral betterment' of individuals. It is every bit as much the case, however, that nobody can claim to *know*, with any degree of certainty, either that it could not be achieved, or that its effects of moral betterment would be negligible.

This cannot be known from where we stand. It is a speculation as empty as any more utopian. Although for obvious reasons not the focus of this essay, the fact is that the human record is replete also with acts of moral heroism and moral excellence, and with ordinary, unspectacular day-to-day decency. Countless human beings live their whole lives without killing or maiming or torturing or otherwise severely harming their fellow beings. Mutual human sympathy and beneficence run both deep and wide. What the future balance might be between these better tendencies and the worse ones, in conditions putatively more encouraging to the former, cannot confidently be known. Given this, to add one's voice to the chorus disparaging ideas of progress just contributes some small further weight to the many obstacles to progress, helping by a little more to ensure that it is not only not inevitable, but is, even as a possibility, more distant and more difficult.

To teach, for example, that Auschwitz gives us the truth about human nature – not merely a truth, the truth – simply serves to strengthen what truth it, unhappily, does have. At the limit the Holocaust then becomes, more than a tragic, ghastly event with its own historicity and conditions, the symbol of inexorable human *fate*, in a reversal of the very idea of progress. Humanity's accumulating crimes live on, not, and as they ought to, as a memory of the evil men and women can do, of what has to be guarded against, fought. They live on, in the minds of all those who succumb to learning this as 'the truth', in the shape of the thought that such is what we are and have to be. This is an option that is not only not appealing. It is repellent. We cannot give up on utopian hope or socialism. We cannot give up on progress. They are not *less* apt in light of what we know about the bad side of human nature. They are more necessary.

For one other thing may be added finally. To accept the world as it (more or less) is, is to help to prolong a state of grave danger. This world, accommodating and countenancing too much of what ought not to be tolerated – plain, persistent injustice, stark, avoidable human suffering – is a world very receptive to present and future atrocity, a world over populated with bystanders. It is one in which the idea is harder and harder to resist that just anything at all may be done to people while others look on; and there be no consequence. As long as the situation lasts, it degrades the moral culture of the planet. It poisons the conscience of humankind.[26]

NOTES

1. The arguments reported here and in the paragraphs immediately following are from Ralph Miliband, *Socialism for a Sceptical Age* (Cambridge: Polity, 1994), pp. 58–62.
2. See my *Marx and Human Nature* (London: Verso, 1983), and *Solidarity in the Conversation of Humankind* (London: Verso, 1995) especially ch. 2.
3. Anna Pawelczynska, *Values and Violence in Auschwitz* (Berkeley: University of California Press, 1979), p. 4.
4. Tadeusz Borowski, *This Way for the Gas, Ladies and Gentlemen* (London: Penguin, 1976), p. 175.
5. Cited in Lawrence Langer, *Holocaust Testimonies* (New Haven: Yale University Press, 1991), p. 59.
6. Richard L. Rubenstein, *The Cunning of History: the Holocaust and the American Future* (New York: Harper & Row, 1987), p. 92, italics removed.
7. Arthur A. Cohen, *The Tremendum: a Theological Interpretation of the Holocaust* (New York: Continuum, 1993), pp. 15–21, 46–7. For an account

of Cohen, see Dan Cohn-Sherbok, *Holocaust Theology* (London: Lamp Press, 1989), pp. 68–79.

8.   Robert Nozick, *The Examined Life* (New York: Simon & Schuster, 1989), pp. 236–42.

9.   Elie Wiesel, *One Generation After* (New York: Random House, 1970), p. 46.

10. The theses of Hannah Arendt – *Eichmann in Jerusalem* (London: Penguin, 1977) – and, more lately, Zygmunt Bauman – *Modernity and the Holocaust* (Cambridge: Polity, 1989) – are widely known. See also in this connection: Gitta Sereny, *Into That Darkness* (London: Andre Deutsch, 1991); Christopher R. Browning, *Ordinary Men* (New York: HarperCollins, 1993); John Sabini and Maury Silver, 'On Destroying the Innocent with a Clear Conscience', in Joel Dimsdale, ed., *Survivors, Victims, and Perpetrators* (Washington: Hemisphere, 1980), pp. 329–58, and reprinted in their *Moralities of Everyday Life* (Oxford: Oxford University Press, 1982), pp. 55–87; Herbert Kelman, 'Violence without Moral Restraint', *Journal of Social Issues*, 29/4 (1973), 25–61; and Henri Zukier, 'The Twisted Road to Genocide: On the Psychological Development of Evil During the Holocaust', *Social Research*, 61 (1994), 423–55.

11. Primo Levi, *The Drowned and the Saved* (London: Abacus, 1989), pp. 28–9.

12. Levi, *The Drowned and the Saved*, pp. 32–3.

13. Levi, *The Drowned and the Saved*, pp. 25–6.

14. Levi, *The Drowned and the Saved*, pp. 27, 33.

15. See Ferdinando Camon, *Conversations with Primo Levi* (Marlboro, Vt. The Marlboro Press, 1989), pp. 19–20.

16. Camon, *Conversations with Primo Levi*, p. 20; Hanna Lévy-Hass, *Inside Belsen* (Brighton: Harvester, 1982), p. 41; Viktor E. Frankl, *Man's Search for Meaning* (London: Hodder & Stoughton, 1987), pp. 87, 136.

17. Sereny, *Into That Darkness*, p. 208.

18. Miliband, *Socialism for a Sceptical Age*, p. 61. Emphasis added.

19. Miliband, *Socialism for a Sceptical Age*, p. 61 – and see above.

20. Miliband, *Socialism for a Sceptical Age*, p. 61.

21. Miliband, *Socialism for a Sceptical Age*, p. 60.

22. David Rousset, *The Other Kingdom* (New York: Reynal and Hitchcock, 1947), p. 168; Livia E. Bitton Jackson, *Elli: Coming of Age in the Holocaust* (London: Grafton, 1984), p. 120; Charlotte Delbo, *Auschwitz and After* (New Haven and London: Yale University Press, 1995), p. 11; Levi, *The Drowned and the Saved*, p. 33; Wiesel, *One Generation After*, p. 47.

23. Henry Friedlander, 'Postscript: Toward a Methodology of Teaching about the Holocaust', in Henry Friedlander and Sybil Milton, eds, *The Holocaust: Ideology, Bureaucracy, and Genocide* (New York: Kraus International, 1980), p. 324; and Henri Zukier, 'The Twisted Road to Genocide', p. 424.

24. Cf. Levi, *The Drowned and the Saved*, p. 27 – notwithstanding the 'sociological pessimism' there registered.

25. Outstanding in this connection is Terrence Des Pres, *The Survivor* (New York: Oxford University Press, 1976).

26. This essay is drawn, slightly modified, from work in progress, which will appear in due course as a book on the Holocaust to be published by Verso.

9 The Enlightenment, the Nation-state and the Primal Patricide of Modernity

Robert Wokler

Critics of a so-called 'Enlightenment Project', however striking the differences between them, characteristically subscribe in one way or another to two fundamental propositions. They believe, on the one hand, that in replacing dogmatic faith with dogmatic reason the Enlightenment loved the thing it killed and framed the secular world of modernity within an ideological mould which merely turned Christianity inside out, in the service of absolutist principles of another sort. They imagine that it made science the new religion of mankind and offered terrestrial grace or happiness to its true believers alone. That in essence is the thesis of Carl Becker's *Heavenly City of the Eighteenth-century Philosophers*, first published in 1932, and in its more political manifestations, such as in Jacob Talmon's *Origins of Totalitarian Democracy* or Simon Schama's *Citizens*,[1] much the same proposition informs their authors' interpretation of the excesses of the French Revolution.

On the other hand, the same critics of an Enlightenment Project, to the extent that they seek to explain the moral underpinnings of the world which they inhabit themselves, also commonly trace its conceptual roots to eighteenth-century philosophy. They are convinced that modernity was bred from the loins of the Enlightenment, out of its notions of the rights of man and its principles of liberty, equality and fraternity, which brought the age of feudalism to a close. If they are communitarians or postmodernists, they seldom hesitate to blame the Enlightenment for having conceived that monstrous child which our civilization has become, since they believe that, even while disposing of original sin, the *philosophes* of the eighteenth century actually committed it. The attempts of eighteenth-century thinkers to free human nature from the shackles of tradition are alleged to have given rise either to the empty desolation of atomistic individualism or to schemes of social engineering on a vast scale, or indeed to both at once. Such propositions, in different permutations, inform Max Horkheimer's and Theodor Adorno's *Dialektik der Aufklärung*, Alasdair MacIntyre's *After Virtue* and Zygmunt Bauman's *Modernity and the Holocaust*.[2]

161

I mean to show in this chapter that both propositions – that the Enlightenment loved the thing it killed, and that modernity springs from the Enlightenment – are false. The first claim, I shall argue, utterly misconstrues the nature of the Enlightenment Project, supposing that there was one, with respect to the religious doctrines which its adherents opposed. The second proposition, I shall contend, misdescribes modernity, in so far as it presumes that the French Revolution enabled the philosophy of the Enlightenment to take its currently predominant form. I shall aim to establish how the modern nation-state, which I take to be an invention of the French Revolution, not only distorted but betrayed the Enlightenment Project in the very course of its legislators' attempts to fulfil its noblest ambitions in a particular way, which was unheralded in any pre-revolutionary constitutional scheme. For my purposes here, I shall adopt the language of Freud in his *Moses and Monotheism* where he maintains that the redemption of man's original sin by way of Christ's absorption of the guilt of his people through his death at their hands had been prefigured by the forgotten event of the Jews' killing of Moses, who was their first Messiah. Out of this primal parricide the Jewish people was born, and with it their collective guilt, he claims.[3] My treatment of the genesis of the nation-state, untimely plucked from the womb of the Enlightenment rather than germinated out of its seed by design, follows Freud. The primal patricide of modernity, as I describe it here, constitutes the murder of the Enlightenment Project, the destruction of the international republic of letters by way of the birth of the nation-state, conceived as a form of republic whose members are bound together in a quite different way. On my reading of its principles, the Enlightenment Project was not fulfilled or realized in the course of the French Revolution but, on the contrary, suffered a kind of cot death through strangulation by way of the zealous embrace of admirers who loved it too well but unwisely, once they seized the opportunity to put its ideals into practice. I do not agree that the Enlightenment loved the thing it killed, but I hope to show here that modernity killed the thing it loved.

I suppose I ought first to admit that in all the years I have attended international colloquia on the Enlightenment, I have never heard a single contribution addressed to a so-called 'Enlightenment Project'. On the contrary, genuine scholars of the period characteristically disaggregate such global terms, so as to situate ideas only in their specific and local contexts, with reference to all their rich particularity and texture. And yet in failing to confront those social theorists who view their domain writ large and on stilts, specialists of Enlightenment thought risk rendering their own research irrelevant to much of contemporary moral philosophy and conceptual history that ought to be informed by it. The *philosophes* were determined not only to interpret the world but, so far as it lay in their power, to change it, to improve it or combat its decay. They were public moralists,[4] secular crusaders, the *engagés volontaires* of reason and light. In attempting here to contradict their critics, and to exculpate them, and indeed Rousseau as well, from responsibility for the sinister trappings of a political world which I believe was not prefigured in their doctrines, I hope to show how the moral landscape of modernity, in having too much escaped their influence, remains in need of it, if only because the duty of men and women of goodwill to breathe life into a patient with scant prospects of survival if uncared for is perennial.

II

How, then, shall we define the 'Enlightenment Project'? Plainly not by consulting a dictionary, since the French language has never had a term for *enlightenment* at all, while the *Oxford English Dictionary* still defines it as 'superficial intellectualism' marked by 'insufficient respect for authority and tradition'. For good measure, it adds that a *philosophe* is 'one who philosophizes erroneously'. Should we begin, rather, with the so-called 'High Enlightenment' of a Fontenelle or Diderot, or instead with the 'Low Enlightenment' of Grub Street pamphleteers? Should we perhaps start with the *frühe Aufklärung* of Christian Wolff or, alternatively the *spätere Aufklärung* of Lessing? Would it be better first to look at the central figures who formed the so-called 'Party of Humanity', or to work our way back from the peripheries of the Counter-Enlightenment?[5] We could initially take our lead from Voltaire, plainly the godfather of the Enlightenment Project, unless of course we happen to live in the United States of America, which grants that title instead to Benjamin Franklin, or in Japan, which instead worships Adam Smith. If for some commentators the Enlightenment Project appears to have embraced the Grand Tour, for others it can be better understood as having issued from the head of a single man who never travelled thirty paces outside of Königsberg. And if instead of Kant we prefer the company of the man who probably exercised the greatest influence of all eighteenth-century thinkers – that is, Montesquieu – we might reflect whether his attachment to the physical laws of human nature makes him a universalist in matters of science, or whether, by contrast, his attention to the variety of social institutions renders him a cultural pluralist, and hence, perhaps, no protagonist of the Enlightenment Project at all.

Our task is not really so difficult as it might seem. When in doubt about the meaning of ideas, it is always sensible to begin with facts, and even in intellectual history the most reliable facts often turn out to be dates. Archbishop Ussher who, in the seventeenth century, established beyond doubt that the world had been created by God at 8 a.m. on Saturday, 22 October, in the year 4004 BC has long held my admiration. I shall presently try to show that we can date the advent of the age of modernity with similar precision, and while there is scant evidence to suggest that the Enlightenment Project was invented in a single day, it seems to me that there is virtually unanimous agreement among commentators that the principal contributors to it flourished in a specifiable period. Whether we take the Enlightenment Project to have been launched by Locke's *Essay Concerning Human Understanding* of 1690 and completed by Condorcet's *Esquisse d'un tableau des progrès de l'esprit humain* of 1795, or, alternatively, inaugurated by the Revocation of the Edict of Nantes in 1685 and completed by the *Déclaration des droits de l'homme* of 1789, our conception of the whole age of Enlightenment encompasses just that century of European history. To put my point another way, a perfectly acceptable temporal definition of the Enlightenment Project would embrace the period delimited by two seminal works which have sought to define the passage of *l'âge classique* into *l'âge moderne*, by way of the transfiguration of the European mind after about 1680, on the one hand, and the invention of the human sciences in the 1790s, on the other – that is, Paul Hazard's *La crise de la conscience européenne* of 1935 and Michel Foucault's *Les mots et les choses* of 1966.[6] Somewhere within the intellectual worlds or movements delimited by Hazard and Foucault lies the Enlightenment Project, as I see it. Swirling beneath their main philosophical currents the moral and political tributaries out of which the French Revolution was to be spawned should be detectable, for it is those tributaries which so many of our leading social theorists of the twentieth century have come to identify as forming the Enlightenment incubus of modernity. Why do I hold them to be utterly mistaken? What do our standard chronologies of eighteenth-century intellectual history tell us about the real nature of the Enlightenment Project?

Simply this. That above all else, in the countries in which it flourished, it was committed to principles of religious toleration. In France, we may date its inception from the year 1685, when, first, the Revocation of the Edict of Nantes by Louis XIV, and subsequently his acceptance of the papal Bull *Unigenitus* of 1713, inaugurated a century-long quarrel between Catholic assenters and dissidents, and between ultramontane monarchists, on the one hand, and gallican clerics and parliamentarians, on the other, which was to issue in the remonstrances of the *parlements* and their expulsion by Louis XV, followed by the suppression of the Jesuits and ultimately Louis XVI's convocation of the Assembly of Notables in 1787, succeeded by the Revolution of 1789. That history of the institutionalization of political and theological intolerance coincides with the whole history of the French Enlightenment itself, as opposition to the Revocation united *philosophes* of all denominations. From Montesquieu's *Lettres persanes* to Diderot's *Supplément au voyage de Bougainville*, sceptics in France denounced theological controversy and the persecution of heretics, often condemning, like Rousseau in the *Contrat social* or Voltaire in his *Traité sur la tolérance*, the refusal of French Catholic priests to administer the sacraments to Protestants, which thereby disenfranchised them of all their civil rights.

Under the reign of a Catholic king in England, religious dissenters in the 1680s fared little better than did Protestants in France, and it is as much with reference to the same issue – either by way of Locke's *Letter Concerning Toleration*, or William and Mary's *Act of Toleration*, both dating from 1689, that the English Enlightenment may be said to have been inaugurated as well. The idea of toleration lies at the heart of the philosophy of Locke in virtually all the domains which engaged his attention, and it was by embracing that idea and the civic culture which gave rise to it that enlightened *philosophes* in France who described themselves as lovers of freedom emulated both his achievement and his country's success. In England it came to be accepted in both official and literary circles that civil disorder was best kept at bay through the state's indifference to matters of religious belief rather than its imposition of a uniformitarian faith, so that at the beginning of the eighteenth century the English Enlightenment had thus already taken a political form, whereas in France it was to remain more radical, because disenfranchised from the prevalent institutions of both the state and the church.

As well as in England and France, the Enlightenment of course also flourished in Holland, and for much the same reason. Immediately following the Revocation of the Edict of Nantes, the most important writings bearing testimony to its impact were those of French Protestants who either fled to Holland from France for their safety or, like Pierre Bayle, had been victims of the dissolution of Huguenot academies even prior to 1685. It was also in Holland that Spinoza put his case for the liberty of opinion; it was in Holland, while in exile, that Locke drafted his own account of the need for freedom of conscience; and it was from Holland that England's new king and queen, committed to religious toleration above all else, would descend. The religious purification of the French nation after

1685 – what might today be termed its 'ethnic cleansing' – did not take the murderous form of the St Bartholomew's Day massacre more than a hundred years earlier. But like all such campaigns it gave rise to a diaspora, to a brain drain and an outcast culture which abroad fermented more richly than it had managed under relative tranquillity at home. As much as from any other philosophical, political or economic source, it was from the precipitation of that brain drain, and the depth of the reaction to it among intellectuals in France, that the French Enlightenment of the eighteenth century was formed. Religious intolerance kindled the Enlightenment Project.

Seventeenth- and eighteenth-century arguments for toleration were of course developed from many Reformation and humanist sources as well.[7] But in the Enlightenment the case was advanced by its proponents in fresh idioms, with new weapons and a new vitality. It was put forward in campaigns to reform the criminal law and secure the abolition of torture. It began to figure within theories of human perfectibility, whose advocates identified the acceptance of theological dogmas, not as belief but as superstition. In the eighteenth century, religious conviction came to be denounced as blind faith, at once barbarous and irrational. Europe's leading *philosophes* could then suppose, contrary not only to Hobbes and Mandeville but also to Scripture, that human nature was fundamentally good. Alternatively, they could be persuaded that it was selfish but sociable, or that it was made of a pliant clay which could be cast in infinitely perfectible ways. What they could not accept, because it was no longer philosophically correct to do so, was the theological doctrine of original sin, now regarded as a myth invented by clerics to regulate the salvation of gullible souls. At the heart of their commitment to the progressive education of mankind lay a crusade against all the dark forces of idolatry. Through the *Encyclopédie* and the book trade as a whole, progressive thinkers of the age of Enlightenment sought to build an eighteenth-century Crystal Palace of the human mind, accessible to readers of all vernacular languages, as transparent as the open book of nature. By contrast, they held the arcane dogmas of Christian theology responsible for fanaticism and hypocrisy throughout human history – for wars of religion, for the Inquisition, for bigotry virtually everywhere.

If such notions comprise the kernel of what we mean, or ought to mean, when we speak of the Enlightenment Project, then the most inescapable truth which must be confronted by those of us who inhabit the age of modernity is that our civilization shows only limited traces of the Enlightenment Project's influence. Like that long day's journey into night which descended upon the culture of ancient Rome, our century, in Gibbon's phrase, bears witness to 'the triumph of barbarism and religion'.[8] The Enlightenment Project has been our god that failed.

III

In order to establish that modernity killed the thing it loved – or, as I conceive it here, that the nation-state strangled the Enlightenment Project to
which it was wedded – I should like next to show that its affection was in
fact genuine and that, in certain respects at least, it truly believed itself to
have embraced Enlightenment principles. To my mind, virtually all the
rhetoric of modernity, turning round images of newly enfranchised
people's democracies as they cast off the yoke of feudalism, can be found
in the Enlightenment. Let me offer just one illustration of what I mean,
which I invoke because it draws together some of the most central figures
of both the Enlightenment and the post-French Revolutionary worlds,
including d'Alembert, Diderot and Goethe, but above all, Rousseau, who
came to be regarded as the French Revolution's Moses, and Hegel, whose
Phänomenologie des Geistes may be described as modernity's Sermon on
the Mount.

The passage I have in mind comes from Rousseau's *Confessions*, which
he probably drafted in 1767, when he spent a largely miserable winter in
north Staffordshire, not far from Manchester, where I have sometimes felt
able to share his discomfort even while attempting to recover his thoughts.
Reflecting about events which had transpired in October and November
1753, around the time his *Lettre sur la musique française* was published,
Rousseau makes the following claim: 'The [Paris] Parlement had just been
exiled; the fermentation was at its height; there were signs of an imminent
uprising. My work appeared; all at once every other dispute was forgotten;
only the danger to French music remained, and the sole uprising that
occurred took place against me. So great was the reaction that the nation
never recovered from it. Thus, whoever reads that my brochure may have
prevented the outbreak of a revolution in the state will imagine himself in
a dream. Nevertheless, that is exactly what happened.'[9] Lack of space prevents me from addressing the full significance of these remarks, but let me
just note that Rousseau's comments turn around two interconnected sets of
events, on the one hand the success of a company of Italian musicians who
for two seasons performed mainly Neapolitan *opera buffa* at the Paris
Opéra; on the other, the expulsion by King Louis XV of the magistrates of
the Parlement de Paris in May 1753, largely because of its gallicanism and
defiance of the Papal Bull *Unigenitus* of 1713, which had attempted to
prohibit the practice of Jansenism in France.

I have already referred to the significance of *Unigenitus* in the context
of Enlightenment campaigns for religious toleration after the Revocation
of the Edict of Nantes. Like other confrontations with the Crown in the

course of the eighteenth century, the crisis of the Parlement in 1753 was at once political and theological, but on this occasion it happened to coincide with, and become embroiled in, an ostensibly quite different controversy about matters of music and language, known as the *Querelle des Bouffons*, which was launched in 1752 by a performance at the Paris *Opéra* of Pergolesi's *La Serva padrona*. That very slight Italian *opera buffa* entranced both its listeners and most of its reviewers, mainly on account of its simplicity and sweetness in contrast with the overbearing tragic opera, *Acis et Galathée* by Lully, court composer to King Louis XIV, with which it had been billed the same evening. In a sense the whole of the *Querelle des Bouffons* can be encapsulated in the difference between these two operas, of which Lully's was solemn, with a regal theme drawn from ancient myth, embellished with richly textured orchestration, while Pergolesi's was mainly melodic, with a plot that was bourgeois and contemporary. Above all, *La Serva padrona* was chanted in the mellifluous open vowels of the Italian language, while *Acis et Galathée* was articulated through the heavy vowels and nasal consonants of French. Virtually all the leading *philosophes* in Paris at the time, including Voltaire, Grimm and Diderot, wrote about it and in each case endorsed the cause of Italian *opera buffa* as against French *tragédie lyrique*. So too of course did Rousseau, whose *Lettre sur la musique française* concludes with the assertion that, on account of the unmusicality of their language, the French have no real music and cannot have any. If ever they do, he adds with a flourish, that will be so much the worse for them.[10]

Supporters of French opera and French culture took great offence at such remarks, and against the *philosophes* in general, whom they decried as upstart Germans, renegade Swiss and muddle-headed mathematicians. To this day, there are loyalist Frenchmen who perceive the doctrines of the eighteenth-century *philosophes* collectively in just these terms. As Rousseau reports, there was indeed a great public surge of anger against him, which provoked the orchestra of the *Opéra* to hang him in effigy and prompted the marquis d'Argenson in his *Journal* to comment that the 'swarm of enemies' which he had stirred up was 'becoming a national conflict.'[11] Six years later d'Alembert would reflect on how Rousseau and his friends had ignited a spark which had since grown to a great blaze in France. They had come to be perceived as members of a society covenanted to destroy Religion, Authority, Morality and Music all at once, says d'Alembert, with Rousseau at the head of a seditious party.[12] In 1753, in effect, Rousseau was for the first time perceived to be a threat to the French nation.

But why? What could be so incendiary about his preference and that of other *philosophes* for Italian over French opera? Let me briefly try to explain. If we turn to Diderot's *Neveu de Rameau*, which first appeared in print in 1805 in the German translation by Goethe, we shall find the following lines: '"Feel how the softness of the Italian language ... lends itself to the art of song ... and how by contrast the musical expression of the French tongue is stiff, heavy, pedantic and monotonous", remarks the nephew. "One fine day the foreign god elbows out the native idol, and bang! crash!, topples it". In spite of everything the Jansenists say, he adds, that transplant quietly ferments an alternative culture which displaces the old.' Shortly afterwards, and long before Diderot's text was ever printed in French, these lines and a few others were incorporated by Hegel in his *Phänomenologie des Geistes*, where he put his own gloss on them in concluding that 'Memory alone ... preserves the dead form of ... Spirit's previous shape as a vanished history. ... the new serpent of wisdom raised on high for adoration has in this way painlessly cast merely a withered skin'.[13] In October 1806, at a time of great tension in his own life, at the very moment that the World-Spirit of modernity – that is, Napoleon Bonaparte – was with his *Grande Armée* laying siege to Jena, Hegel, within that city's walls, found himself captivated by the *Neveu de Rameau*, perhaps the chief literary masterpiece of the whole Enlightenment. Virtually turning the pages of that book with one hand and transcribing Diderot's remarks with the other, he incorporated them within his own text of the *Phänomenologie des Geistes*, without adding so much as a footnote[14] to make plain their source, as if through Goethe he had managed to imbibe Diderot's spirit and philosophy. In Diderot, Hegel recognized a kindred soul and in effect embraced Diderot's own statement of the metamorphosis of World Spirit in the course of the *Querelle des Bouffons*, such as *he* had witnessed it himself, not astride a horse but on the stage. The very terms Hegel employed as the rubric of the section of his *Phänomenologie* in which he incorporated Diderot's text, *Sich entfremdete Geist*, figured as Goethe's own translation from the French – *aliénation d'esprit* – employed by Diderot to characterize the condition of the nephew at the most dramatic moment of the dialogue in which he pantomimes French and Italian operatic arias. Here, *in nuce*, was the lacerated consciousness, the *zerrissenes Bewußtsein*, of modernity itself.[15]

If we turn next to Rousseau's reflections on the same subject, we find him insisting not only upon the gentleness of the Italian language as so much better suited to musical expression than the bark and bray of French, but also on the proposition that all modern languages which have come to be divorced from music are inimical to freedom. The corruption of our music and language provides an accurate portrait of the utterly degraded state into which our societies have fallen, he concludes in his *Essai sur l'origine des langues*. Conversation has become covert, political discourse has become barren, and we have all succeeded in bringing our original manner of speaking up to date only by becoming the speechless auditors of those who rule by diatribes and recitations from the pulpit. While our southern forebears had at first sung *Aimez-moi* to one another and subsequently their northern conquerors had cried out *Aidez-moi*, in the world of modernity that we inhabit ourselves, all of us now only mutter *Donnez de l'argent*.[16]

Where today, asks Rousseau in his *Lettre sur les spectacles*, is the concord of citizens? Where is public fraternity? In his *Gouvernement de Pologne*, similarly, he calls upon Polish youth to follow the example of the people of Rome rather than emulate the decadence of the French, so as to become accustomed to 'equality' and 'fraternity' as citizens of a truly free state. For while liberty had once been linked with equality and fraternity, our contemporary institutions of representation and finance had destroyed fraternity, on the one hand, and equality on the other, so that in the modern world, shorn of its ancient associations, liberty had in effect come to mean nothing more than the pursuit of private gain. Rousseau's critique of French music and culture thus drew him in the direction of both ancient Rome and modern Italian opera as a means of bringing together *liberté*, *égalité* and *fraternité* once more.

In passing through the *Querelle des Bouffons* and the French Revolution of 1753 which did not take place, we can thus wend our way to the French Revolution of 1789. Couched in terms of music and language lies the impassioned rhetoric of the age of Enlightenment that modernity came to love, the imagined community of *Roma redivivus*, giving rise to the charge of Mme de Staël and other liberals who did not welcome it that Rousseau 'n'a rien découvert, mais il a tout enflammé',[17] the passions, the senses, the Terror. From the point of view of his critics, of course, first Robespierre and then Bonaparte were henceforth to make plain that Rousseau's notion of the general will would always come to mean the general's will. But while it was *his* language and imagery which would rightly earn for him the status of chief poet and acknowledged legislator of the age of modernity inaugurated by the Revolution that did take place, let me conclude these comments about French and Italian music by citing, not Rousseau himself but d'Alembert, in particular his text, *De la liberté de la musique*, of 1759.

There is a kind of fatality attached in this century to everything we have received from Italy, he writes. Everything from *Unigenitus* to the music of *Les Bouffons* has caused us great trouble. Would it not be possible for us to settle our differences with the Italians, to keep their music and send back all the rest? What d'Alembert admired about *opera buffa* is here portrayed in much the same terms as those of other *Encyclopédistes* earlier – that is, the perfect accord between the Italian language and the music in which it is sung, and the concentration upon a clear melodic line rather than its harmonic accompaniment. This makes Italian music more free in its expression than our own, he claims. *Les Bouffons* had in effect come to France, chanting the language of liberty. And how were their supporters regarded? Look in a dictionary, and you will find there the terms *bouffoniste*, *republican*, *atheist*, even *materialist*, used interchangeably. Is it not time, asks d'Alembert, that in a century in which so many works have been devoted to free trade and free marriages, we should now also put a plea on behalf of the freedom of music? All liberties hang together and are equally dangerous, according to our political leaders, he concludes: 'The liberty of music presupposes that of feeling; the liberty of feeling requires freedom of thought; freedom of thought entails freedom of action; and freedom of action brings about the ruin of states. Preserve opera as it is, therefore, if we wish to conserve the kingdom; and let us put a brake on the freedom of thought if we do not wish that of speech to follow it.'[18]

IV

I must not of course exaggerate the extent to which the *philosophes*' convergence with Rousseau in his critique of French music and culture aligned their philosophy to the rhetoric that he above all other thinkers bequeathed to the French Revolution. In many respects, he was the Enlightenment Project's fiercest adversary in the eighteenth century and not one of its proponents. If the French Revolutionary commitment to one nation, *une et indivisible*, can be said to have had some basis in his philosophy, it had much less justification in theirs. The public celebration of a great and unique civil religion that drew all subjects together appealed to them far less than did a multiplicity of religions, each practised at home. In what might be termed their deconstruction of the universalist pretensions of Christian dogmas by way of critical theory, they looked back to seventeenth-century England's *Act of Toleration* and its *Declaration of Right* rather than forwards to the French Revolution's *Déclaration des droits de l'homme et du citoyen*. In the 1790s their followers imagined that if France had been able to enjoy a similar bloodless revolution around the same time as the Glorious Revolution of England, the minds of Frenchmen might have been changed without it having proved necessary to cut off their heads.

In exculpating the *philosophes* of the Enlightenment from responsibility for the Revolution which is said to have sprung out of their doctrines, I do not only mean that they were reformers instead of revolutionaries, who indeed sought to avert a revolutionary crisis which many of them perceived as imminent, rather than to promote it. I have in mind also the fact that virtually none of their constitutional programmes of reform came to be realized anywhere in the age of modernity which their ideas are said to have spawned. For unless it is the legal despotism of Le Mercier de la Rivière, not a single major scheme of government conceived by Enlightenment thinkers – not classical republicanism or its modern derivatives meant for large states, not enlightened monarchy, nor democracy, nor the re-establishment of the ancient constitution, nor the mixed constitution, nor the separation of powers – has come to prevail anywhere in the age of the nation-state sired by the French Revolution. The Enlightenment Project is as blameless for the predominant political divisions of modernity as it is for modernity's religious and ethnic strife. Politically no less than theologically, it offered us a multiplicity of gods that failed.

In order to prove that modernity killed the thing it loved, I therefore really need to show that it put to death that which it loved most of all – in effect, that the French Revolutionary nation-state, which was apparently cast in the image of Rousseau's philosophy, betrayed it. As is implied in the very title of Mercier's work of 1791, *Rousseau, considéré comme l'un des premiers auteurs de la Révolution*, Rousseau was of course the spiritual guide of a regenerated France. He pointed the way to the promised land. But while his *Contrat social* would come to be esteemed as the holy writ of the French Revolution, its most central tenets were to be repudiated in the age of modernity launched by the political upheavals of 1789. Even in adopting much of his rhetoric, France's revolutionary leaders deliberately abandoned most of his principles and, at each stage of their deliberations, triumphantly opposed everyone who endorsed them. The political system they devised not only destroyed the Enlightenment Project but also, by design, suffocated the most fundamental strictures of that system's primordial founder. Like Freud's conception of the birth of the Jewish people, even like Rousseau's birth, which cost his mother her life, the first modern nation-state that ostensibly embraced his doctrines suppressed them. In the act of its self-creation, modernity killed the Rousseauist ideals to which it purportedly subscribed. Ours is the age not only of the primal patricide but of the primal parricide as well.

Let me explain, by way of contextualizing Hegel's philosophical account of the genesis of modernity in its political form, as he explains it in another section of his *Phänomenologie des Geistes*, addressed to the subject of absolute freedom and terror. As I read him, Hegel is the Archbishop Ussher of modernity, who not only identified the date of its explosive birth correctly but in fact witnessed it himself and, in penetrating its internal logic, entered the very mind of God, which of course for him meant the plan, or reason, of human history. In its political form, as he explains it, modernity was born with the establishment of the French National Assembly on 17 June 1789, from which of course it follows immediately that, from the day of its creation to the Fall of the Bastille on 14 July, modernity can only have enjoyed four weeks of innocence.

On 17 June 1789, the deputies of the Estates General, which had been convoked the previous autumn by King Louis XVI, resolved that they were no longer assembled at the monarch's behest but were rather agents of the national will (*le vœu national*), entrusted with the task of representing the sovereignty of the people of France. The three estates thereby constituted themselves as a single *Assemblée nationale*, bearing sole authority to interpret the people's general will. It is in this way that political modernity came to be born, in France, through the establishment of a unicameral parliament corresponding to a unitary will and the creation of a unified state designed to give voice to an undifferentiated nation. Herein lay the establishment of the first genuinely modern state, in the sense in which it has become a nation-state, plucked from the womb of the *ancien régime* by its own offspring, who in transfiguring their delegated powers and hence their own identity, brought a new world into being. The United States of America, whose Constitution had been framed a fraction earlier, by contrast never formed one nation and at first scarcely formed one state.

Since the motion that thus generated the National Assembly had been put, initially to the delegates of the Third Estate alone, by the abbé Sieyès, it may be said that Sieyès is the father of the nation-state, standing to the whole of political modernity as does God to his Creation. His incendiary tract, *Qu'est-ce que le tiers état?*, published in January 1789, not only prefigured much of the debate that was to lead to the establishment of the National Assembly and then its abolition of the vestiges of feudalism on 4 August 1789; in its first printing it also introduced the expression *la science sociale* to the history of social philosophy and the human sciences, thereby lending some support, of which Foucault was unaware, to his thesis that the epistemic transformation of the classical into the modern age began in the 1790s.[19] Striving perhaps even harder than God had done to ensure that his handiwork flourished, Sieyès set himself the task, over the next several years after the nation-state had been born, of serving as its nursemaid and counsellor as well. No one has contributed more to shaping the modern world's political discourse. Hegel, who, as I have already

own. Joined together with his conception of the unity of the representer – that is, the sovereign – as outlined in his *Leviathan*,[23] the modern state since the French Revolution requires that the represented – that is, the people as a whole – be a moral person as well, national unity going hand in hand with the political unity of the state.

Sieyès never failed to oppose Rousseauist notions of republicanism in the National Assembly, because he recognized what he took to be the threat to the expression of the nation's general will which might be constituted by the people if they did not comprise a single nation whose government pronounced upon public policy with just one voice. It was of the essence of his plan that the nation in assembly spoke for all the people and must never be silenced by the people themselves. Over the past two hundred years the nation-state has characteristically achieved that end because it represents the people, standing before them not just as monarchs had done earlier, as the embodiment of their collective will, but rather by assuming their very identity, bearing the personality of the people themselves.[24] While a small number of genuinely multinational states have in that period been established as well and continue to flourish, the majority of peoples everywhere now comprise nations which, by way of their representatives, are politically incorporated as states. All peoples that have identities form nation-states. What Sieyès did not foresee was that in the age of modernity heralded by his political philosophy, a people might not survive except by constituting a nation-state. In the age of modernity, it has proved possible for the nation-state to become the enemy of the people.

To the Hobbesian theory of representation, the nation-state adds the dimension of the comprehensive unity of the people, the representer and represented together forming an indissoluble whole, the state now identical with the nation, the nation bonded to the state, each understood through the other. As Hannah Arendt rightly noted in her *Origins of Totalitarianism*, it has been a characteristic feature of the nation-state since the French Revolution that the rights of man and the rights of the citizen are the same.[25] By giving real substance and proper sanction to the various declarations of the rights of man within the framework of its own first constitutions, the French revolutionary nation-state invented by Sieyès joined the rights of man to the sovereignty of the nation. It defined the rights of man in such a way that only the state could enforce them and only members of the nation could enjoy them. Yet so far from putting into practice the universal rights of man long advocated by proponents of cosmopolitan enlightenment, the modern nation-state was to ensure that henceforth only persons comprising nations which formed states could have rights, and since the French Revolution the history of modernity has characteristically been marked by the abuse of human rights on the part of nation-states which alone have the authority to determine the scope of those rights and their validity.

Not only individuals but whole peoples which comprise nations without states have found themselves comprehensively shorn of their rights. At the heart of the Enlightenment Project, which its advocates perceived as putting an end to the age of privilege, was their recognition of the common humanity of all persons. For Kant, who in Königsberg came from practically nowhere and went nowhere else at all, to be enlightened meant to be intolerant of injustice everywhere, to pay indiscriminate respect to each individual, to be committed to universal justice, to be morally indifferent to difference. But in the age of the nation-state, it is otherwise. Thanks ultimately to the father of modernity, ours is the age of the passport, the permit, the right of entry to each state or right of exit from it which is enjoyed by citizens that bear its nationality alone. For persons who are not accredited as belonging to a nation-state in the world of modernity, there are few passports and still fewer visas. To be without a passport or visa in the modern world is to have no right of exit or entry anywhere, and to be without a right of exit or entry is to risk a rite of passage to the grave. That above all is the legacy bequeathed to us from the political inception of the modern age on 17 June 1789. It was then, it seems to me, that the metempsychosis of modernity began, when in attempting to sculpt Pygmalion's statue we began instead to manufacture Frankenstein's monster, and when whole peoples without states – above all the Jews – would be doomed if ever such a creature should rise up against them. I have said that Becker's *Heavenly City of the Eighteenth-century Philosophers* bears false testimony to the proposition that the Enlightenment Project loved the thing it killed. Let me now add that Ernst Cassirer's magisterial study, from a Kantian perspective, of *Die Philosophie der Aufklärung*, produced in that same year – 1932 – at the dusk of the Weimar Republic by one of the first Jewish chancellors of a German university, makes plainer than any other work I know, how modernity has killed the thing it loved.

By accident of birth, most readers of this collection will have been fortunately spared the sheer horror of even witnessing that experience. But if in my too Eurocentric manner I dare parochially to ignore the barbarous atrocities that have occurred these past few years in Cambodia, Rwanda and Algeria, I can still remind them of the ethnic cleansing of Bosnia and Kosovo. 'Never again' was our shared resolution, forty years ago, on behalf of which many of the foundational institutions of the European Community were established. Yet there again, indeed, we find ourselves, and virtually no political figure on the continent of Europe deserves any credit for having brought that slaughter to its current halt, or pause. Without assistance from America, could we have averted the ethnic cleansing of Bosnia? We might have required some courage, but I do not think the path we should have taken, and which it was entirely within our power to take, is obscure. Instead of acquiescing to Lord David Owen, we should have joined Voltaire and indeed all the *philosophes* of the age of Enlightenment who opposed the ethnic cleansers of their day, following the Revocation of the Edict of Nantes and the Papal Bull *Unigenitus*. Since our faults lie in ourselves and not our stars, there is nothing in the history of human affairs, including the Holocaust, that was not avertible. Such is the burden of guilt which those who fail to act must always carry. It may also be the chief lesson that we have still to learn from the *engagés volontaires* of the age of Enlightenment, the international brigade of the eighteenth-century republic of letters, who, unlike most of us today, felt themselves charged with Voltaire's commitment to *écraser l'infâme* – that is, to root out bigotry and to pursue it across all borders, since the moral boundaries of the modern nation-state are not impermeable.[26]

NOTES

1.   Cf. Becker, *The Heavenly City of the Eighteenth-century Philosophers* (New Haven: Yale University Press, 1932), pp. 102–3 (in the twenty-fourth printing of 1964); Talmon, *The Origins of Totalitarian Democracy* (London: Secker & Warburg, 1952), pp. 3–11; and Schama, *Citizens: a Chronicle of the French Revolution* (London: Viking, 1989), pp. 441–55 and 619–39.

2.   Cf. Horkheimer and Adorno, *Dialektik der Aufklärung: Philosophische Fragmente* (Amsterdam: Quevedo, 1947), pp. 5–57 and 100–43; MacIntyre, *After Virtue: a Study in Moral Theory* (London: Duckworth, 1981), pp. 38–59; and Bauman, *Modernity and the Holocaust* (Cambridge: Polity Press, 1989), pp. 1–30. I shall address at least some of the already vast literature on this subject in *The Enlightenment Project and its Critics*, of which a kind of prefatory outline, bearing the same title, appears in Sven-Eric Liedman (ed.), *The Postmodernist Critique of the Project of Enlightenment*, *Poznań Studies in the Philosophy of the Sciences and the Humanities*, 58, 13–30.

3.   See Freud, *Moses and Monotheism* (London: Hogarth Press, 1939), pp. 58–64 and 130–45. Pursuing a line of argument from his *Totem and Taboo* of 1912 inspired mainly by Darwin, Freud here develops an account of sexual aggression and collective parricide within a primeval horde. As René Girard has remarked in chs 3 and 8 of *La Violence et le sacré* (Paris: Bernard Grasset, 1972), there is a critical hiatus in Freud's treatment of the

subject in *Totem and Taboo*, in particular, where, by contrast with *Moses and Monotheism*, he makes no reference or allusion to Sophocles' *Œdipidus Rex*. For an illuminating reading of the later text and its notion of primal parricide from the perspective of its insurance of males' sex rights over females, see Carole Pateman, *The Sexual Contract* (Cambridge: Polity Press, 1988), ch. 4, pp. 77–115. These, for me quite new, dimensions of my subject, which in effect embrace a Freudian version of an essentially Foucauldian account of epistemic change couched in the language of Hegel's reading of the Terror, I owe in large measure to Eric Santner.

4. The expression forms the title of Stefan Collini's *Public Moralists: Political Thought and Intellectual Life in Britain* (Oxford: Clarendon Press, 1981).

5. I have in mind here, of course, the work of Robert Darnton, Peter Gay and Isaiah Berlin, respectively. See, for instance, Darnton, *The Literary Underground of the Old Regime* (Cambridge, Mass.: Harvard University Press, 1982); Gay, *The Party of Humanity* (Princeton: Princeton University Press, 1959); and Berlin, 'The Counter-Enlightenment', in his *Against the Current* (London: Hogarth Press, 1979), pp. 1–24.

6. See especially the preface to Hazard's *La crise de la conscience européenne (1680–1815)* (Paris: Boivin, 1935), and Foucault's *Les mots et les choses* (Paris: Gallimard, 1968), chs 8 and 10.

7. Above all, perhaps, in the campaigns on behalf of the freedom of worship of Erasmians, Socinians and Anabaptists.

8. Edward Gibbon, *The Decline and Fall of the Roman Empire*, ed. J.B. Bury (London: Methuen, 1909–29), ch. lxxi, 7.321.

9. Rousseau, *Confessions*, livre VIII, *Oeuvres complètes* (Gallimard: Bilbiothèque de la Pléiade, 1959–95), I.384.

10. See Rousseau, *Lettre sur la musique françoise*, *Oeuvres complètes*, V.328. On the *Querelle des Bouffons*, see especially Lionel de la Laurencie, 'La grande saison italienne de 1752: Les bouffons', *Revue musicale S.I.M.* (1912), 8.6.18–33 and 8.7–8.13–22. Most of the contributions to this dispute have been assembled by Denise Launay in her three-volume collection entitled *La Querelle des Bouffons* (Geneva: Minkoff, 1973).

11. René Louis de Voyer, marquis d'Argenson, *Journal et mémoires*, ed. J.B. Rathery (Paris: Vve Jules Renouard, 1859–67), 8.180.

12. See d'Alembert, *De la liberté de la musique*, in *La Querelle des Bouffons*, 3.2210.

13. Cf. Diderot, *Le Neveu de Rameau*, ed. Jean Fabre (Genève: Librairie Droz, 1977), pp. 81–2; Diderot, *Rameaus Neffe*, ed. Goethe with a commentary by Richard Münnich (Weimar: Gustav Kiepenheuer, 1964), pp. 131–2; and Hegel, *Phänomenologie des Geistes*, in his *Gesammelte Werke* (Hamburg: Felix Meiner, 1968–), 9.295-6.

14. In the *Phänomenologie*, Hegel cites a total of three passages from *Rameaus Neffe*. Although they are in his text designated with quotation marks, the footnote references to Diderot were appended by the editor.

15. For a fuller treatment of the subject of this paragraph, see the second section ('Diderot and the lacerated consciousness of modernity'), in my 'French Revolutionary Roots of Political Modernity in Hegel's Philosophy' (see n. 26 below). Both there and here I am indebted to James Hulbert's 'Diderot in the Text of Hegel: a Question of Intertextuality', in *Studies in Romanticism*

(1983), 22.267-91, and especially James Schmidt's 'The Fool's Truth: Diderot, Goethe, and Hegel', in the *Journal of the History of Ideas* (1996), 57.625-44.

16.   See Rousseau's *Essai sur l'origine des langues*, chs 10 and 20, *Oeuvres complètes*, V.408 and 428.

17.   Germaine Necker, Mme de Staël, *De la littérature considérée dans ses rapports avec les institutions sociales* (Paris: Maradan, [1800]), 2.33.

18.   d'Alembert, *De la liberté de la musique*, in *La Querelle des Bouffons*, 3.2217.

19.   See Sieyès, *Qu'est que le tiers-état?*, ed. Robert Zappieri (Geneva: Droz, 1970), p. 151. In all subsequent editions, for *la science sociale* Sieyès substituted the expression *la science de l'ordre social*. His inaugural use of the term is noted by Brian Head in 'The Origins of "La Science sociale" in France, 1770–1800', *Australian Journal of French Studies* (1982), 19.115–32. In *Les mots et les choses* (see pp. 238 and 263), Foucault contends that 1795 was a pivotal year within the wider period of twenty or thirty years that comprises the epistemic metamorphosis of modernity. I have addressed these issues in my 'Saint-Simon and the Passage from Political to Social Science', in Anthony Pagden (ed.), *The Languages of Political Theory in Early Modern Europe* (Cambridge: Cambridge Universty Press, 1987), pp. 325–38, and in 'The Enlightenment and the French Revolutionary Birth Pangs of Modernity' (see n. 26 below).

20.   See Hegel's *Politischen Schriften* (Frankfurt: Suhrkamp, 1966), p. 310. It must be noted, however, that Hegel here refers, not to Sieyès' role in establishing the National Assembly in 1789, but to his authorship of the constitution of the year VIII, which he drafted as provisional consul a decade later, following the bloodless *coup d'état* of the eighteenth Brumaire of Napoleon Bonaparte that marked the transition of France's revolutionary government from the *Directoire* to the *Consulat*. As First Consul, Bonaparte altered Sieyès' scheme to suit his own advantage and ambition.

21.   Hegel, *Phänomenologie des Geistes*, p. 320.

22.   With respect to the political symbolism of this subject, see especially Annie Duprat, *Le roi décapité: Essai sur les imaginaires politiques* (Paris: Éditions du cerf, 1992).

23.   In particular, in ch. 16 of this text, which I take to be of seminal significance with respect to its prefiguration, in theory, of the modern practice of representative democracy to the extent that representative democracy provides for the popular election of absolutist governments.

24.   A particularly notable treatment of this subject can be found in David Runciman's *Pluralism and the Personality of the State* (Cambridge: Cambridge University Press, 1997).

25.   See Arendt, *The Origins of Totalitarianism*, first published in 1951, 2nd edn (London: Allen and Unwin, 1958), pp. 230–1.

26.   This essay draws extensively from a number of my publications, in which can be found fuller references to both my primary and secondary sources: most distantly, 'La Querelle des Bouffons and the Italian Liberation of France', in *Studies in the Eighteenth Century*, 6, special issue of *Eighteenth-Century Life* (1987), 11, n.s. 1.94–116, and 'Rousseau's Two Concepts of Liberty', in George Feaver and Frederick Rosen (eds), *Lives, Liberties and*

the Public Good (London: Macmillan, 1987), pp. 61–100; most recently, 'The French Revolutionary Roots of Political Modernity in Hegel's Philosophy, or the Enlightenment at Dusk', *Bulletin of the Hegel Society of Great Britain* (1997), 35.71–89; 'The Enlightenment and the French Revolutionary Birth Pangs of Modernity', in Johan Heilbron et al. (eds), *The Rise of Social Science and the Formation of Modernity*, *Sociology of the Sciences: Yearbook 1996* (1998), XX.35–76; and 'Contextualizing Hegel's Phenomenology of the French Revolution and the Terror', in *Political Theory* (1998), 26.33–55. Part of the second section as well as the final paragraph are adapted from my 'Ethnic Cleansing and Multiculturalism in the Enlightenment', to be published in Ole Peter Grell and Roy Porter (eds), *Toleration in Theory and Practice in the Eighteenth Century* (forthcoming, Cambridge University Press). A different version of the text, delivered as my fellow's lecture at the Collegium Budapest in November 1997, is scheduled to appear around October 1999 in that institution's own series of working papers and occasional lectures. For his comments and suggestions, too few of which I have been able to heed, I am especially grateful to Alistair Edwards.

10 Critique and Enlightenment: Michel Foucault on 'Was ist Aufklärung?'

Maurizio Passerin d'Entrèves

> Foucault saw himself as perpetuating the principle whereby philosophers "enlighten" their present, which Kant introduced in his classic 1784 paper that defines Enlightenment as an emancipation from self-imposed "immaturity." But while Foucault may have tried to enlighten our present, he was hardly a figure of *the* Enlightenment. Indeed he is often taken as the great modern counter-Enlightenment philosopher and historian. More precisely, Foucault's nominalism is directed against the *universalism* of the Enlightenment … In reversing, dispersing, and criticizing what was taken to be universal, Foucault attacks what, in the present, has come to be regarded as *the* Enlightenment.[1]

One of the last writings Foucault was able to complete before his death in June 1984 was an essay entitled 'What is Enlightenment?' This was meant to be delivered at the University of California, Berkeley in the spring of 1984 as part of a seminar on modernity and the Enlightenment whose participants would have included Jürgen Habermas, Charles Taylor, Richard Rorty, Hubert Dreyfus and Paul Rabinow. The seminar never took place, due to Foucault's death, and the essay thus became a sort of testament of Foucault's stance toward the Enlightenment and, more specifically, toward Kant's answer to the question '*Was ist Aufklärung?*' formulated in 1784 in the pages of the *Berlinische Monatsschrift*. But Foucault's interest in Kant's answer to the question 'What is Enlightenment?' went back at least a decade. He had in fact composed an article entitled 'Qu'est-ce que la critique? [Critique et *Aufklärung*]' which was delivered as a lecture before the Société française de Philosophie in May 1978, and devoted the opening lecture of a course at the Collège de France in 1983 to an assessment of Kant's essay on the Enlightenment and his attitude to the French Revolution.[2] In these essays Foucault presented what may be called a qualified defence of the Enlightenment, in particular, of its critical attitude to the present which he termed a 'philosophical ethos'. In offering a qualified endorsement of the Enlightenment 'ethos' of critique, Foucault appeared to betray his earlier understanding of the Enlightenment as the age that paved the way for the 'sciences of man', i.e. the sciences of discipline and normalization, of surveillance and control of bodies and souls, of marginalization and exclusion of the deviant, the abnormal, the insane. 'In the history of the sciences,' he wrote, 'it is a matter at bottom of examining a reason, the autonomy of whose structures carries with it a history of dogmatism and despotism – a reason, consequently, which can only have an effect of emancipation on condition that it manages to liberate itself from itself ... Two centuries later, the Enlightenment returns: but not at all as a way for the West to take cognizance of its present possibilities and of the liberties to which it can have access, but as a way of interrogating it on its limits and on the powers which it has abused. Reason as despotic enlightenment.'[3]

Judged against the tenor of this statement, Foucault's later pronouncements strike a discordant note. In his 1984 essay 'What is Enlightenment?' he characterizes it as a 'permanent reactivation of an attitude – that is, of a philosophical ethos that could be described as a permanent critique of our historical era.'[4] Not surprisingly, a number of commentators have explored this tension or contradiction in Foucault's attitude toward the Enlightenment, and reached fairly similar conclusions. Habermas, for instance, ends his brief eulogy of Foucault with the following observation:

> Only a complex thinking produces instructive contradictions ... He contrasts his critique of power with the 'analytic of truth' in such a fashion that the former becomes deprived of the normative yardsticks that it would have to borrow from the latter. Perhaps the force of this contradiction caught up with Foucault in this last of his texts, drawing him again into the circle of the philosophical discourse of modernity which he thought he could explode.[5]

Richard Bernstein claims that many responses are possible to Foucault's contradictory stance toward the Enlightenment, for example, that he changed his mind, that he adopted a more conciliatory tone, that he was rewriting his own history, and so on. Perhaps, he says, 'we can give a different, more sympathetic reading of what Foucault is doing,' a reading that enables us to get a better grasp of his critical project, but that still leaves us with a number of unresolved problems, chief among which is the lack of an adequate evaluative perspective from which to specify what is uniquely dangerous about modernity and its techniques of normalization.[6] Thomas McCarthy, for his part, recognizes that Foucault's 'belated affirmation' of the philosophical ethos of the Enlightenment 'signals important changes in Foucault's understanding of his critical project,' but claims that neither

Foucault's 'social ontology of power', nor his later concern with techniques of 'self-fashioning' provide 'an adequate framework for critical
social inquiry'.[7]

I would like in what follows to provide an equally critical but nuanced
perspective on Foucault's attitude to the Enlightenment. For this purpose
I will offer a detailed examination and assessment of Foucault's essays
on Kant and the Enlightenment, starting with his 1978 article 'Qu'est-ce
que la critique?'

ENLIGHTENMENT VERSUS GOVERNMENTALITY

The aim of this article was to examine the emergence in the early modern
era of a 'critical attitude' in response to the development of a system of
power that Foucault called 'governmentality'. In 1978 and 1979 Foucault
had given a number of lectures on the question of governmentality at the
Collège de France in which he analysed the development of a set of political strategies and techniques that aimed at governing individuals in a
continuous, regular and permanent fashion.[8] These techniques and strategies of governmentality were the product of two different conceptions of
political power: the Christian model of pastoral rule and the Greek model
of the self-determining polis. Out of these two conceptions there arose the
rationale underpinning the modern doctrine of 'reason of state'.[9] Such a
rationale entrusted political authorities with a power to survey, control and
discipline individuals which had previously been the prerogative of religious authorities. Foucault's studies on governmentality offered a historical genealogy of those techniques of political control and surveillance that
would eventually culminate in the modern forms of disciplinary power so
well documented in his pioneering book *Discipline and Punish*. But, as we
know from that book, each form of power generates its own form of resistance, so Foucault's account of the emergence of governmentality involves
at the same time an account of the emergence of the specific form of resistance which this new form of power instigates or makes possible. The
lecture 'Qu'est-ce que la critique?' is devoted precisely to providing an
account of the distinctive form of resistance to governmentality. In this
lecture Foucault argues that resistance to governmentality did not take the
form of an absolute opposition. The answer to the question 'how to gov-
ern?' which dominated political discourse in the early modern era did not,
in fact, take the form of 'how not to be governed'. Rather, it crystallized
around a set of more specific issues, such as: 'how not to be governed
like that, by that, in the name of principles such as that, in view of such

objectives and by the means of such procedures'.[10] For Foucault, this attempt to question or challenge the particular forms in which the 'art of governance' is exercised signals the emergence of the modern notion of critique – which Foucault characterizes as 'the art of not being governed in such a manner'.[11]

This questioning or resistance to governmentality is directed both at the spiritual authority of the church and at the temporal authority of civil rulers: their claim to speak with authority is met with a resistance which takes the form of a questioning of their power to define the truth for the subject. As Foucault puts it, 'the focus of critique is essentially the bundle of relations which tie ... power, the truth, and the subject.'[12] Thus, while governmentality subjects individuals to a power that lays claim to truth, critique is 'the movement by which the subject gives itself the right to interrogate the truth with respect to its effects of power and interrogate power with respect to its discourse of truth.'[13] Critique is thus best characterized as 'the art of voluntary inservitude' (an ironic and purposeful reversal of the title of Etienne de La Boétie's political tract of 1550, *Le Discours de la Servitude Volontaire*), as 'a thoughtful indocility' which aims at 'desubjectification' within the 'politics of truth'.[14]

After having provided this account of the origins of the idea of critique, Foucault turns to an examination of Kant's definition of Enlightenment, a definition that he considers very pertinent to the issue explored in the first part of the lecture, namely, the mutual implication of critique and governmentality. Kant's definition of Enlightenment is as follows:

> *Enlightenment is man's emergence from his self-incurred immaturity. Immaturity* is the inability to use one's own understanding without the guidance of another. This immaturity is *self-incurred* if its cause is not lack of understanding, but lack of resolution and courage to use it without the guidance of another. The motto of enlightenment is therefore: *Sapere aude!* Have the courage to use your *own* understanding![15]

Four aspects of Kant's definition are seen as relevant to Foucault's own discussion of the intertwining of critique and governmentality. First, the Enlightenment is defined as the opposite to a state of immaturity or tutelage. Second, this state of immaturity is seen as the incapacity to use one's own understanding without the guidance of another (heteronomy). Third, Kant suggests a connection between an excess of authority, on the one hand, and a lack of courage and resolution, on the other. Finally, the domains in which the contest between a state of immaturity and one of enlightenment takes place are those highlighted by Foucault in his discussion of the opposition of critique to governmentality, namely, religion, law, and conscience.

Kant's definition of Enlightenment thus bears a close affinity to the issues raised in Foucault's essay. Moreover, according to Foucault, Kant's defence of enlightenment was not blind to the interplay between critique and power. The Enlightenment's motto: '*Sapere aude!*' – have the courage to use your own reason – was counterbalanced by the injunction, attributed to Frederick the Great, to: '*Argue* as much as you like and about whatever you like, *but obey!*' By counterposing these two claims, and by accepting as legitimate the restrictions imposed on the private use of reason, Kant seems to acknowledge the limits of critique. The courage to know is at one and the same time the courage to recognize the limits of reason. Such a reason finds its legitimate employment only in its public use, by which Kant means the use 'which anyone may make of it *as a man of learning* addressing the entire *reading public.*'[16] And the interweaving of argument and obedience contained in the quote attributed to Frederick II indicates Kant's awareness of what Foucault calls the 'play of power and truth'. Obedience to the sovereign is made legitimate by being grounded on the autonomy of reasoning subjects. The activity of critique is a play of power and truth (of obedience and argument) in so far as it gives the subject the power to determine itself, to retain its autonomy while acknowledging the authority of the sovereign.

Having explored the links between Kant's definition of Enlightenment and his own conception of critique (i.e. 'the art of voluntary inservitude'), Foucault considers, in the final part of the lecture, the fate these ideals underwent in the nineteenth century. According to Foucault, the history of the nineteenth century can be seen as carrying on the critical project which Kant identified with the Enlightenment, but with critique now turned at Enlightenment itself. Three crucial developments are seen as motivating this reorientation of critique toward the original ideals of the Enlightenment. First, the development of positivist science. Second, the emergence of a teleological (viz. Hegelian) and technocratic (viz. Saint-Simonian) conception of the state. Third, the binding together of positive science and the state into a 'science of the state'.[17]

Faced with these developments, can the enlightenment ideal of a critique of arbitrary political power be sustained? Can the critique of governmentality be effective once reason, in the form of positivist science, has been shown to be intimately connected to the excesses of state power? Foucault identifies two responses to this dilemma. The first, developed in Germany in the writings of the Hegelian Left, Weber, and the Frankfurt School, takes the form of a critique of positivism, scientism and instrumental reason, seen as the handmaidens of an insidious form of power. The second, developed in France in the works of historians and philosophers of science such as Cavaillés, Bachelard and Canguilhem, takes the form of a critical inquiry into the factors conducive to the emergence and eventual predominance of one particular form of rationality. Here the question that is raised is what Foucault calls the '*réciproque et l'inverse*' of the original aspirations of the Enlightenment, namely: 'How is it that rationalization is conducive to a desire for power?'[18]

This question had also been at the centre of the Frankfurt School's critique of instrumental reason, and Foucault acknowledged the deep affinity that existed between his genealogical inquiries and the work of the Frankfurt School.[19] Both had been concerned with the question that Kant addressed for the first time in 1784 ('What is Enlightenment?') and both could be seen as continuing the interrogation of reason initiated by Kant. In the case of Foucault, such interrogation must now take the form of 'historico-philosophical' investigations which examine 'the relations between the structures of rationality that articulate true discourses and the mechanisms of subjectification which are bound to them.'[20] The question 'What is Enlightenment?' invites now the question: 'What is it that I am, the me which belongs to this humanity, perhaps to this fragment ... to this instant of humanity which is subjected to the power of truth in general and of truths in particular?'[21]

The aim of the 'historico-philosophical' inquiries which address this new question is, as Foucault puts it, to 'desubjectivize philosophical questions by recourse to historical content,' and 'to free the historical contents by an interrogation of the effects of the power of this truth'.[22] These inquiries will concern themselves with that extended epoch which constitutes 'the moment of formation of modern humanity', with '*Aufklärung* in the broad sense of the term, of that period without fixed dates to which Kant, Weber, and others, make reference, of those multiple entries by which it may be defined, such as the formation of capitalism, the constitution of the bourgeois world, the establishment of the state system, [and] the foundation of modern science with its correlative techniques.' Thus, to pose today the question as to 'What is "What is Enlightenment?"' is, Foucault concludes, 'to encounter the historical problematic of our modernity'.[23]

ENLIGHTENMENT AND REVOLUTION

Foucault's 1983 lecture, translated in English with the title 'Kant on Enlightenment and Revolution', indicates a slight change of direction.

Enlightenment is no longer viewed as being closely tied to the idea of critique, as exemplifying the attitude which had emerged in response to the techniques and strategies of governmentality. Rather, the focus now is on the Enlightenment as a period in history marked by a novel awareness of its own presentness and singularity. Kant's essay on the Enlightenment introduces 'a new type of question in the field of philosophical reflection', namely, 'the question of the present, of the contemporary moment' which is without precedent in the history of philosophy.[24] In Kant's essay, Foucault maintains, 'one sees philosophy... problematizing its own discursive present-ness: a present-ness which it interrogates as an event, an event whose meaning, value and philosophical singularity it is required to state, and in which it is to elicit at once its own *raison d'être* and the foundation of what it has to say' (KER, 89).

Foucault now stresses the link between the new kind of philosophical reflection inaugurated by the Enlightenment and the focus on modernity. 'Philosophy as the problematization of a present-ness,' he writes, 'the interrogation by philosophy of this present-ness of which it is a part and relative to which it is obliged to locate itself: this may well be the characteristic trait of philosophy as a discourse of and upon modernity' (KER, 89).

Foucault also emphasizes the fact that with the emergence of the Enlightenment there appears a new way of posing the question of modernity, 'no longer within a longitudinal relationship to the Ancients, but rather in what one might call a "sagital" relation to one's own present-ness' (KER, 90). The Enlightenment is, in fact, the first age which named itself the Enlightenment (*Aufklärung*); in this sovereign act of naming itself 'a cultural process of indubitably a very singular character... came to self-awareness' (KER, 90). The Enlightenment is the first epoch which 'names its own self' and which, rather than simply characterizing itself against other epochs as 'a period of decadence or prosperity, splendour or misery', views itself as a period with its own special mission and purpose (KER, 90).

Foucault then proceeds to examine Kant's essay of 1798, *The Contest of Faculties*, focusing on Kant's discussion of the French Revolution. He argues that there is a deep connection between the 1784 essay 'What is Enlightenment?' and the 1798 essay, in so far as both were concerned with exploring the meaning of the present, of the contemporary moment. In 1784, he writes, Kant 'tried to answer the question put to him, "What is this *Aufklärung* of which we are a part?" and in 1798 he answered a question which contemporary reality posed for him... This question was "What is the Revolution?"' (KER, 91).

Kant's analysis of the French Revolution is pursued in the context of attempting to answer the broader question 'Is the human race continually improving?' In order to answer this question, one had to identify an event in human history that would indicate, or be a sign of, the existence of a permanent cause which guides mankind in the direction of progress. Such a cause had to be permanent in the sense that it had to be shown to be operative throughout the course of human history. Hence the event that will enable us to decide whether the human race is constantly improving must be a sign that is *rememorative* (showing that the alleged cause of progress has been operative in the past), *demonstrative* (demonstrating that it is active in the present), and *prognostic* (indicating that it will also operate in the future). Only then will we be sure that the cause which makes progress possible has not just acted at a particular moment in time, but guarantees a general tendency of the human race as a whole to advance in the direction of progress.[25]

Kant found the sign of such a progress in the event of the French Revolution, an event which he identified not with 'those momentous deeds or misdeeds of men which make small in their eyes what was formerly great or make great what was formerly small', but with 'the attitude of the onlookers as it reveals itself *in public* while the drama of great political changes is taking place.'[26] In the 'universal yet disinterested sympathy' that the public openly shows toward one set of protagonists, regardless of the cost it may carry to themselves, Kant finds evidence of human progress. 'Their reaction,' he writes, 'because of its *universality*, proves that mankind as a whole shares a certain character in common, and it also proves, because of its *disinterestedness*, that man has a moral character, or at least the makings of one. And this does not merely allow us to hope for human improvement; it is already a form of improvement in itself, in so far as its influence is strong enough for the present.'[27] In sum, it is not the success or failure of the Revolution, but rather the '*sympathy* which borders almost on enthusiasm' with which it was received by the non-participating spectators, that provides a sign that the human race is improving.

This sympathy cannot be caused, Kant says, 'by anything other than a moral disposition within the human race'. This moral disposition manifests itself in two ways: (1) the *right* of every people to give itself a republican constitution, and (2) the *aim* of submitting to those conditions enshrined in a republican constitution by which war may be averted.[28]

It is clear, as Foucault remarks, that these two elements are also central to the process of enlightenment, that the Revolution 'does indeed complete and continue the process of *Aufklärung*', and that, to this extent, 'both

Aufklärung and Revolution are events which can never be forgotten' (KER, 94). Or, as Kant puts it:

> Even without the mind of a seer, I now maintain that I can predict from the aspects and signs of our times that the human race will achieve this end [of giving itself a republican constitution which will prevent offensive wars], and that it will henceforth progressively improve without any more total reversals. For a phenomenon of this kind which has taken place in human history *can never be forgotten*, since it has revealed in human nature an aptitude and power for improvement of a kind which no politician could have thought up by examining the course of events in the past.[29]

Moreover, anticipating the sceptical challenge,

> even if the intended object behind the occurrence we have described were not to be achieved for the present, or if a people's revolution or constitutional reform were ultimately to fail, or if, after the latter had lasted for a certain time, everything were to be brought back onto its original course ... our own philosophical prediction still loses none of its force. For the occurrence in question is too momentous, too intimately interwoven with the interests of humanity and too widespread in its influence upon all parts of the world for nations not to be reminded of it when favourable circumstances present themselves, and to rise up and make renewed attempts of the same kind as before.[30]

Thus, even if the Revolution may miscarry, its very existence attests to a permanent human disposition or potentiality that cannot be ignored: it is the guarantee for future history that the human race will continue to improve.

Now, just as Kant was not concerned to provide a justification for the success or failure of the French Revolution, but to interpret the significance of that event for the present, so Foucault is not concerned with determining 'what part of the Revolution should be retained and set up as a model'. Rather, as he puts it, 'it is to know what is to be done with that will to revolution, that "enthusiasm" for the Revolution, which is quite different from the revolutionary enterprise itself' (KER, 95).

This statement is rather striking and liable to divergent interpretations. The employment of a term such as 'the will to revolution' to characterize the enthusiasm displayed toward the event by sympathetic spectators bears strong Nietzschean traces (the 'will to revolution' as a synecdoche of the 'will to knowledge,' and thus of the 'will to power'). This is, in effect, how Habermas interprets it in his eulogy of Foucault. 'For Foucault,' he writes, 'the challenge of the Kant texts he has chosen is to decode that will once contained in the enthusiasm for the French Revolution, namely, the will-to-knowledge ... Up to now, Foucault traced this will-to-knowledge in modern power-formations only to denounce it. Now, however, he presents it in a completely different light, as the critical impulse worthy of preservation and in need of renewal.'[31]

This is indeed a legitimate reading of Foucault's statement, but an equally legitimate one is to stress that the 'will to revolution' is not a synonym of the 'will to power', but a synonym of a 'will to freedom' understood in a prosaic, non-Nietzschean sense. Such a will to freedom would transgress against the limits of the given and provide a space for the refashioning of subjectivity. I shall take up this issue later in my discussion of Foucault's essay 'What is Enlightenment?' For now it is sufficient to notice that Foucault saw revolution and revolt (the example he used was that of the Iranian Revolution) as the means whereby subjectivity 'introduces itself into history and gives it a breath of life'.[32] Revolution, in this sense, provides the opportunity for such a 'will to freedom' to interrupt the continuum of history and to refashion subjectivity in a novel way.

Foucault concludes his essay by noting that the two questions – 'What is Enlightenment?' and 'What is the Revolution?' – are the two forms under which Kant posed the question of his own present. They are also, he maintains, 'the two questions which have continued to haunt, if not all modern philosophy since the nineteenth century, at least a great part of it' (KER, 95). But he is quick to point out that it is not a question of preserving alive and intact the heritage of the Enlightenment. 'It is not the legacy of *Aufklärung* which it is our business to conserve,' he writes, 'but rather the very question of this event and its meaning, the question of the historicity of the thought of the universal, which ought to be kept present and retained in mind as that which has to be thought' (KER, 95).

'The historicity of the thought of the universal': here Foucault's historicism and nominalism come to full view. What matters for him is to relativize and contextualize those historical factors that since the eighteenth century have enabled the 'thought of the universal' (of the necessary, the obligatory, the transcendental) to prevail over the 'thought of the singular' (of the contingent, the arbitrary, the merely empirical), and to disqualify and subjugate the latter. The urge to demystify the privilege accorded to the 'universal' in the tradition stemming from the Enlightenment is reasserted in the concluding paragraphs of the essay, where Foucault draws a distinction between two critical traditions initiated by Kant. The first, which he calls an 'analytic of truth', is preoccupied with defining 'the conditions under which a true knowledge is possible'. This is the tradition initiated by Kant's *Critique of Pure Reason*. The second, which he terms 'an ontology of the present, an ontology of our-selves', is concerned with the question: 'What is our present? What is the contemporary field of possible experience?' (KER, 96). This other tradi-tion, which he sees emerging in Kant's essay on the Enlightenment and his reflections on the French Revolution, abandons the search for those uni-versal conditions that determine whether sentences can be true or false, and concerns itself exclusively with the question of actuality, namely, the question of our present and its field of possible experience. In separating the 'ontology of the present' from the 'analytic of truth' in such a radical fashion Foucault lays himself open to Habermas's charge, to wit, that he deprives himself of the normative standards that the former must unavoid-ably borrow from the latter. A more generous reading, however, would point out that the ontology of the present and of ourselves favoured by Foucault is meant to open up a space for reflection, for a critical interro-gation that destabilizes our currently accepted ways of being, of doing, of thinking. It is to these questions that Foucault turns his attention in the last of the essays he devoted to Kant. Let us then look closely at what he has to say.

ENLIGHTENMENT AS TRANSGRESSION

In his 1984 essay 'What is Enlightenment?' Foucault attempts to formu-late an answer to the very same question that was posed to Kant in 1784 by the German periodical *Berlinische Monatsschrift*. In his view, '*Was ist Aufklärung?*' marks the entry into the history of thought 'of a question that modern philosophy has not been capable of answering, but that it has never managed to get rid of, either... From Hegel through Nietzsche or Max Weber to Horkheimer or Habermas, hardly any philosophy has failed to confront this same question, directly or indirectly' (WE, 32).

Foucault argues that Kant was not the first philosopher who had sought to reflect on his own present. Throughout Western history philosophers have posed the question of the present and, broadly speaking, their answers have taken three forms:

1) The present was seen as belonging to an era of the world marked by inherent characteristics (the present as a definite world era, exemplified in Plato's *Statesman*);
2) The present was interrogated in order to discover signs of a forthcom-ing event (the present as a threshold, exemplified in St Augustine's *The City of God*);

3) The present was conceived as a point of transition toward the dawning of a new world (the present as an accomplishment, exemplified in Vico's *La Scienza Nuova*).

Kant's originality consisted in inaugurating a new way of thinking about the relation between philosophy and the present. For Kant, the Enlightenment is 'neither a world era to which one belongs, nor an event whose signs are perceived, nor the dawning of an accomplishment. Kant defines *Aufklärung* in an almost entirely negative way, as an *Ausgang*, an "exit", a "way out" ... He is not seeking to understand the present on the basis of a totality or of a future achievement. He is looking for a difference: What difference does today introduce with respect to yesterday?' (WE, 34). Enlightenment is not conceived within the framework of a progressive teleology of history. Rather, it is seen as a process that releases us from self-incurred immaturity, a process that is at the same time an individual task and obligation. It is 'a process in which men participate collectively' and 'an act of courage to be accomplished personally' (WE, 35). Enlightenment means the striving for maturity and responsibility (*Mündigkeit*). It represents the moment 'when humanity is going to put its own reason to use, without subjecting itself to any authority' (WE, 38). And it is precisely at this moment, Foucault remarks, stressing the connection between Kant's essay on the Enlightenment and the three *Critiques*, that 'the critique is necessary, since its role is that of defining the conditions under which the use of reason is legitimate in order to determine what can be known, what must be done, and what may be hoped' (WE, 38). It is only when the legitimate employment of reason has been defined, in both the theoretical and practical spheres, that its autonomy can be assured. Thus, the critique is 'the handbook of reason that has grown up in Enlightenment; and, conversely, the Enlightenment is the age of the critique' (WE, 38).

Foucault sums up his assessment of Kant's essay by noting how this text is located at the crossroads of 'critical reflection' and 'reflection on history'. By this he means not simply that it represents a reflection by Kant on the contemporary status of his own philosophical enterprise. Rather, he means to highlight the fact that 'it is the first time that a philosopher has connected in this way, closely and from the inside, the significance of his work with respect to knowledge, a reflection on history, and a particular analysis of the specific moment at which he is writing and because of which he is writing.' In this respect, 'it is in the reflection on "today" as *difference* in history and as *motive* for a particular philosophical task that the novelty of this text appears ... to lie' (WE, 38, emphases added). Kant's text on the Enlightenment thus provides the outline of what Foucault calls 'the attitude of modernity' (WE, 38).

It is at this point that Foucault's essay takes a rather unexpected turn. He claims that modernity should be seen as an attitude rather than as a period in history – 'a mode of relating to contemporary reality; a voluntary choice made by certain people; in the end, a way of thinking and feeling.' Such an attitude is a way of 'acting and behaving that at one and the same time marks a relation of belonging and presents itself as a task. A bit, no doubt, like what the Greeks called an *ethos*' (WE, 39). In order to characterize such an attitude or ethos, Foucault turns to a discussion of Baudelaire's essay 'The Painter of Modern Life'. Baudelaire was one of the first to recognize that modernity meant an awareness of the discontinuity of time, of a break with tradition, that it induced 'a feeling of novelty, of vertigo in the face of the passing moment' (WE, 39).[33]

In his essay Baudelaire defined modernity as 'the ephemeral, the fleeting, the contingent', and stressed that these elements must 'on no account be despised or dispensed with'.[34] One had no right to despise the present. Rather, one had to adopt a certain attitude toward it, an attitude which recaptured something eternal in the fleeting moment. As an example, Baudelaire cites the work of Constantin Guys, who was able to 'extract from fashion whatever element it may contain of poetry within history, to distil the eternal from the transitory.'[35] The attitude of modernity makes it possible, in Foucault's words, 'to grasp the "heroic" aspect of the present moment … it is the will to "heroize" the present' (WE, 40). This 'heroization' of the present, Foucault pointedly remarks, is ironical. It does not treat the passing moment as sacred in order to preserve it, nor does it involve collecting it as a fleeting and interesting curiosity. Rather, the ironic heroization of the present is an act of *transfiguration*. Transfiguration 'does not entail an annulling of reality, but a difficult interplay between the truth of what is real and the exercise of freedom' (WE, 41). In this interplay, 'natural' things become 'more than natural', and 'beautiful' things 'more than beautiful'. It is in this sense of a transfigurative interplay of freedom and reality that Foucault characterizes the attitude of modernity, its ironic heroization of the present. 'For the attitude of modernity,' he writes, 'the high value of the present is indissociable from a desperate eagerness to imagine it, to imagine it otherwise than it is … Baudelairean modernity is an exercise in which extreme attention to what is real is confronted with the practice of a liberty that simultaneously *respects* this reality and *violates* it' (WE, 41, emphases added).

As we shall see, this is very much the attitude or ethos that Foucault adopts *vis-à-vis* the present: simultaneously to respect it in its singularity and to violate it in its claim to embody universality (whether such universality pertains to the structure of reason, the logic of history, or the truths of human nature). His stance is indeed one of transgression, one that he set out brilliantly in his preface to Georges Bataille's *oeuvre* in 1963.[36] The same can be said of his attitude to the self. Drawing again on Baudelaire, he claims that modernity is not simply a form of relationship to the present; it is also 'a mode of relationship that has to be established with oneself' (WE, 41). 'To be modern,' he writes, 'is not to accept oneself as one is in the flux of the passing moments; it is to take oneself as object of a complex and difficult elaboration: what Baudelaire, in the vocabulary of his day, calls *dandysme*' (WE, 41). The deliberate attitude of modernity is tied to an 'indispensable asceticism'. The dandy 'makes of his body, his behaviour, his feelings and passions, his very existence, a work of art.' Modern man does not seek 'to discover himself, his secrets and his hidden truth; he is the man who tries to *invent* himself'. He is constantly faced with the task of '*producing* himself' (WE, 41–2, emphases added).

Foucault's attitude to the present is thus closely tied to his attitude to the self: just as the former must, ultimately, take the form of a possible transgression, so the latter must take the form of an original production and invention of the self, a self-fashioning or '*souci de soi*'. There is no 'human nature' to discover or unearth, no 'human essence' to be freed or unshackled. There is only the constant, ever-renewed task to create ourselves freely, to pursue and give new impetus to 'the undefined work of freedom' (WE, 46).

This attitude or ethos of self-fashioning which is to be freely adopted by each subject is certainly congruent with Baudelaire's reflections on the dandy, but is by no means congruent with Kant's position. As Thomas McCarthy has perceptively pointed out, 'the representation of autonomy as aesthetic self-invention eliminates the universality at the heart of [Kant's] notion, the rational *Wille* expressed in norms binding on all agents alike.'[37] Foucault was fully aware of the distance separating his ethics of self-fashioning from any morality based on universal criteria. As he declared in his last interview: 'The search for a form of morality acceptable to everybody, in the sense that everyone should submit to it, strikes me as catastrophic.'[38] He never inquired whether a form of morality based on universal principles *freely agreed to* by all subjects, a morality that provided a general framework of principles of justice within which individuals would be free to pursue their own particular conceptions of the good life, would be equally pernicious.

Foucault, in effect, wanted to adhere to an ethos of transgression and aesthetic self-fashioning ('Couldn't everyone's life become a work of art?', he declared in a 1983 interview with Hubert Dreyfus and Paul Rabinow)[39] and attempted to trace such a modernist ethos, via Baudelaire, to Kant's reflections of the Enlightenment. He wished to emphasize 'the extent to which a type of philosophical interrogation – one that simultaneously problematizes man's relation to the present, man's historical mode of being, and the constitution of the self as an autonomous subject – is rooted in the Enlightenment' (WE, 42). Preserving the legacy of the Enlightenment, however, does not mean 'faithfulness to doctrinal elements, but rather the permanent reactivation of an attitude – that is, of a philosophical ethos that could be described as a *permanent critique of our historical era*' (WE, 42, emphasis added).

Foucault goes on to offer a positive characterization of this ethos, after having contrasted it negatively with what he calls the enlightenment blackmail of being either for or against the Enlightenment, and with the conflation of Enlightenment with humanism.[40] Such a philosophical ethos, he writes, 'may be characterized as a *limit-attitude*...Criticism indeed consists of analyzing and reflecting upon limits. But if the Kantian question was that of knowing what limits knowledge had to renounce transgressing, it seems to me that the critical question today has to be turned back into a positive one: in what is given to us as universal, necessary, obligatory, what place is occupied by whatever is singular, contingent, and the product of arbitrary constraints?' (WE, 45). And, reiterating the theme that has been at the centre of my reading of Foucault's attitude to the Enlightenment, he asserts that the point is 'to transform the critique conducted in the form of necessary limitation into a practical critique that takes the form of a *possible transgression*' (WE, 45, emphasis added).

This is a philosophical ethos with a marked affinity to Georges Bataille, to Nietzsche, to the surrealist revolt against the stultifying bourgeois standards of cognition and action, of knowledge and morality. It is an ethos of transgression which revolts against all that is normative, all that which, in Foucault's understanding, leads to 'normalization', to the regime of surveillance and control, of disciplinary power. In its most extreme version, this transgressive ethos, as Habermas has pointed out, 'is addicted to the fascination of that horror which accompanies the act of profaning, and is yet always in flight from the trivial results of profanation.'[41]

Foucault did not, in the end, embrace this version of an ethos of transgression. Although he did actively seek for certain 'limit-experiences'[42] in both his work and in his life, he was more concerned, ultimately, with testing the 'contemporary limits of the necessary' (WE, 43). In the context of his reflections on Kant and the Enlightenment, this meant a reappraisal and reformulation of the concept most central to the Enlightenment, namely, the concept of critique. 'Criticism,' he tells us, 'is no longer going to be practiced in the search for formal structures with universal value, but rather as a historical investigation into the events that have led us to constitute ourselves and to recognize ourselves as subjects of what we are doing, thinking, saying' (WE, 45–6). Such criticism is '*genealogical* in its design' and '*archaeological* in its method'. Archaeological, 'in the sense that it will not seek to identify the universal structures of all knowledge or of all possible moral action, but will seek to treat the instances of discourse that articulate what we think, say, and do as so many *historical events*' (WE, 46, emphasis added). Genealogical, 'in the sense that it will not deduce from the form of what we are what it is impossible for us to do and to know; but it will separate out, from the contingency that has made us what we are, the possibility of *no longer being, doing, or thinking what we are, do, or think*' (WE, 46, emphasis added). In this respect, criticism 'is seeking to give new impetus, as far and wide as possible, to the undefined work of freedom' (WE, 46).

Foucault is quite aware that this liberating criticism, this work done 'at the limits of ourselves', must be experimental, so that it may be able 'both to grasp the points where change is possible and desirable, and to determine the precise form this change should take' (WE, 46). This criticism must also give up the hope of ever acceding 'to any complete and definitive knowledge of what may constitute our historical limits' (WE, 47). The criticism of limits and the possibility of moving beyond them are always limited; but rather than being a drawback, we should acknowledge that this is what enables us always to begin again. Criticism, in other words, must be constantly reactivated: only in this way can it provide an impetus to our 'undefined work of freedom'.

We can see from these statements how Foucault's ethos of critique remains bound to certain limits even while it attempts to transgress or subvert them. It is this which distinguishes his position from the one taken by the more radical exponents of an ethos of transgression. And yet, it is the figure of Nietzsche, rather than that of Kant, that provides the major source of inspiration for Foucault's notion of critique. As he puts it in the concluding reflections on the meaning of that critical interrogation on the present and on ourselves inaugurated by Kant:

> The critical ontology of ourselves has to be considered not, certainly, as a theory, a doctrine, nor even as a permanent body of knowledge that is accumulating; it has to be conceived as an attitude, an ethos, a philosophical life in which the critique of what we are is at one and the same time the historical analysis of the *limits* that are imposed on us and an experiment with the possibility of *going beyond them*. (WE, 50, emphases added)

EPILOGUE: NIETZSCHE OR KANT?

A few comments before closing. It is indeed a peculiar feature of the discussion around Foucault's work on Kant and the Enlightenment that a number of American commentators have tried to interpret it as somehow a return to the fold of a reasonable, accommodating community of 'enlightened' inquiry. Dreyfus and Rabinow, for instance, characterize Foucault's ironic stance toward the present as one that encourages a 'conflict of interpretations'. They suggest that 'the archaeological step back that Foucault takes in order to see the strangeness of our society's practices does not mean that he considers these practices meaningless. Since we share cultural practices with others, and since these practices have made us what we are, we have, perforce, some common footing from which to proceed, to understand, to act. But that foothold is no longer one which is universal, guaranteed, verified, or grounded.' It follows, therefore, that 'what makes one interpretive theory better than another... has to do with articulating common concerns... while leaving open the possibility of "dialogue", or better, a conflict of interpretations, with other shared discursive practices used to articulate different concerns.'[43]

This is what I would call the American 'taming' of Foucault. In the hands of such interpreters, Foucault's transgressive stance begins to look 'human, all too human'. What is missing in such a reading is Foucault's Nietzscheanism, for whom the project of autonomy pursued by Enlightenment thinkers from Kant to Habermas requires as a corrective a strong dose of 'inhuman thoughts'. Foucault's critical ontology of ourselves, his ethos of transgression and aesthetic self-fashioning are indeed much closer to Nietzsche's vision of a transvaluation of values than to Kant's notion of maturity (*Mündigkeit*).[44] Let us not betray Foucault's inheritance by making him appear as, ultimately, a child of the Enlightenment. As the 'masked' and ironic philosopher that he was, he deserves better treatment from us.

NOTES

1.   John Rajchman, *Michel Foucault: the Freedom of Philosophy* (New York: Columbia University Press, 1985), p. 59.
2.   See J. Schmidt and T.E. Wartenberg, 'Foucault's Enlightenment: Critique, Revolution, and the Fashioning of the Self', in *Critique and Power:*

Recasting the Foucault/ Habermas Debate, ed. M. Kelly (Cambridge, MA: MIT Press, 1994), pp. 283–314. I am indebted to this article for providing a reconstruction of Foucault's 1978 article on the Enlightenment ('Qu'est-ce que la critique?').

3. M. Foucault, 'Georges Canguilhem: Philosopher of Error', trans. G. Burchell, *Ideology and Consiousness*, no. 7 (Autumn 1980), pp. 51–62, at p. 54. This essay was written as an introduction to G. Canguilhem, *Le Normal et la Pathologique* (Paris: PUF, 1966). A translation of the same essay is available in G. Canguilhem, *The Normal and the Pathological*, trans. C. Fawcett (New York: Zone Books, 1989), pp. ix–xx. A somewhat different French version later appeared as 'La vie: l'expérience et la science', *Revue de métaphysique et de morale*, 90 (1985), pp. 3–14.

4. M. Foucault, 'What is Enlightenment?', trans. C. Porter, in *The Foucault Reader*, ed. P. Rabinow (New York: Pantheon Books, 1984), pp. 32–50, at p. 42. Page references to this article will be given in round brackets in the text, preceded by the abbreviation WE.

5. J. Habermas, 'Taking Aim at the Heart of the Present', trans. S. Brauner and R. Brown, in *Foucault: a Critical Reader*, ed. D.C. Hoy (Oxford: Blackwell, 1986), pp. 103–8, at pp. 107–8.

6. R. Bernstein, 'Foucault: Critique as a Philosophic Ethos', in *Critique and Power*, op. cit., pp. 211–41, at pp. 222, 227.

7. T. McCarthy, 'The Critique of Impure Reason: Foucault and the Frankfurt School,' in *Critique and Power*, pp. 243–82, at pp. 259, 272.

8. M. Foucault, 'Omnes et Singulatim: Towards a Criticism of "Political Reason"', in *The Tanner Lectures on Human Values*, vol. 2, ed. S. McMurrin (Salt Lake City: University of Utah Press, 1981), pp. 225–54. This essay is also included under the title 'Politics and Reason', in *Michel Foucault: Politics, Philosophy, Culture*, ed. L.D. Kritzman (New York: Routledge, 1988), pp. 57–85. M. Foucault, 'Governmentality', trans. R. Braidotti, in *The Foucault Effect: Studies in Governmentality*, eds G. Burchell, C. Gordon and P. Miller (Chicago: University of Chicago Press, 1991), pp. 87–104.

9. Foucault remarks that: 'Our societies proved to be really demonic, since they happened to combine these two games – the city-citizen game and the shepherd-flock game – in what we call the modern states.' M. Foucault, 'Omnes et Singulatim', p. 239.

10. M. Foucault, 'Qu'est-ce que la critique? [Critique et *Aufklärung*],' *Bulletin de la Société française de Philosophie*, 84 (1990), pp. 35–63, at pp. 37–8. Translation in *What is Enlightenment? Eighteenth-Century Answers and Twentieth-Century Questions*, ed. J. Schmidt (Berkeley: University of California Press, 1996).

11. Ibid., p. 38.

12. Ibid., p. 39.

13. Ibid.

14. Ibid.

15. I. Kant, 'An Answer to the Question: "What is Enlightenment?"', in *Kant's Political Writings*, ed. H. Reiss (Cambridge: Cambridge University Press, 1970), pp. 54–60, at p. 54.

16. Ibid., p. 55.

17. M. Foucault, 'Qu'est-ce que la critique?', p. 42.

18.   Ibid., p. 44.
19.   See the 1983 interview with Gérard Raulet, 'Critical Theory/Intellectual History', trans. J. Harding, in *Michel Foucault: Politics, Philosophy, Culture*, ed. L.D. Kritzman (New York: Routledge, 1988), pp. 17–46; another translation is available with the title 'How Much Does it Cost for Reason to Tell the Truth?', trans. M. Foret and M. Martius, in *Foucault Live: Interviews 1966–1984*, ed. S. Lotringer (New York: Semiotext(e), 1989), pp. 233–56.
20.   M. Foucault, 'Qu'est-ce que la critique?', p. 45.
21.   Ibid., p. 46.
22.   Ibid.
23.   Ibid.
24.   M. Foucault, 'Kant on Enlightenment and Revolution', trans. C. Gordon, *Economy and Society*, vol. 15, no. 1 (Feb. 1986), pp. 88–96, at p. 88. Page references to this article will be given in round brackets in the text, preceded by the abbreviation KER. There is also a translation of the same lecture by A. Sheridan, entitled 'The Art of Telling the Truth', in *Michel Foucault: Politics, Philosophy, Culture*, pp. 86–95.
25.   I. Kant, 'The Contest of Faculties,' in *Kant's Political Writings*, pp. 176–90, at p. 181.
26.   Ibid., p. 182.
27.   Ibid., emphases added.
28.   Ibid., pp. 182–3.
29.   Ibid., p. 184.
30.   Ibid., p. 185.
31.   J. Habermas, 'Taking Aim at the Heart of the Present', p. 107.
32.   M. Foucault, 'Is it Useless to Revolt?', trans. J. Bernauer, *Philosophy and Social Criticism*, vol. 8, no. 1 (Spring 1981), pp. 1–9, at p. 8. See also M. Foucault, 'Iran: the Spirit of a World Without Spirit', trans. A. Sheridan, in *Michel Foucault: Politics, Philosophy, Culture*, pp. 211–24.
33.   Habermas also draws on Baudelaire to characterize the new attitude of modernity. He claims that: 'The spirit and discipline of aesthetic modernity assumed clear contours in the work of Baudelaire ... Aesthetic modernity is characterized by attitudes which find a common focus in a changed consciousness of time ... The new time consciousness ... does more than express the experience of mobility in society, acceleration in history, of discontinuity in everyday life. The new value placed on the transitory, the elusive, and the ephemeral, the very celebration of dynamism, discloses the longing for an undefiled, an immaculate and stable present.' J. Habermas, 'Modernity versus Postmodernity', trans. S. Benhabib, *New German Critique*, no. 22 (Winter 1981), pp. 3–14, at pp. 4–5.
34.   Charles Baudelaire, *The Painter of Modern Life and Other Essays*, trans. J. Mayne (London: Phaidon Press, 1964), p. 13.
35.   Ibid., p. 12.
36.   See M. Foucault, 'Préface à transgression', *Critique*, 195–6 (1963), pp. 751–69; translated as 'A Preface to Transgression', trans. D.F. Bouchard and S. Simon, in *Language, Counter-Memory, Practice*, ed. D.F. Bouchard (Ithaca. NY: Cornell University Press, 1977), pp. 29–52. In that preface he claimed that 'transgression is not related to the limit as black to white, the

prohibited to the lawful, the outside to the inside.' Rather, transgression 'forces the limit to face the fact of its imminent disapperance' (ibid., pp. 34–5). For a useful discussion of this aspect of Foucault's thought, see D.R. Hiley, *Philosophy in Question* (Chicago: University of Chicago Press, 1988), pp. 106–10.

37. T. McCarthy, 'The Critique of Impure Reason: Foucault and the Frankfurt School', in *Critique and Power*, p. 269.

38. M. Foucault, 'The Return of Morality', trans. T. Levin and I. Lorenz, in *Michel Foucault: Politics, Philosophy, Culture*, pp. 242–54, at pp. 253–4.

39. M. Foucault, 'On the Genealogy of Ethics: an Overview of Work in Progress', in *The Foucault Reader*, pp. 340–72, at p. 350.

40. As regards the former, he maintains that: 'One has to refuse everything that might present itself in the form of a simplistic and authoritarian alternative: you either accept the Enlightenment and remain within the tradition of its rationalism ... or else you criticize the Enlightenment and then try to escape from its principles of rationality' (WE, 43). As regards the latter, he argues that: 'The humanist thematic is in itself too supple, too diverse, too inconsistent to serve as an axis for reflection ... I believe that this thematic ... can be opposed by the principle of a critique and a permanent creation of ourselves in our autonomy ... From this standpoint, I am inclined to see Enlightenment and humanism in a state of tension rather than identity ... We must escape from the historical and moral confusionism that mixes the theme of humanism with the question of the Enlightenment' (WE, 44–5).

41. J. Habermas, 'Modernity versus Postmodernity', p. 5.

42. For a stimulating discussion of Foucault's fascination with 'limit-experiences', see J. Miller, *The Passion of Michel Foucault* (New York: Simon and Schuster, 1993).

43. H.L. Dreyfus and P. Rabinow, 'What is Maturity? Habermas and Foucault on "What is Enlightenment?"', in *Foucault: a Critical Reader*, pp. 109–21, at p. 115.

44. For a contrasting 'French' reading that stresses Foucault's debt to Nietzsche, see G. Deleuze, *Foucault*, trans. P. Bové (Minneapolis: University of Minnesota Press, 1988) and V. Descombes, *Modern French Philosophy*, trans. L. Scott-Fox and J.M. Harding (Cambridge: Cambridge University Press, 1980).

11 The Enlightenment, Contractualism and the Moral Polity

Vittorio Bufacchi

This chapter explores the legacy of the Enlightenment on contractualism. It is often remembered that in recent years there has been a revival of interest in the social contract theory; indeed it is hard to disagree with Alan Hamlin and Philip Pettit's claim that 'contractarianism in one form or another is perhaps the dominant contemporary approach to normative political theory'.[2] Of course, contemporary social contract theories are significantly different from their ancestors. During the period of its prevalence in the seventeenth and eighteenth centuries the social contract was employed principally to give an account of political obligation and political legitimacy, while more recently it has been revived in order to justify principles of social justice or even to account for the nature of morality.[3]

I want to suggest that the present resurrection of the social contract is far from being complete. Contrary to what has been suggested by critics of liberalism,[4] I believe the social contract can make a valuable contribution to the debate on the desirable attributes of the good polity. The focus of the chapter will be on two different contractarian moral conceptions of society, or moral polity. I will argue that the antithetical conceptions of the moral polity within contractarianism are traceable to tensions within the so-called Enlightenment project.

I. THE ENLIGHTENMENT AND ITS MANY CHILDREN

Defining the Enlightenment is notoriously difficult. The standard definition points to rationalism as the common currency of the Enlightenment Project (assuming that there was such a thing as the Enlightenment Project). This is the way the Enlightenment Project has been defined by its most ardent critics, for example by authors who adhere to the school of postmodernism such as Jacques Derrida and Jean-François Lyotard,[5] or the communitarian writings of Alasdair MacIntyre.[6] In fact, the picture of the Enlightenment its critics have drawn is simplistic and misleading.

Above all, one must be careful not to caricature the uncritical endorsement of reason, and in particular instrumental rationality, in the Enlightenment Project. Within what may be termed the Enlightenment Project there were those who had powerful reservations about rationalism, who questioned the optimism of the entire enterprise, who doubted the newly discovered blind faith in the power of reason, and even challenged the desirability of this new faith.[7]

The resulting picture of the Enlightenment is clearly more complex than that of its critics, but at the same time unquestionably more faithful to historical reality.[8] The so-called Enlightenment Project seems to be endorsing a paradox, where reason is praised but with major reservations. Nevertheless, if we want to assess the legacy of the Enlightenment in contemporary political theory, we have no choice but to subscribe to this more complex portrait of the Enlightenment.

Accounting for the legacy of the Enlightenment has been a major preoccupation for both its sympathizers and enemies. It appears to be a widely held view that something called 'modernity' is the most enduring legacy of the Enlightenment Project. In fact 'modernity' and Enlightenment are often used interchangeably.[9] While at one level I would not want to contradict this trend, I also feel that the vagueness and unintelligibility of the term 'modernity' makes this arguably the most useless (but sadly also most popular) analytic concept in contemporary social and political theory. If there were only one essentially contested concept, 'modernity' must certainly be the best candidate. Thus leaving aside 'modernity', can anything more specific be said about the legacy of the Enlightenment in political theory? Who are the children of the Enlightenment? Perhaps we can start by saying that the Enlightenment made liberal thought possible.[10] This statement is undeniable, but still not very helpful. After all, that the liberal cord is made up of many threads is also indisputable. The truth is that the so-called Enlightenment Project had many 'liberal' children. One of these was utilitarianism: David Hume, Adam Smith and Francis Hutcheson were influential figures of the Scottish Enlightenment, and precursors of what later became known as utilitarianism. More significantly, Jeremy Bentham himself, who of course was the principal architect of utilitarianism, should also be included under the banner of Enlightenment thinkers.[11]

Of course it would be incorrect to assume that utilitarianism is the only child of the Enlightenment. The idea of a social contract, so heavily criticized by utilitarian thinkers,[12] is also a legitimate child of the Enlightenment. As Will Kymlicka rightly points out, it is during the Enlightenment that contractarian thinking first achieved prominence. The social contract provided an alternative to the standard account of moral obligations, which in pre-Enlightenment thought was dominated by appeals to natural or divine order.[13]

In this chapter, I will leave utilitarianism aside and focus instead on the contractarian legacy of the Enlightenment. My aim is to show that the ambiguity of the Enlightenment on the question of reason is fully reflected in the contemporary neo-contractualist literature. First, I will show that the social contract captures many of the aspirations of the so-called Enlightenment Project. I will then focus on the contractarian approaches of two key figures in the Enlightenment Project, Hobbes and Kant, whose respective contracts are grounded on opposing conceptions of reasons. Finally, I will argue that the way contemporary neo-contractarian thinkers deliberate on the normative evaluation of society fully reveals the complex nature of the Enlightenment.

II. THE IDEA OF A SOCIAL CONTRACT

Before we can start our analysis of social contract theories, we need a working definition of the contractarian enterprise: *A social contract is an agreement based on the consent of every individual to regulate the benefits of social cooperation.*[14] It may be useful to analyse in more depth some of the key terms in this statement. There are two terms which constitute the framework of any contractarian theory: agreement and social cooperation. Although there cannot be a social contract without an agreement, not just any agreement will satisfy the requirements of a social contract. The agreement upon which all contractarian theories rest is grounded on *the consent of every individual*. This alerts us to three further characteristics of a social contract: first, that there is a bias towards individualism; second, that social contract theories are universalist in aspiration; third, that the validity of the social contract rests upon what people would consent to. The idea of consent is crucial, indeed it is on this point that we see the family resemblance between the Enlightenment and the social contract. The consent of every individual would not have any binding force, hence the agreement would not have any legitimacy, unless every individual who takes part in the agreement had the power to reason. In other words, it is consent based on reason that liberals in general, and contractarians in particular, are keen on.[15]

Social cooperation is the other key term in our definition of the social contract. Social cooperation can be interpreted in two ways: instrumentally (as a means necessary to satisfy individual ends) or as an ideal (as an end in itself). According to the instrumental approach, social cooperation

Figure 11.1

per se has no intrinsic worth; instead cooperation is to be valued exclusively in terms of the benefits it yields to the individuals involved. Alternatively, social cooperation can be approached as an ideal in itself, encompassing the values of mutual aid, reciprocity and fraternity. These two conceptions of social cooperation, namely instrumental and ideal social cooperation, are the battlefield where opposing theories of justice fight for supremacy.

The search for the nexus between agreement and social cooperation is the common denominator which unites a number of disparate and disjointed writers under the insignia of contractualism. I want to suggest that all contractarian models, notwithstanding their irreducible differences, follow a two-stage process: Stage 1 represents the moment of agreement based on individual consent, while Stage 2 represents the goal of social cooperation. Thus the format of a traditional social contract argument can be represented schematically as in Figure 11.1.

The point worth emphasizing here is that in the traditional debate a fundamental point of contention between different social contract theorists concerned opposing views of both the agreement (based on different conceptions of reason) and social cooperation (based on different accounts of what this entails).

III. HOBBES AND KANT

My analysis of the traditional social contract will focus on the theories of Hobbes and Kant. Although I am primarily interested in Hobbesian and Kantian views of the social contract as ideal-types, rather than in the most faithful interpretation of their texts,[16] one may query the legitimacy of assuming that Hobbes and Kant were indeed Enlightenment and contractarian thinkers. While there is no doubt that Kant was very much at the heart of the Enlightenment project,[17] Hobbes's position, in view of the fact that he predates the period from 1690 to 1790 characteristically held to define the Enlightenment, is more precarious. It is true that there are some aspects of Hobbes's political theory that most (if not all) adherents of the Enlightenment Project condemned, namely his pessimistic conception of human nature. Yet if we follow Kant's definition of the Enlightenment, then Hobbes must surely be considered part of the Enlightenment. Kant famously proclaimed that the Enlightenment motto is: *Sapere Aude!* Have the courage to use your own reason, or in other words the ability to use one's understanding without guidance from others.[18] Now reason, especially of a scientific nature, was of course at the centre of Hobbes's political thought; perhaps there was no other Enlightenment figure who was more critical of scholasticism than Hobbes. Considering that Hobbes was perhaps the first modern political theorist who deliberately attempted to ground moral beliefs and the political order on rational foundation, I would suggest that Hobbes was, at least in spirit, very much an Enlightenment thinker.[19]

Were Hobbes and Kant contractarian thinkers? On this question Kant and Hobbes swap positions. Hobbes's prominence in the history of social contract tradition is overall undisputed.[20] On the other hand, Kant's position is more problematic. Although the received view in Anglo-American circles is that Kant was a social contract theorist, recently this position has come under close scrutiny from those who favour an interpretation of Kant's ethics based on an account of obligation rather than contract.[21] Nevertheless, considering that contemporary contractarians thinkers are greatly influenced by Kant, in what follows I will simply leave this debate aside and assume that Kant did have a theory of the social contract.

Finally why, of all social contract theorists, focus on Hobbes and Kant? In my choice of these two thinkers, I am following the example of a growing number of scholars who have become convinced that Hobbes and Kant stand at opposite ends of the contractarian spectrum. As Will Kymlicka points out:

> There are two basic forms of contemporary social contract theory ... One approach stresses a natural equality of physical power, which makes it mutually advantageous for people to accept conventions that recognize and protect each other's interests and possessions. The other approach stresses a natural equality of moral status, which makes each person's interests a matter of common or impartial concern ... I will call proponents of the mutual advantage theory 'Hobbesian contractarians', and proponents of the impartial theory 'Kantian contractarians' for Hobbes and Kant inspired and foreshadowed these two forms of contract theory.[22]

Given that Hobbes and Kant theories represent the two most clear antithetical positions within the social contract tradition, our next step is to analyse in greater detail their respective theories in terms of what they have to say about the notions of agreement and social cooperation.

A. Hobbes's Social Contract

Hobbes's rejection of all metaphysical foundations of politics is well documented. In lieu of metaphysics Hobbes prescribes a scientific account of politics, hence he defends a mechanistic account of sensation, and the belief that human motivations, including conceptions of good and evil, can be reduced to appetites and aversions.[23]

Hobbes's scientific approach to politics and morality helps us fully to understand his conception of agreement (Stage 1 in Figure 11.1). The 'agreement', according to Hobbes, is not morally loaded, since individuals in the state of nature are beyond moral consideration. In fact as we shall see, with the exception of one moral imperative ('preserve your own life'), morality follows from the agreement; it does not precede it. In Hobbes's social contract individual consent to the agreement is not based on a moral motivation, if by these we understand incentives not reducible to self-interest.[24] It follows that in the Hobbesian state of nature the type of reason behind individual consent to an agreement is best captured by the notion of instrumental rationality rather than a sense of justice.[25] Instrumental rationality refers to means–end reasoning, grounded on selfish motivations.

Hobbes's conception of rational agreement, devoid of unselfish moral motivations, is determining for his conception of social cooperation, in fact from a moral point of view the most salient moment in Hobbes's contractarian procedure occurs at the stage of social cooperation (Stage 2 in Figure 11.1). Hobbes's denial of moral motives and moral standards is reflected in his accounts of the state of nature and the laws of nature. Concerning the state of nature, Hobbes points out that this hypothetical state is once again beyond moral evaluation.[26] The same applies with respect to Hobbes's account of natural laws.[27] If the state of nature is beyond moral appraisal, and the laws of nature are not moral imperatives, it follows that, according to Hobbes, there is no right and wrong prior to human agreement. Similarly justice is determined by human agreement, not by moral absolutes prior to such agreement:

> For where no covenant hath preceded, there hath no right been transferred, and every man has right to every thing; and consequently, no action can be unjust. But when a covenant is made, then to break it is unjust; and the definition of injustice, is no other than the not performance of covenant. And whatsoever is not unjust, is just.[28]

To recapitulate, according to Hobbes the moment of agreement, being stripped of unselfish moral connotations, can only be grounded on the

STAGE 1   STAGE 2

Rational Agreement ——▶ Instrumental Social Cooperation

Figure 11.2   Hobbesian social contract.

bargaining of individual agents. The only possible outcome from this rational agreement is what I earlier described as instrumental social cooperation (see Figure 11.2).

In order to understand the Hobbesian idea of instrumental social cooperation, we must ask ourselves what individual agents in the state of nature could agree to. As everyone will pursue a rational strategy of advancing their individual interests, the only acceptable form of social cooperation is one where everyone makes a gain, where such gain is measured with respect to the non-cooperative point. It follows that people seeking rational agreement would only find conditions of mutual advantage generally agreeable. Instrumental social cooperation is revealed in the idea of mutual advantage; furthermore it is the idea of mutual advantage that ensures that the agreement is unanimous. As we shall see, this idea of social cooperation as mutual advantage has been taken up by contemporary neo-Hobbesian contractarian theorists.

B. Kant's Social Contract

One of the distinguishing attributes of Kant's social contract is that the moment of 'agreement' is morally loaded. In seeking an agreement individual agents are moved by predetermined moral motivations. As we shall see, this has important implications for Kant's idea of social cooperation, in fact to the extent that the moment of agreement comes prior to and therefore determines the terms of social cooperation, the latter becomes infused with moral ideals.

Kant's most clear account of the social contract comes from his essay 'On the Common Saying: "This May be True in Theory, but it does not Apply in Practice"'. Here Kant deals with the relationship of theory and practice in three separate areas: morality, politics and the cosmopolitical sphere. The second of these ('On the Relationship of Theory and Practice in Political Right') is a direct attack on Hobbes's *De Cive*, and where Kant discusses his view of the social contract, and how it differs from Hobbes's.

Kant distinguishes between two types of social contract: as the basis of a society (*pactum sociale*) and as a basis of a civil state, i.e. a commonwealth (*pactum unionis civilis*). The former is more general, and it refers to a union of many individuals for some common end which they all share. The latter is more specific, and it refers to a union as an end in itself which they all ought to share. Needless to say that Kant defends the latter type of social contract as pertinent to the civil or political state, and he sees Hobbes as his major adversary, since Hobbes fails to distinguish between a society and a civil state:[29]

The civil state … is based on the following *a priori* principles:

1. The *freedom* of every member of society as a *human being*.
2. The *equality* of each with all the others as a *subject*.
3. The *independence* of each member of a commonwealth as a *citizen*.

These principles are not so much laws given by an already established state, as laws by which a state can alone be established in accordance with pure rational principles of external human right.[30]

The distinction Kant makes between society and civil state captures the distinction I made in section II between instrumental social cooperation and ideal social cooperation. Thus while Hobbes, as we have seen, is advocating instrumental social cooperation (society), Kant is championing ideal social cooperation (civil state). The difference in their respective conceptions of social cooperation can be traced back to their opposing views on agreement in general, and reason in particular.

Unlike Hobbes, Kant is able to load the concept of agreement with moral undertones. That is because he holds to a different conception of reason than that of Hobbes. We have seen that according to Hobbes, reason is solely instrumental rationality. Alternatively Kant tells us that reason also implies acting on a universal maxim.[31] Reason is ultimately about the con-nection between duty and autonomy: to be autonomous is to freely accept the moral law, and actions are performed in accordance to duty. As Robert Audi explains, duty performs a double function: it provides a motive *to* per-form the act and it constitutes the agent's actual reason *for* performing it. It follows that 'Kant not only postulates normative foundations of rational action, he also gave them both a priori status and motivational power'.[32]

The morally informed moment of agreement has important implications for Kant's idea of social cooperation. In fact we find that as a result of his conception of agreement, the terms of social cooperation in Kant's social contract reveal a normative quality: namely, because individuals have an intrinsic value, they ought to be treated as end-in-themselves. In his *Groundwork of the Metaphysics of Morals*, Kant refers to this formula of social cooperation as the Kingdom of Ends. Starting from the assumption that a 'kingdom' refers to a systematic union of different rational beings

STAGE 1   STAGE 2

Moral Agreement————▶ Ideal Social Cooperation
                              (Kingdom of Ends)

Figure 11.3   Kantian social contract.

under common law, Kant explains the idea of a Kingdom of Ends as follows:

> For rational beings all stand under the *law* that each of them should treat himself and all others, *never merely as a means, but always at the same time as an end in himself.* But by so doing there arises a systematic union of rational beings under common objective laws – that is, a kingdom.[33]

To recapitulate, Kant's social contract is grounded on *a priori* moral principles, hence it is the moral agreement (i.e. an agreement based on a moral conception of reason) that determines the type of social cooperation being pursued (see Figure 11.3). In the last analysis, what distinguishes Kant from Hobbes is their different conceptions of the nature of morality: according to Kant morality is summoned at the moment of agreement,[34] while for Hobbes morality is evoked after the agreement, at the later stage of defining social cooperation.[35] Hobbes's and Kant's diverse conceptions of agreement and reason are fully reflected in their conflicting conceptions of social cooperation and the moral polity.

So far two opposing interpretations of the social contract have been analysed, formulated respectively by Hobbes and Kant. I have tried to argue that the best way of understanding the difference between Hobbes and Kant is in terms of their different conceptions of agreement (especially the interpretation of reason) and social cooperation. In what follows, I want to argue that, more specifically, their opposing conceptions of social cooperation still form the basic axioms for contemporary debates on the normative assessment of society.

IV. GAUTHIER AND RAWLS

The two opposing conceptions of social contract advanced by Hobbes and Kant, discussed in section III above, have shaped the recent debate on the moral polity. Thus we find that David Gauthier has followed Hobbes in advocating an ideal of social cooperation grounded on mutual advantage, whereas John Rawls has followed, at least in part, in the footsteps of Kant in formulating his notion of a well-ordered society.

A. Gauthier on Mutual Advantage

The idea of social cooperation as mutual advantage championed by Hobbes implies that all those who participate in the cooperative venture will stand to benefit from it. The most influential advocate of social cooperation as mutual advantage in contemporary debates is undoubtedly David Gauthier. What distinguishes Gauthier from most other contemporary moral philosophers is his steadfast determination to develop a theory of morals as part of the theory of rational choice.[36] Gauthier wants to argue that rational choice cannot be distinguished from moral choice: 'Morality, as we shall see, can be generated as a rational constraint from the non-moral premises of rational choice.'[37]

One of the cardinal assumptions on which Gauthier's libertarian theory of justice rests is that a contractarian views society as a cooperative venture for mutual advantage, where the willing allegiance of each rational person can be secured if and only if each person is to expect greater benefit from the society than she could expect in a non-social state of nature. Gauthier goes as far as to suggest that individual returns from social cooperation be in some way proportionate to the level of contribution being made.[38]

What is interesting to note here is that the idea of social cooperation for mutual advantage finds justification in the instrumental conception of reason, namely rational choice. Gauthier identifies rationality with the maximization of utility, where utility is defined in terms of preference satisfaction.[39] He is also very explicit in distinguishing his conception of practical reason from that endorsed by Kant and neo-kantians.[40] According to Gauthier, it is the rationality of the agreement that vindicates the view of social cooperation as mutual advantage. The basic axioms of Gauthier's position are that it is in general possible for a society to afford each person greater benefit compared to a non-social 'state of nature', and that only a society founded on the assumption of mutual benefit could be seen as acceptable by every rational individual. Thus although not all actual societies need be cooperative ventures, nor actual persons uninterested in their fellows, the fact remains that mutual benefit is a pre-condition for morally legitimate social cooperation.

B. Rawls on the Well-ordered Society

There are four distinct features of a well-ordered society, according to Rawls.[41] While all four play an important part in his argument, for the issues being discussed in this chapter the first two are arguably more important than the latter; therefore I shall focus exclusively on these attributes. The first feature is that a well-ordered society is one that is effectively regulated by a public conception of justice. This implies that each citizen accepts, and knows that the others accept, the same conception of justice; that the basic institutions of the society satisfy this conception of justice and are believed by everyone to satisfy it; that this public conception of justice is based upon reasonable beliefs established by widely-accepted methods of inquiry. The second feature is that citizens in a well-ordered society are, and recognize themselves as being, free and equal moral persons. This implies that citizens are recognized as having two basic moral powers: first, the capacity to understand, to apply and to act from (and not merely in accordance with) the principles of justice,[42] and secondly the capacity to form, to revise, and rationally to pursue a conception of the good.[43] The third and fourth features are respectively that in a well-ordered society the circumstances of justice will obtain, and that a well-ordered society is stable with respect to its conception of justice.

Rawls also tells us that his conception of a well-ordered society is closely analogous to, but not identical with, Kant's notion of a Kingdom of Ends: 'think of the notion of a well-ordered society as an interpretation of the idea of a kingdom of ends thought of as a human society under circumstances of justice'.[44] Having established the approximate affinity between Rawls and Kant on the issue of social cooperation,[45] we now shift our attention to the type of agreement, and in particular the conception of reason, that lies behind Rawls's notion of a well-ordered society. I believe that Rawls's well-ordered society cannot be grounded on instrumental rationality, instead it must necessarily be sustained by a Kantian conception of reason. Furthermore, contrary to what his critics have said, I believe Rawls does endorse something closely resembling Kant's conception of reason.[46]

I am referring to Rawls's distinction between reasonableness and rationality. Rawls argues that the concept of reasonableness is autonomous and independent from the notion of rationality, and ought to be defined on different grounds than rationality: the reasonable expresses a conception of the fair terms of cooperation, while the rational expresses a conception of each participant's rational advantage, in other words what as individuals each participant is trying to advance.[47] The reasonable (unlike rationality) has a moral underpinning,[48] making reasonableness and fairness closely related. Rational agents lack the moral sensibility that underlies the desire to engage in fair cooperation,[49] or in other words they lack a sense of justice and fail to recognize the independent validity of the claims of others.[50] On the other hand reasonable persons desire a social world in which they, as free and equal, can cooperate with others on terms all can accept.[51]

Rawls even goes as far as to suggest that the reasonable and the rational do not stand on equal rank, instead:

> [T]he Reasonable presupposes and subordinates the Rational ... The Reasonable subordinates the Rational because its principles limit, and in a Kantian doctrine limit absolutely, the final ends that can be pursued.[52]

It is important to remember that according to Rawls, Kant's notion of reason (*vernünftig*) covers both the terms 'reasonable' and 'rational'.[53] In my view, it is the idea of reasonableness (and the moral motivation that it entails), and not instrumental rationality, that does most of the work behind his conception of a well-ordered society. After all, the reasonable presupposes and subordinates the rational. As we shall see, Rawls's Kantian conception of reason is, in the last analysis, what distinguishes his understanding of a moral society from Gauthier and other Hobbesian philosophers.

V. THE MORAL POLITY: MUTUAL ADVANTAGE vs. A WELL-ORDERED SOCIETY

So far I have argued that there are two competing conceptions of social cooperation, which can be traced back to two conflicting approaches in the social contract tradition: (a) the neo-hobbesian idea of social cooperation as mutual advantage, grounded on the idea of instrumental rationality; (b) the neo-Kantian idea of a well-ordered society based on a 'Kantian' idea of reason. In what follows, I will argue that these two conceptions of society are incompatible, and that from a moral point of view, the idea of a well-ordered society is to be preferred to the idea of social cooperation as mutual advantage.

In order to see the incompatibility of mutual advantage and a well-ordered society, we need to look no further than Rawls's theory of justice. It is interesting to note that although Rawls explicitly acknowledges the influence of Kant on his moral theory, and the fact that Rawls clearly states that his intention was to formulate a non-Hobbesian social contract theory,[54] there is ample textual evidence to suggest that Rawls is in fact embracing certain aspects of Hobbes's social contract, namely a conception of social cooperation as mutual advantage.[55] In the last analysis, we find that in *A Theory of Justice* Rawls appeals to two separate but related conceptions of social cooperation: (a) as promoting mutual advantage and (b) as endorsing a well-ordered society.[56] Indeed in Rawls's theory these two conceptions of social cooperation are tightly knit together, to the extent that they become indivisible: 'In [justice as fairness] we think of a well-ordered society as a scheme of cooperation for reciprocal advantage.'[57] What Rawls fails to see, and what I have attempted to argue so far in this chapter, is that the concepts of mutual advantage and of a well-ordered society reflect two radically different theories of the social contract, therefore portraying two radically different conceptions of morality and of the moral polity.

Samuel Freeman has made an interesting attempt to isolate Rawls's conception of social cooperation from Gauthier's by focusing on the differences in their respective notion of mutual advantage. He points out that while Rawls and Gauthier share the idea of social cooperation for mutual advantage, they differ in the characterization of this basic idea. Thus according to Freeman, Gauthier's notion of cooperation for mutual advantage involves no irreducible moral elements; instead the only valid conception of cooperation is one of efficiently coordinated activity for each person's benefit. On the other hand, Rawls's idea of cooperation as mutual advantage endorses irreducible moral notions, which implies that Rawls's conception of social cooperation has a dual aspect: as each individual's rational good, and as an independent moral component, characterized in Rawls by the notion of fair terms and what is reasonable.[58]

While I share Freeman's view that there is a difference between Gauthier and Rawls on the issue of social cooperation, I think Freeman is wrong to look for that distinction within the notion of mutual advantage. That is to say, I don't think there is any difference in the way Gauthier and Rawls understand mutual advantage. Instead, the difference between Gauthier and Rawls is that social cooperation for mutual advantage is Gauthier's *only* conception of social cooperation, while Rawls appeals also to another conception of social cooperation, namely a moral conception, enclosed in the idea of a well-ordered society – not surprisingly the concept of a well-ordered society is absent from Gauthier's moral theory.

Perhaps one way of explaining the peculiar fact that Rawls holds two conflicting ideas of social cooperation, as mutual advantage and as a well-ordered society, is that Rawls needs both conceptions for different reasons, that is to say these two conceptions of social cooperation perform different functions in his theory. Thus while social cooperation for mutual advantage is important to Rawls in order to establish the circumstances of justice, the idea of a well-ordered society reflects Rawls's ethical idea of justice. Leaving aside the question of *why* Rawls attempts to reconcile a Kantian notion of a well-ordered society with a Hobbesian notion of mutual advantage, in what follows I shall focus on the fact that Rawls's attempted reconciliation between mutual advantage and a well-ordered society is doomed to fail.

The impossibility of endorsing both conceptions of social cooperation stems from the incompatibility of ends between mutual advantage and a well-ordered society. Thus while it is possible for a well-ordered society to promote institutions that make social cooperation between different individuals mutually advantageous, it is not unlikely for a well-ordered society to infringe the condition of mutual benefit, and vice versa. In other words, sometimes a well-ordered society will not follow the canons of mutual advantage, and similarly, promoting mutual advantage may contradict the notion of a well-ordered society. When this happens, one has no choice but to choose between mutual advantage and a well-ordered society.

The tension between mutual advantage and a well-ordered society can best be seen in terms of the moral premise of impartiality. Both Gauthier and Rawls argue that impartiality is characteristic of morality itself, yet the notion of equality and impartiality which is captured by the idea of a well-ordered society differs radically from the concept of equality and impartiality we find in the idea of mutual advantage. On one level, both Gauthier and Rawls agree that impartiality implies not discriminating against the interest of anyone; in fact both authors refer to impartiality in terms of the Archimedean point, yet they have radically opposed conceptions of what this may entail.

Thus we find that in Gauthier's theory impartiality is derived from the condition of rationality and mutual advantage: according to Gauthier impartiality simply means that everyone should be guaranteed equal or equivalent shares, and since mutual advantage advances the interest of each agent, mutual advantage is by definition impartial.[59] Contrary to Gauthier, in Rawls's theory impartiality is derived from the model-conception of the person as a free and equal moral person. According to Rawls impartiality is essentially about finding a basis of agreement that is acceptable from all points of view, a notion which is captured by Rawls in one of his early articles that preceded *A Theory of Justice* in terms of 'the recognition of one another as persons with similar interests and capacities engaged in a common practice'.[60]

The two conceptions of impartiality advanced by Rawls and Gauthier are not always compatible. Guaranteeing equal or equivalent shares is not necessarily acceptable from all points of view; in fact as Gauthier points out, his theory has nothing to say about equalizing or meeting needs. Thus Gauthier famously sees no injustice in the case of the poor woman starving at the gate of the rich man feasting on caviar and champagne.[61] It goes without saying that Rawls would not agree with Gauthier on this point, since the social system that allows an old woman to starve at the gate of a rich man would not be acceptable from the point of view of the old woman. It follows that just as Gauthier and Rawls defend their respective theories on the basis of diverse understanding of impartiality, similarly their respective conceptions of social cooperation are not easily compatible.

Another way of stating the difference between Gauthier and Rawls on the question of social cooperation is to say that Gauthier is interested in *the benefits* of social cooperation, while Rawls is interested in *the terms* of social cooperation. In the words of Rawls: 'Social cooperation is not merely coordinated social activity efficiently organized for some overall collective end. Rather, it presupposes a notion of fair terms of cooperation.'[62] The *terms* of social cooperation are the object of Rawls's conception of a well-ordered society, while the *benefits* of social cooperation are the object of Gauthier's conception of social cooperation as mutual advantage. One may benefit from social cooperation even if the terms are unacceptable. Exploitation may be mutually beneficial to both the exploited and the exploiter, but it is unacceptable in terms of a well-ordered society. It is when acceptable terms of social cooperation clash with the benefits of social cooperation that one has to decide which conception of social cooperation is to be preferred.

The idea that fair terms of social cooperation ought to be preferred to the benefits of social cooperation finds a fervent adherent in Thomas Scanlon. One of the differences between Scanlon's contractualism and Rawls's regards their different conception of social cooperation. While Rawls's original position reflects the priority of mutual advantage over the well-ordered society, Scanlon contends that social cooperation is determined above all by the motive for impartial moral concern, while mutual advantage is secondary. According to Scanlon what is important to stress is the ethical dimension of social cooperation: that social cooperation among equals is to be valued for its own sake and not exclusively for its benefits. The point is that according to Scanlon there is more to social cooperation than mutual advantage. As Scanlon points out:

> Membership in a cooperative association of equals, in which the needs of all are provided for and in which each is motivated to contribute by his perception of the needs of the group and his obligations to it, may itself be counted an important and valuable good.[63]

In other words social cooperation among equals has an independent moral value separate from the benefits that can result from it. This does not mean that social cooperation as mutual advantage plays no part in Scanlon's contractualism, but simply that he subordinates the criterion of mutual advantage to the idea of agreement on a footing of equality. It follows that according to Scanlon, and contrary to Gauthier's specification, principles of social justice ought to be grounded on the moral motivation to endorse impartiality, not on the pursuit of moral advantage based on rational self-interest.

VI. CONCLUSION: THE LEGACY OF THE ENLIGHTENMENT

The Enlightenment Project posed a question: what is the normative foundation of society? Contractualism provides two answers. If we follow the Hobbesian tradition, the moral polity is defined in terms of social cooperation for mutual advantage. Alternatively if we follow the Kantian tradition, we end up with the idea of a well-ordered society. Although they both stem from contractarian reasoning, these two conceptions of the moral polity are antithetical, endorsing as part of their justification radically opposing ideas of reason. Mutual advantage is based on instrumental rationality, while the well-ordered society assumes a Kantian conception of reason.

These two conceptions of social cooperation, as mutual advantage and as a well-ordered society, are not simply antithetical but also irreconcilable. Rawls's failure to unite both conceptions of the moral polity under the same roof is in no way an indication of his philosophical incompetence, but of the infeasible nature of the enterprise he embarked on.

I believe there are two lessons to be learned from the above discussion of two opposing social contract traditions, and Rawls's failure to reconcile them. First of all, to the extent that the social contract is an offspring of the Enlightenment project, the contemporary controversy between contractarian philosophers captures the complexity of the Enlightenment Project. Contrary to the standard approach, there is not one Enlightenment Project, which is defined *à la* MacIntyre by a boundless faith in the powers of rationality. Instrumental rationality, found in Hobbes, Hume and Bentham alike, is not the only way Enlightenment thinkers defined reason. There is also the Kantian conception of reason, which as we have seen is enveloped in moral considerations. Unless we recognize that there are multiple conceptions of reason in the Enlightenment Project, we would be forced to endorse the unflattering conclusion that within the contractarian camp the legacy of the Enlightenment is captured by Gauthier's conception of social cooperation for mutual advantage. Instead in this chapter I have argued that the Rawlsian idea of a well-ordered society, grounded in something resembling the Kantian conception of reason (namely the idea of reasonableness), is as much a legitimate legacy of the Enlightenment Project as Gauthier's theory. Rational choice accounts of the social contract are not the only valid or legitimate foundations for delineating the moral fabric of society.

Secondly, Rawls's effort to reconcile Hobbesian and Kantian social contracts can be construed as an attempt to unify the Enlightenment under one coherent project. This cannot be done, because in the last analysis the Enlightenment cannot be confined to a logically coherent project. As Wokler reminds us:

> It may be thought that the diversity of thinkers linked with that whole assemblage is too great, or the tensions between them too profound, to allow any ascription of a generic identity or common purpose to them, and eighteenth-century scholars who have failed to uncover any such 'project' or 'movement' or even 'the Enlightenment' after a lifetime's research devoted to the subject could be forgiven their exasperation when confronted by so great a leap and quick fix.[64]

That, in part, explains the enduring appeal of the Enlightenment.

NOTES

1.   I am grateful to all the contributors to this volume for their comments on earlier drafts of this paper.
2.   A. Hamlin and P. Pettit (eds), *The Good Polity* (Oxford: Blackwell, 1989), p. 11.
3.   I will discuss contractarian accounts of social justice later on in this paper. For an illuminating attempt to argue that contractualism can be employed at the level of philosophical enquiry in order to explain the nature of morality, see T. Scanlon, 'The Aims and Authority of Moral Theory', *Oxford Journal of Legal Studies*, 12, no. 1, 1992.
4.   Chandran Kukathas reminds us that according to Sandel and Wolff, 'liberalism has long been derided as a political philosophy which lacks any theory of society, the implication being that it can therefore contribute very little to the discussion of questions concerning the nature of the good society and the place of the individual in the social order'. C. Kukathas, *Hayek and Modern Liberalism* (Oxford: Clarendon Press, 1989), p. 85.
5.   The same is true of the young Michel Foucault, although in the light of some of his final essays, his position on this question is more ambiguous. On Foucault and the Enlightenment, see M. Passerin d'Entrèves' paper in this volume.

6. MacIntyre defines the Enlightenment Project in terms of the attempt to provide a rational foundation for and justification of morality. A. MacIntyre, *After Virtue* (London: Duckworth 1985), p. 43.
7. For example Adam Smith and David Hume in Scotland, and Voltaire in France.
8. For a critique of MacIntyre's assessment of the Enlightenment, see R. Wokler, 'Projecting the Enlightenment', in J. Horton and S. Mendus (eds), *After MacIntyre* (Cambridge: Polity Press, 1994).
9. See J. Habermas, *The Philosophical Discourse of Modernity*, trans. F. Lawrence (Cambridge: Polity Press, 1987).
10. See J. Waldron's 'Theoretical Foundations of Liberalism', in his *Liberal Rights: Collected Papers 1981–1991* (Cambridge: Cambridge University Press, 1993).
11. Iain Hampsher-Monk reminds us that although Bentham is often thought as an English nineteenth-century thinker, 'in fact his roots lie deep in the eighteenth-century European Enlightenment'. I. Hampsher-Monk, *A History of Modern Political Thought* (Oxford: Blackwell, 1992), p. 307. See also J.H. Burns, 'From Radical Enlightenment to Philosophic Enlightenment', *The Bentham Newsletter* (June 1984).
12. Referring to the social contract, Bentham says that 'The indestructible prerogatives of mankind have no need to be supported upon the sandy foundations of a fiction'; quoted in D. Boucher and P. Kelly, 'The Social Contract and its Critics: an Overview', in Boucher and Kelly (eds), *The Social Contract from Hobbes to Rawls* (London: Routledge, 1994), p. 21. Curiously the twentieth century has produced utilitarian contractarians, like John Harsanyi and Russell Hardin.
13. See W. Kymlicka, 'The Social Contract Tradition', in P. Singer (ed.), *A Companion to Ethics* (Oxford: Blackwell, 1993).
14. In formulating this definition of the contractarian enterprise I have found two recent articles by Samuel Freeman very helpful: 'Reason and Agreement in Social Contract Views', *Philosophy and Public Affairs*, 19, no. 2, 1990, and 'Contractualism, Moral Motivation, and Practical Reason', *The Journal of Philosophy*, 88, no. 6, 1991.
15. See Waldron, 'Theoretical Foundations of Liberalism', pp. 43–50.
16. In other words I am not suggesting that my interpretation of Hobbesian and Kantian philosophy captures the intentions of Hobbes and Kant when writing their works.
17. See A. Baumeister's 'Kant: the Arch-enlightener', in this volume.
18. See I. Kant [1784], 'An Answer to the Question: What is Enlightenment?', in *Perpetual Peace and Other Essays* (Cambridge: Hackett, 1983).
19. 'The eighteenth century doctrine of the state and society only rarely accepted without reservations the content of Hobbes's teaching, but the form in which Hobbes embodied this content exerted a powerful and lasting influence'. E. Cassirer, *The Philosophy of the Enlightenment* (Princeton: Princeton University Press, 1951), p. 19.
20. There are of course exceptions to this rule. See J. Hampton, *Hobbes and the Social Contract Tradition* (Cambridge: Cambridge University Press, 1986), and R. Hardin, 'Hobbesian Political Order', *Political Theory*, 19, no. 2, May 1991.

21.   See K. Flikschuh, 'On Kant's *Rechtslehre*', *European Journal of Philosophy*, 5, no. 1, April 1997.

22.   Kymlicka, 'The Social Contract Tradition', p. 188. Analogous accounts to Kymlicka's can also be found in J. Hampton, 'Two Faces of Contractarian Thought', in P. Vallentyne (ed.), *Contractarianism and Rational Choice* (New York: Cambridge University Press, 1991), p. 33, and M. Lessnoff, 'Introduction: Social Contract', in M. Lessnoff (ed.) *Social Contract Theory* (Oxford: Blackwell, 1990), p. 15.

23.   T. Hobbes [1651] *Leviathan*, edited by C.B. Macpherson (Harmondsworth: Penguin, 1968), p. 24; all emphasis omitted.

24.   Self-preservation is thus both a moral imperative and a selfish motivation.

25.   This is the interpretation one finds in D. Gauthier, *The Logic of Leviathan* (Oxford: Clarendon Press, 1969); J. Hampton, *Hobbes and the Social Contract Tradition* (New York: Cambridge University Press, 1986); and G. Kavka, *Hobbesian Moral and Political Theory* (Princeton: Princeton University Press, 1986). For an alternative account, see R. Tuck, *Hobbes* (Oxford: Oxford University Press, 1989).

26.   Hobbes, *Leviathan*, p. 63.

27.   It should be said that in the seventeenth century the language of natural laws often implied moral imperatives, especially in the works of those following in the Christian and Aristotelian tradition. Hobbes adopts the notion of natural law, but strips it of all moral connotations.

28.   Hobbes, *Leviathan*, p. 71; all emphasis omitted.

29.   The reason why Kant is keen to discredit Hobbes's social contract is essentially the following: he feels that under Hobbes's contract the head of state has no contractual obligation towards the people, while Kant wants to emphasize that the people too have inalienable rights against the head of state. It is because Kant believes in such inalienable rights that his contract is based on *a priori* principles.

30.   I. Kant, 'On the Common Saying: "This May be True in Theory, but it Does not Apply in Practice"', in *Kant: Political Writings* (Cambridge: Cambridge University Press, 1991), p. 74; emphasis in original.

31.   'But reason provides a concept which we express by the words *political right*. And this concept has binding force for human beings who coexist in a state of antagonism produced by their natural freedom ... Thus it is based on *a priori* principles, for experience cannot provide knowledge of what is right, and there is a *theory* of political right to which practice must conform before it can be valid.' Kant, 'On the Common Saying', p. 86; emphasis in original.

32.   R. Audi, *Practical Reasoning* (London: Routledge, 1989), p. 188. For a more thorough analysis of reason in Kant, see Audi, ch. 3. For an excellent overview of Kant's ethics, see O. O'Neill, 'Kantian Ethics', in P. Singer (ed.), *A Companion to Ethics* (Oxford: Blackwell, 1993).

33.   I. Kant, *Groundwork of the Metaphysics of Morals*, trans. H.J. Paton as *The Moral Law* (London: Hutchinson, 1953), p. 74; emphasis in original.

34.   This again raises the question of whether Kant is a social contract theorist. I shall leave this question unanswered.

35.   As Jean Hampton rightly points out, according to Hobbes: 'morality is a human-made institution, which is justified only to the extent that it

effectively furthers human interests'. Hampton, 'Two Faces of Contractarian Thought', p. 36.

36. Gauthier points out that a similar project has been entertained by Rawls and Harsanyi, although he rightly explains that the claims made by Rawls and Harsanyi of this effect 'are stronger than their results warrant'. D. Gauthier, *Morals by Agreement* (Oxford: Oxford University Press, 1986), p. 4.

37. Gauthier *Morals by Agreement*, p. 4. Gauthier is clearly trying to deduce the *ought* (moral choices) from the *is* (rational choices).

38. Gauthier, *Morals by Agreement*, p. 152.

39. 'But in identifying rationality with the maximization of a measure of preference, the theory of rational choice disclaims all concern with the ends of action. Ends may be inferred from individual preferences; if the relationship among these preferences, and the manner in which they are held, satisfy the conditions of rational choice, then the theory accepts whatever ends they imply.' Gauthier, *Morals by Agreement*, p. 26.

40. Gauthier, *Morals by Agreement*, p. 6.

41. Here I am following Kenneth Baynes's simple but accurate analysis. See K. Baynes, 'Constructivism and Practical Reason in Rawls', *Analyze & Kritik*, 14, 1992. I am grateful to Maurizio Passerin d'Entrèves for pointing out this article to me.

42. In other words, citizens can be effectively motivated by the appropriate conception of justice.

43. In other words, citizens have their own conceptions of the good which motivate them and give them a sense of purpose in life.

44. J. Rawls, 'A Well-Ordered Society', in P. Laslett and J. Fishkin (eds), *Philosophy, Politics and Society*, fifth series (Oxford: Blackwell, 1979), p. 18. The original title of this piece was 'A Kantian Conception of Equality', *The Cambridge Review*, Feb. 1975.

45. Rawls is the first to admit that there is a discrepancy between his own theory, which he describes as Kantian, and Kant's own theory. See Rawls, 'A Well-Ordered Society', p. 18.

46. I am referring to Onora O'Neill's claim that 'Rawls's constructivism assumes a quite different account of rationality from Kant's. Rawls identifies the principles that *would* be chosen by instrumentally rational beings to whom he ascribes certain sparsely specified ends – not the principles that *could* consistently be chosen regardless of particular ends.' O'Neill, 'Kantian Ethics', p. 184. I think what O'Neill says is true of Rawls's *A Theory of Justice*, although he has moved away from that position since 1971, especially in his 1980 Dewey Lectures on 'Kantian Constructivism and Moral Theory'.

47. J. Rawls, 'Kantian Constructivism in Moral Theory', *The Journal of Philosophy*, 77, no. 9, 1980, p. 528.

48. 'Reasonable persons, that is, … persons who have realized their two moral powers.' J. Rawls, 'The Domain of the Political and Overlapping Consensus', *New York University Law Review*, 64, no. 2, 1989, p. 236.

49. Rawls, *Political Liberalism*, p. 51.

50. Ibid., p. 52.

51. Ibid., p. 50.

52. Rawls, 'Kantian Constructivism in Moral Theory', p. 530.

53.   Rawls, 'Themes in Kant's Moral Philosophy', in E. Förster (ed.), *Kant's Transcendental Deductions* (Stanford: Stanford University Press, 1989), pp. 87–8.

54.   'As the text suggests, I shall regard Locke ... Rousseau ... and Kant ... as definitive of the contract tradition. For all of its greatness, Hobbes's *Leviathan* raises special problems.' J. Rawls, *A Theory of Justice* (Oxford: Oxford University Press, 1972), p. 11n.

55.   Rawls claims that a contractarian views society as 'a cooperative venture for mutual advantage'. J. Rawls, *A Theory of Justice*, p. 4. Not surprisingly David Gauthier is happy to echo Rawls regarding the question of social cooperation.

56.   On Rawls's two theories of justice, see B. Barry, *Theories of Justice* (Berkeley: University of California Press, 1989). The argument that follows was strongly influenced by Barry's analysis.

57.   J. Rawls, *A Theory of Justice*, p. 33. With this formula Rawls is probably trying to capture Kant's notion of *vernünftig*, which as we have seen covers both the reasonable (a well-ordered society) and the rational (a scheme of cooperation for reciprocal advantage).

58.   S. Freeman, 'Reason and Agreement in Social Contract Views', p. 124.

59.   The complexity of Gauthier's account of impartiality are analysed by D. Copp, 'Contractarianism and Moral Skepticism', in Vallentyne (ed.), *Contractarianism and Rational Choice*. See also M. Moore, 'Gauthier's Contractarian Morality', in Boucher and Kelly (eds), *The Social Contract from Hobbes to Rawls*, who argues that Gauthier fails to reconcile the two elements of his moral theory, namely the rationality requirement and the impartiality requirement.

60.   J. Rawls, 'Justice as Fairness', *Philosophical Review*, 67, 1958, p. 182.

61.   See Gauthier, *Morals by Agreement*, p. 218.

62.   J. Rawls, 'Social Unity and Primary Goods', in A. Sen and B. Williams (eds), *Utilitarianism and Beyond*, p. 164. 'Justice as fairness starts from the idea that society is to be conceived as a fair system of cooperation': J. Rawls 'Justice as Fairness: Political not Metaphysical', *Philosophy and Public Affairs*, 14, no. 3, 1985, pp. 232–3.

63.   T. Scanlon, 'Liberty, Contract, and Contribution', in G. Dworkin et al. (eds), *Markets and Morals* (London and New York: John Wiley & Sons, 1977), p. 58.

64.   R. Wokler, 'Projecting the Enlightenment', p. 115.

Index